BEYOND THIS HARBOR

Goodnight, Great Summer Sky

Goodnight, great summer sky
world of my childhood and the star-struck sea.

White chaise from that ancestral southern
porch my raft,
white goose-down quilt my ballast,
under Orion on the green-waved lawn
I float, high—
new moon, old craft
tide strong as ever to the sheer horizon.

Over the seawall, on the dock
Andromeda their strict and jeweled guard
as tall Orion—seas and lawns ago—
chose to be mine,
our children sleep: Alexandra, Tom
under their folded goose-wing sails
true friends in dream,
the folly wrangle of their sibling day
outshone by starlight.

Calm island evening, never-ending sea—
our lovers' rages, too, are quiet,
drowned.

Miracle of midsummer, the trust of dark
sails us beyond this harbor.

BEYOND THIS HARBOR

ADVENTUROUS TALES
OF THE HEART

Rose Styron

 ALFRED A. KNOPF · NEW YORK · 2023

THIS IS A BORZOI BOOK
PUBLISHED BY ALFRED A. KNOPF

Copyright © 2023 by Rose Styron

All rights reserved.
Published in the United States by Alfred A. Knopf,
a division of Penguin Random House LLC, New York, and distributed
in Canada by Penguin Random House Canada Limited, Toronto.

www.aaknopf.com

Knopf, Borzoi Books, and the colophon
are registered trademarks of Penguin Random House LLC.

Grateful acknowledgment is made to Farrar, Straus and Giroux for permission
to reprint an excerpt from "One Art" from *Poems* by Elizabeth Bishop.
Copyright © 2011 by The Alice H. Methfessel Trust.
Publisher's Note and compilation copyright © 2011 by Farrar, Straus and Giroux.
Reprinted by permission of Farrar, Straus and Giroux. All Rights Reserved.

Library of Congress Cataloging-in-Publication Data
Names: Styron, Rose, author.
Title: Beyond this harbor : adventurous tales of the heart / Rose Styron.
Description: First edition. | New York : Alfred A. Knopf, 2023.
Identifiers: LCCN 2022046087 (print) | LCCN 2022046088 (ebook) |
ISBN 9780525659020 (hardcover) | ISBN 9780525659037 (ebook)
Subjects: LCSH: Styron, Rose. | Poets, American—Biography. |
Human rights workers—United States—Biography. | Styron, William, 1925–2006—Family.
Classification: LCC PS3569.T89 Z46 2023 (print) | LCC PS3569.T89 (ebook) |
DDC 811/.54 [B]—dc23/eng/20230103
LC record available at https://lccn.loc.gov/2022046087
LC ebook record available at https://lccn.loc.gov/2022046088

All photographs are from the author's collection.

Front- and spine-of-jacket image by Kilimanjaro STUDIOz / Alamy; back-of-jacket images:
(clockwise, from top) Rose Styron by Jeanna Shepard. Courtesy of Jeanna Shepard and the
Vineyard Gazette; Amnesty International march, courtesy of the author; Styron family by
Peter Simon; Rose and William Styron, courtesy of the author
Jacket design by Jenny Carrow

Manufactured in the United States of America

First Edition

For our four extraordinary, loving children:
Susanna, Paola, Tom, and Alexandra
and for their splendid, caring children:
Emma, Lilah, Tavish, Tommy, Lulu, Gus, Huck, and Sky

Contents

1 Chile · 3

2 Baltimore and Beyond · 20

3 Meeting Bill: Before and After · 46

4 Settling in Roxbury · 66

5 Roxbury Years · 91

6 Buying the Vineyard House · 95

7 Friendships · 102

8 Roman Holiday with Family · 122

9 Nat Turner, Frankfurt, Moscow, Uzbekistan · 128

10 Amnesty International · 143

11 More Wildlife Adventures · 168

12 The Council on Foreign Relations · 175

13 Reebok and Human Rights Watch and Amnesty · 181

14 My Orwellian Year · 196

15 Intrigue in Eastern Europe · 216

16 The Best of Friends: Kay Graham,
   "Les Girls," Mike Wallace, and Art Buchwald · 227

17 Poetry's Return, Belfast, Doolin, Dublin · 239

18 The Women's Refugee Commission
    Trip to Bosnia   ·   250

19 Impromptu Dinner Parties, Martha's Vineyard,
    and Havana   ·   258

20 Bill's Second Depression   ·   276

21 Bill's Burial and Memorial   ·   295

22 Past Missions and Moving Forward   ·   302

23 Selling Roxbury, Life on the Vineyard Full-Time   ·   312

24 Vineyard Celebrations   ·   328

    Acknowledgments   ·   333

BEYOND THIS HARBOR

1

Chile

TWO WEEKS THAT CHANGED MY LIFE, from being a poet, wife, and mother to becoming an activist, occurred starting before New Year's and in early January 1974. My oldest daughter, Susanna, and I found ourselves in a hotel swimming pool on the outskirts of Santiago, Chile, tossing a big red beach ball around with some new Chilean women friends. As far as anyone knew, we were two innocent American tourists, unaware that we'd chosen the saddest time in Chile's history to do our vacationing there. At least that was the impression I hoped we were making on the government agents who were no doubt spying on us. I feared that if they discovered our true reason for being there, my daughter's and my lives, and those of our new Chilean friends, might be in serious peril.

Four years earlier, in free and open elections, the people of Chile had chosen Salvador Allende, a medical doctor and Marxist, as their president. Hoping to cure some of the country's chronic economic woes and narrow the huge gap between its very wealthy elite and its very poor citizens, Allende nationalized banks and the copper mines, and raised wages for the working class. This made him many enemies among Chile's business elite.

In the United States, meanwhile, President Nixon's national security advisor, Henry Kissinger, determined that a Marxist government in Latin America could not be tolerated. The CIA, which had been carrying out covert operations in Chile since the 1960s, helped to instigate a military coup. That coup came on the fateful date of September 11, 1973, when General Augusto Pinochet led a swift, brutal U.S.-backed takeover of the government. President Allende died in the siege of La Moneda, the seat of government and presidential palace in the capital city of Santiago. Pinochet's junta launched its "dirty war"—a vicious reign of terror against anyone in Chile, foreigner or citizen, accused of participating in, supporting, or just being possibly sympathetic to the Allende government.

Allende's cabinet members vanished into torture centers spread out around the country and as far away as the Chilean Antarctic Territory. Tens of thousands of others whom the new junta accused of being "dissidents" (a new term then was "the disappeared"), including many students and artists, some of them Americans, were among them. Not long after the coup in Chile, I got a phone call from Ginetta Sagan, a senior figure at London-based Amnesty International, an organization I had joined in 1969. Ginetta told me that First Lady Hortensia Allende was to speak at the UN in February 1974, and I'd been chosen by Amnesty International to go to Chile and bring back all the data I could gather on Allende's ministers who had been killed or were imprisoned since the coup. This information would substantiate Mrs. Allende's report to the UN. I was also to seek the whereabouts of artists and American students arrested and dragged into the infamous Estadio Nacional de Chile, the huge soccer stadium in Santiago that the junta had converted into a detention camp.

Why did they choose me to go? I was a poet and mother, married to the novelist William Styron, not a secret agent. But that was why, I guess. I could plausibly pose as an innocent American tourist, just taking in the sights—unlikely as it was that anyone sane would choose to vacation in Chile at that moment. I agreed almost instantly. Since joining Amnesty, I had helped to monitor the status of political prisoners on other continents and raise public pressure to free them. I'd met Ginetta in 1972 at a Paris conference where Amnesty launched its Campaign for the Abolition of Torture. This would be my first undercover work for the organization. I had no sense of fear. If I had realized how dangerous it might be, I would not have taken my daughter along.

Ginetta flew to New York from San Francisco where she then lived with her American husband to meet with me, brief me, and give me names and contact numbers to memorize. She was tiny—her nickname was Topolino (Little Mouse)—but she had a lion's heart. She was a teenager in Milan during World War II when the Black Brigades of Mussolini executed her Catholic father and sent her Jewish mother to die in Auschwitz. At seventeen, Ginetta became a runner and messenger for the anti-Fascist resistance. Before she was captured and thrown in prison, where she was raped and tortured for forty-five days, she helped some three hundred Jews flee from Italy to the safety of Switzerland.

One night a guard tossed a loaf of bread into her cell; inside was a matchbox and a note from the resistance that said, *"Coraggio! Lavoriamo per te."* ("Courage! We are working for you.") Two German defectors helped her escape to France. The matchbox and the word *Coraggio* became the symbol of Amnesty International, and *Matchbox* became the name of the first Amnesty publication. Ginetta married an American doctor, Leonard Sagan, moved to California, and helped found an Amnesty chapter in San Francisco. Soon seventy-four were founded across the United States. She remained hugely important to the human rights movement up to her death in 2000.

I was also briefed by Bill Wipfler, who was head of the Latin American division of the World Council of Churches. He gave me contacts among the clergy in Chile. Clergy of all faiths were the only group in Chile openly challenging the Pinochet regime. By October 1973 they'd organized the interfaith Comité de Cooperación para la Paz en Chile (Committee of Cooperation for Peace in Chile), later reorganized as La Vicaría de la Solidaridad (Vicariate of Solidarity). At increasing risk to their immunity—in an extremely Catholic country, the junta had to treat priests, bishops, and others very carefully—they were pursuing every legal means available to find people who'd disappeared and try to get them released, as well as putting moral pressure on the government to cease its brutal activities.

One drawback to my going was that although I'd learned some Spanish in high school, I did not speak it well. But Susanna, who was seventeen, had spent several months in Spain. She was a savvy teenager, a freshman at Yale studying Latin American history. Her language skills saved me more than once from getting my contacts or us into major trouble.

Up until then, I almost always traveled with Bill, often annually on vacation with the children to Paris or the Caribbean. I had been involved with Amnesty since late 1968, but had not planned a significant trip without Bill out of North America. Before leaving I spoke to my fine friend Felicia Montealegre, Leonard Bernstein's wife. Felicia was a Chilean actress. Her sister Nancy was married to a wealthy businessman and politician, Arturo Alessandri, who had more than one former president of Chile on his family tree. He was one of the leading conservatives in the country and well-connected to the new regime.

"I'll give you a large bolt of fabric my sister wants for curtains," Felicia said. "You take it with you. I'll call her husband and ask him to pick you up at the airport and take you to their house for lunch. When people see him picking you up and know you're attached to him, it'll be good protection for you."

Susanna and I arrived at the Santiago airport on New Year's Day. Felicia's brother-in-law met us there in a sporty red convertible, which we loaded up with our luggage and the big bolt of cloth sticking up next to Susanna in the rear seat. Arturo drove us to his large house with beautiful walled gardens. He was a most gracious host. We had a splendid lunch. Might he have given us a different reception had he known the real purpose of our visit? Over lunch, I expressed cautious interest in what was going on politically in Chile.

"You people in the U.S. have heard it all wrong," he insisted. "There's no trouble here. There was a flare-up in September, but everything has quieted down now. Things are wonderful with the government. However, Santiago is still rather a mess. You may want to spend a few days here, but then why don't you come join me and Nancy at our estate on the lake? I'm leaving for there tonight. You can come with me, or join us in a few days."

"How nice!" I said. "We have a couple of friends to meet here in Santiago, but maybe we'll take you up on it."

"Great. Come next week and stay as long as you like." He handed me a business card. "This is my own travel agency. It's right around the corner from your hotel. Just go see them and they'll make all the arrangements. I'll mention you to them."

From there, after appreciative goodbyes, Susanna and I went to our hotel. It was in the center of the city—as it happened, it looked across the way at La Moneda, still scarred from the bombs and fires of a few months before. The city was under martial law. The streets were full of armed soldiers and there were very few civilians about. A week earlier, an Italian tourist had been shot and killed just outside our hotel. The city was quiet, tense. After we checked in, I went out trying to contact the people whose names were in my head. I could not find the initial few. The first person to befriend us was the wife of Samuel Araya, a Methodist minister, and the head of Santiago's Theological Institute. Not long after our visit, he would be arrested while teaching a class there, and held for some time in the Estadio. His name had been given to me by the World Council of Churches. His wife was a quiet activist. When I explained our mission, she said, "Okay, I trust you. I'll help you get in touch with my women friends whose husbands have all disappeared." I think she trusted me because I had Susanna with me, and maybe because I seemed naive but determined.

As foreign visitors so soon after the coup, we knew that government agents were monitoring our activities. Our hotel room was most likely bugged, so we would play music or news reports loudly to muffle our voices when we chatted. But we knew we were being watched outside as well. Next to the hotel was a small parking lot where blue government-run taxis lined up. Whenever we came out, one taxi drove forward to pick us up, while another man went to a telephone that was on a pole at the back of the lot and made a call—no doubt reporting that we had left the hotel. Foreigners and dignitaries from other governments stayed in that hotel, so the regime kept close tabs on the comings and goings.

To evade our driver from the hotel, who was surely spying on us, Susanna and I would have him take us to the large department store where we'd duck out on him, go to a back door, and take another cab to our true destination, possibly an appointment with the underground, the clergy. The latter we met in the basement of a Catholic Church–owned building, where they were making copies of all the documentation they had been gathering on the people who had disappeared, including the death certificates of those who'd been assassinated. They hoped we'd be able to smuggle these out of the country.

Mrs. Araya came up with an ingenious scheme for our meeting with her friends, out in the open in an innocuous-looking setting. This was how, a few days later, Susanna and I found ourselves in that little resort swimming pool. The beach ball was a signal to the women Mrs. Araya had arranged for us to meet: the wives of a detained general, an ambassador, a senator, and a defense minister. One by one, in disguise—wigs, hats, glasses, padded bathing suits—they got into the pool to play with us. As we tossed the ball around they shifted their positions, so that the one nearest to me could whisper details of the prison in which her husband was sequestered, how he was being tortured, and his current condition. Amnesty had warned me to write nothing down, but to commit their stories to memory. I instantly asked each one to repeat whatever she told me to Susanna, whose Spanish was impeccable, as was her memory.

Once in the pool I discovered that Isabel Letelier spoke perfect English. Her husband, Orlando, had first been Allende's ambassador to the United States, and then returned to Chile to be his minister of defense. He advised Allende to leave Santiago and not to trust General Pinochet, but Allende didn't believe him. The army had always backed the president, he declared. He was an innocent in his own way. The coup came just a few days later. Allende died and Letelier was arrested. He would be held in various prisons, including a year in cold Punta Arenas (the Chilean gateway to Antarctica), originally founded as a penal colony.

Susanna and I didn't know it, but as we were tossing the beach ball around in the pool, we were being watched not only by government agents but also by people on our side. A group called the Chicago Commission of Inquiry into the Status of Human Rights in Chile was staying at the hotel. A young Chicago journalist named Frank Teruggi Jr. and his New York friend Charles Horman had been arrested soon after the coup. Because of their work for a small magazine called *FIN* (*Fuente Norteamericano de Información*, or *North American Information Source*)—they were accused of being foreign troublemakers. A group from the commission had come to Santiago with Frank

Teruggi Sr. to try to find his son and Charles Horman. Among them were Father Gerard Grant, a Jesuit priest from Loyola University who was vice president of the World Federalist Movement, and a graduate student named Joanne Fox-Przeworski. Joanne had lived in Chile previously and had many friends and contacts there. Knowing their rooms were bugged, they would sit on the roof of the hotel to talk. As Joanne remembers it now, "We were having a meeting on the roof, and I look down and see this attractive blonde tourist in the swimming pool with her daughter, throwing a ball back and forth. I'm thinking, 'Jesus! Who in their right mind would come to Chile for a vacation at this time?'"

Meanwhile, Joanne's group, the Chicago Commission of Inquiry, was meeting with the underground and planning to smuggle out the same sort of documents I was. They told her they were working with another woman from America, but didn't tell her my name, and she didn't make the connection with the blonde tourist in the pool. The Vicaría's plan was that they'd divide the documents among us, and we'd all try to leave Chile with the copied documents hidden on our persons. That way, even if some of us were caught, at least a significant portion of the information would get out.

It was all quite James Bond, and we Americans were amateurs. Joanne remembers helping Father Grant photograph documents in his hotel room. "We were such poor undercover agents that we were using the flash and not realizing that anyone outside could see it. It was so stupid." As I became aware of how serious this mission was, I also became increasingly concerned about the risks—not so much for myself as for Susanna and the people we were getting information from, who may have been placing their lives in our hands. As we gathered more stories, I kept word markers in a tiny notebook. There was simply too much detail to commit to memory. I developed my own private code for these notes, just in case it somehow got into the wrong hands. When I returned home I couldn't decipher half of what I'd scribbled, but it helped me to remember.

One day at the clergy's urging we took a taxi to the beautiful resort city of Valparaíso. The idea was to spend a day away from Santiago acting like tourists, while the Vicaría continued copying documents for us. But the underground in Valparaíso were alerted that we were coming, and hourly, persons met us on the street or the waterfront or in a café and surreptitiously gave us information on what their government and ours were doing. They showed us three stately tall ships docked in the harbor that were being used as political prisons. And beyond them were U.S. Navy ships, indicating not only our military support for the coup but the CIA's covert activities to prepare the way for it—a national truck strike that Kissinger had engineered—which shocked me. In those early months of Pinochet's regime, we Americans did not yet know our government's involvement. My disgust with Kissinger and Nixon would grow as I learned how they secured and supported the Pinochet regime with economic aid, were silent on the atrocities, and refused asylum to Chilean refugees.

The stories Susanna, I, and many others heard and brought out of Chile outraged and sickened people of good conscience around the world. I related some of them in articles for the *New York Review of Books,* and also for *Ramparts* and other publications. There was the lecturer from Argentina and his wife, both held in the Estadio. She was stripped, assaulted, and searched by soldiers looking for "dynamite in her vagina" while she listened to the cries of her husband being beaten nearby. At one point she saw him hung by his arms, naked, being given shocks with an electric goad. Paulina Altamirano, the wife of the leader of Allende's Socialist Party, who was "the most wanted man in Chile" until he managed to escape to Cuba, was arrested and forced to listen to faked tape recordings of her children screaming in agony.

Víctor Jara, the teacher, poet, songwriter, and political activist, was arrested on September 12 and dragged to the Estadio. His captors gave him a guitar and commanded him to play while they broke his fingers. He bravely began to sing "Venceremos" ("We Shall Prevail"), a song of resistance. An officer put a pistol to his head, but Víctor kept singing. Some said they cut out his tongue first. The officer fired, and Víctor fell dead on the stadium steps. They strung his body up as an example to others. In fact, he did become an example, but not the kind they wanted: To this day, he is a hero to the people of Chile and around the world, an example of courage in the face of government brutality. He wrote one last song in the Estadio before his murder, scribbled on a scrap of paper. "Ay, Canto, Qué Mal Me Sales!"

describes the horrors Jara witnessed in his few days there, the killings, and the despairing captives throwing themselves to their deaths from the stands. A fellow captive smuggled it out in his shoe. I was given a similar scrap of paper, blue, with minute writing edge to edge, also smuggled out. Its author was a very young man. I quoted it in my article for the *New York Review of Books*:

In case this anguished message arrives soon in the hands of anyone in my family, I am going to tell what they did with us since Friday the week of January 18, 1974, when civil personnel in the presence of Sr. Guillermo Alvarez K., delegate from CORFO [the Chilean government's economic development agency], "invited" four of us to take part in an interrogation which would last "two hours." We tranquilly got into vehicles, cream and blue . . . They proceeded to put adhesive tape over our eyes and there we understood that it was a kidnapping . . . In a closed truck, blindfolded and tied, we traveled two or three hours . . . I heard the noise of weapons, which chilled me to my soul. I said good-bye to myself with my eyes full of tears for all my loved ones. I thought they were going to shoot us because they put us against wooden beams with our hands up and our legs spread behind. I didn't know what to think. My God, but why do they do this? . . . Monday they took us in a small truck . . . we went down a stairway . . . hooded, our hands tied behind. They made us undress, tied us again, put us in small cells . . . and the inferno of terror began. The first one they took to the torture table emitted not screams, but howls. My body trembled with horror; one could feel the blows and hear the voice of the torturer. "Who painted it? Who went?" . . . I spent many hours there listening to the tortures . . . My turn came. They tied me to a table . . . They passed cables over my naked body. They wet me and began to apply currents to all parts of my body and the interrogator did not ask me, he assured me, "You did this thing." I denied the monstrosities and the blows began to my abdomen, ribs, chest, testicles, etc. I don't know for how long they massacred me, but with the blows in my chest, my throat and bronchial tubes filled up, and it was drowning me. I was dying. They were laughing but assured me they were not kidding and threw acid on my toes.

They stuck me with needles. I was numb. They took me down. I
couldn't breathe . . .

There were secret prisons and detention camps throughout Chile.
At Chacabuco, a mine in the northern desert of Antofagasta (tem-
peratures 110°F by day, 32°F at night), nearly two thousand middle-
level Allende officials, professionals, and relatives of government
ministers were held. Among them was the musician and poet Ángel
Parra, who would survive and become a spokesperson for Chilean
political exiles around the world. At the women's prison in Santiago,
electricity applied to the gums induced delirium; applied to the uterus
of a pregnant woman, it caused brain lesions and miscarriages. Young
pregnant girls had their nipples and genitals burned, their hair pulled
out. Teenagers detained in a concentration camp near Santiago were
subjected to sexual assault, electric shock, and burnings. I was horrified and disgusted. I could not have imagined during my protected,
privileged life such personally inflicted brutality. I have been preoc-
cupied with questions about the mind of the torturer ever since.

When PEN, the international writers' organization of which Bill and
I were members, heard that I was going to Chile, they asked me to do
a mission for them too. On September 23, at the height of the coup,
the Nobel Prize–winning Chilean poet and political activist Pablo
Neruda had died of heart failure. He was nearing seventy and had
been ill with cancer, but there was also the sense that the coup simply
broke his heart. He'd been a progressive all his life, a supporter of
Allende, and for a while he'd been Allende's ambassador to France.
Pinochet banned any public demonstrations at Neruda's funeral, but
thousands defied him and poured into the streets in what was the
first public protest of the new regime. In the initial days of the coup,
government agents had ransacked his house, during which he'd made
the wonderful statement, "Look around. There's only one thing of
danger for you here—poetry." Maybe that was how the story spread
that Neruda's widow, Matilde Urrutia, buried his last manuscript in
concrete on a particular street corner. PEN asked me to try to recover
it and smuggle it out. I did go and look, but saw no signs of fresh

concrete, and nobody in Chile could give me any information. Either the story was a canard, or that manuscript remains buried there still.

One day, when Susanna and I returned to our hotel from one of our fake shopping trips, the elevator operator stopped at the fifth floor instead of the eighth, where our room was. When I pointed out his error, he patronizingly replied, "Oh, Mrs. Horman, you forgot where your room is. It's there." He pointed. Curious, I knocked on the door. The family of Charles Horman, Frank Teruggi's friend, answered. The operator had mistaken me for Charles's wife. (Later, Sissy Spacek would portray her, and Jack Lemmon played Charles's father in Costa-Gavras's 1982 film *Missing*.) They were the only other Americans staying at the hotel.

Charles's body turned up at the city morgue soon after I met the Hormans. He had apparently been executed in the stadium some weeks earlier. So had his friend Frank Teruggi of Chicago.

After two weeks of meeting extraordinary people, hearing their stories, and witnessing incredible scenes, it was time for Susanna and me to leave so that we could get Mrs. Allende the information for her UN presentation. The underground was finishing up the copying of all the documents they wanted me to smuggle out. I had our tickets on a Braniff Airways flight in my pocket. This was when I was most frightened for my daughter. If I were caught, she would surely be arrested with me. And then what?

For our last day in Chile, a particularly gray one, we accepted an invitation to a lunch swim party at the home of the chief executive of the Ford Foundation outside Santiago. There would be other Americans there to provide some cover, and it seemed like a good place for the courier from the Vicaría, a young priest named Fernando Salas, to pass me the documents. Then we'd go collect our bags, check out, and fly away. Or so I hoped. So there I was, standing in a swimming pool again, roped into a conversation with an unattractive American I didn't know. I kept watching nervously for Fernando. Meanwhile, the taxi driver who had brought us loitered outside, keeping tabs on us as always. As time passed I began to fear that Fernando had been arrested. Were we next? Losing my cool, I made a snap decision to confide in our hostess, whom I'd instantly liked. She was very sympathetic to my mission, but also concerned.

"You might get picked up," she told me. "They watch us closely. Two of our guests were arrested here last week by the DINA [Pinochet's secret police]. But since they had registered with the American embassy on arrival, they were rescued by an official the next day. So not to worry."

But we hadn't registered with the embassy, I told her. Our government under Nixon was openly cooperative with the Pinochet regime. Alerting our embassy to our presence would have meant almost certain failure.

"Oh dear," she said. "Well, at least let me give you some pointers on how to hide the documents on your person, if your priest can get them to you."

She took me into a private room and presented me with a big leather bag that had a false bottom. "Leave now," she told me. "Go back to your hotel and get your things. Hide any documents in the bottom of the bag, or in your bosom under your bathing suit, with a shirt and sweater on top. Sew some into the hem of your skirt. Then go catch your flight and get out of Chile."

We couldn't wait any longer for Fernando. We got back into our government taxi and returned to the hotel. When we opened the door to our room, we saw it had been ransacked. Suitcases and drawers had been emptied. The room was an unbelievable mess. Our fears mounted. We began packing our bags. Suddenly, the closet door opened and a man stepped out. I thought my heart would fly out the top of my head. But it was Fernando, the brave and handsome young priest whom I will never forget. When he'd seen us drive off in a government taxi he decided it was too risky to follow us to the party, so he'd waited for us in our room instead. When the DINA men entered to search it, he jumped into the closet and was able to lock it somehow from the inside. My heart pounding, I took the documents from him. We stashed some in the bag, sewed some in my skirt, and hid the rest in my well-padded bosom. Then we bade Fernando goodbye and took our bags down to the desk.

"Oh, Mrs. Styron," the receptionist said, beaming. "You'll be happy to know we changed your Braniff ticket to LAN Chile, which only stops in Lima before New York. Much quicker!" Adrenaline rushing, I took the ticket and passed it to the farthest bellboy, with the travel agency's card Felicia Bernstein's brother-in-law had given me two weeks earlier. Pressing dollars in his hand, I said, "Hurry and change this back to Braniff, now." To the man behind the desk I said, "Oh, thanks anyway. But I must meet my friend at Braniff's lounge just before takeoff."

"He's not in Santiago," the receptionist replied.

"He's coming especially from the lake today to give me things to bring his sister in New York," I countered, inventing. Then I grabbed a large postcard from the desk and wrote, under his nose:

To Senator Edward Kennedy:
  Dear Teddy—leaving Santiago—see you in D.C. Friday—if I don't make it (ha! ha!) send a posse to Chile!

Bill and I had been friends with Teddy and all of the Kennedys for years. Teddy had no idea that I was on a mission to Chile, but I figured his name would give this man behind the counter pause. I asked him for a stamp. He read the postcard and looked extremely puzzled, as I'd hoped. When he turned and went behind a curtain to show it to a colleague, Susanna got the tickets from the bellboy. We made our getaway and fled to the airport. On our way out there, I was well aware that we were being tailed by government agents. We were also secretly being followed by new Chilean friends. There wouldn't be anything they could do to stop me being arrested, but at least they could let someone know.

In the terminal, there were two security lines, a male and a female official at the head of each, checking people's bags and persons before they passed through the metal detectors. Susanna cleverly pulled me out of the line as I was waiting apprehensively for a big woman to strip-search me. Susanna pulled me over to her line where a man was in charge. She later told me she had done that because she figured a man would not pat me down as vigorously as a woman would, and she knew I had secured the most important papers under my bathing suit top covered by two shirts and a jacket. Brilliant of her, again! We walked through the metal detector and ran to the gate where the Braniff plane was waiting. It looked beautiful—not least because Alexander Calder, our neighbor uphill in Roxbury, Connecticut, had painted it. A few months before, I'd seen an article in *Time* magazine about his having agreed to paint a Braniff jet with a big, colorful mural that had elements of the American flag and the sunrise in it, and here I was looking at it. "Oh boy," I thought, "Sandy's come to get us!"

Joanne Fox-Przeworski remembers seeing us again at the airport. In fact, she stood in line right beside us, also smuggling documents. Quite by happenstance, she had booked the same flight we had. She'd been instructed to hide her documents in the folder with her ticket. That way, when she raised her arms for the patdown, she'd be holding the documents away from her body. She thought it was terribly risky, and remembers her heart pounding like mad as she stood there, but it worked. Father Grant was also smuggling documents out, hidden under his hat and a toupee.

When we boarded the beautiful Sandy Calder jet, Susanna and I were seated in the last, windowless row. We had the two inner seats. The man who took the aisle seat, blocking us in, was clearly an agent, doubtless of DINA. We could not have escaped had we chosen to try. Susanna and I made a big show of chatting mindlessly about our Chilean vacation on the flight to Lima. We got off at the airport there for the layover before the announced reboarding—and locked ourselves in the ladies' room, where we stayed for two hours, until we were sure the plane (with our bags) had left for New York. We emerged to a nearly emptying terminal, no DINA agent in sight, and got ourselves a very late flight to Dallas.

I called unsuspecting Ted Kennedy from the Dallas airport and told him I was coming back from Chile and had sent him a postcard, suggesting we get together sometime soon to talk about my mission there. When we arrived the next day at JFK, he had sent a young assistant to meet me and asked me to come to Washington on the spot. I said goodbye to Susanna, who returned home to Connecticut after a memorable vacation. Wearing my old travel clothes, I accompanied Teddy's assistant to the event that he was attending. Little did I know it was a big formal party honoring Kissinger. Teddy greeted me, hugged me, and said, "Come with me, Henry Kissinger is arriving at the other end of this room." I looked around at everyone in formal clothes and protested, saying I did not wish to meet Kissinger. Teddy laughed and dragged me to the ramp where Kissinger would soon ascend. As I stood there, he came through a door below and shook the hands of everyone waiting to greet him. Flashbulbs flashing. Photographers recording. Near the top of the ramp, he met me and I refused to shake his hand—to his apparent consternation (but to the photographers' delight!).

Next morning I went to Teddy's office and talked with him about my trip, my disgust with Kissinger's American-led coup. He assured me that he would work to help its victims.

We were safely back in the United States with the precious documents from Chile for Mrs. Allende. She used the information in her speech at the UN. Hortensia and I met in New York and then in Paris at the French Bicentennial, where a musician played as we walked with my longtime mentor Sean McBride, Nobel laureate, founding member of Amnesty, and son of Maud Gonne. Hortensia and I kept in touch for years. I still treasure the glass Chilean compotes she gave me. I don't remember if Susanna and I ever did get our bags back. I am aware now that the mission to Chile was a turning point in my life.

Returning home from Chile in January 1974, I was truly upset that our government was refusing asylum to refugees from Chile and other Latin American "tyrannies" because of Kissinger's doctrine of supporting those regimes to prevent the spread of Communism in the Southern Hemisphere. At that time, a refugee was defined by law as a person who had fled his country because of a well-founded fear of persecution from, essentially, a Communist or left-wing regime. I was told that the only way to change this policy was to persuade the attorney general to use what was called his parole authority to go outside normal immigration procedures. Gerald Ford's attorney general was Edward Levi, formerly the president of the University of Chicago, with a reputation for intelligence and integrity. Ford appointed Levi to restore public confidence in the Department of Justice, which was disgraced after Watergate. My sister-in-law and good friend Amelie, in Bethesda, knew Levi's wife, and I brazenly wrote to her, saying I would like to have a few minutes with her husband. She arranged it.

Thus one day I found myself sitting on a bench at the end of a long, wide corridor with a bright blue carpet leading to the attorney general's office door. I didn't know what I'd say to him. I was winging it. When I was called, I walked the mile of carpet and went through the door. There was the huge desk of the attorney general, with flags and a seal of the United States behind it. A slight, even-featured, balding man in his sixties sat at the desk wearing a bow tie and puffing on a pipe. The only other person in the room was a note-taking special assistant, a young attorney I was not introduced to, seated in the left corner.

Mr. Levi asked what he could do for me, and I started to talk. I talked and talked for about an hour. Levi had exercised his parole authority to allow into this country what grew to be some 150,000 Vietnamese, along with Cambodians and Laotians who were at high risk of being persecuted or killed after Saigon fell because of their association with the United States during its war in Indochina. I wanted to convince Levi that he should use the same authority for victims of the right-wing regime in Chile. I realized I had given him a thousand details he didn't need, about each prisoner and where some were and how they should be brought to the United States.

Mr. Levi had not interrupted me or questioned me once. When I stopped talking he said, "Well, Mrs. Styron, you go home. I will talk to General Chapman, the commissioner of the Immigration and Naturalization Service, and I'll let you know if there's something we can do."

I went home to Roxbury thinking nothing would come of it. Around eleven o'clock that night I got a call from the young man who'd been taking notes.

"The attorney general was very impressed," he told me. "He's talking to General Chapman right now. I think some good may come of this."

(Ten years later, at the home of my next-door neighbors, Sheldon and Lucy Hackney, that young man and I would meet again. I was taken aback when he asked me how Isabel Letelier was faring, and I wondered how he knew I kept up with the widow of Orlando Letelier, who was killed by a car bomb in Washington in 1976. Mark Wolf and I have been co-conspirators ever since. He became a crisis-advising federal judge and also the chief judge of the U.S. district court in Massachusetts. He is also the much-traveled founder of the

International Criminal Court, a frequent headliner in the *Boston Globe* for cases such as Whitey Bulger's, a lover of poetry, and one of my favorite tennis opponents.)

I alerted Teddy Kennedy about my talk with Mr. Levi. Teddy had just gotten a bill through Congress called the Kennedy Amendment, stopping U.S. arms sales to Pinochet's military. He told me he was now ready to develop a parole program to provide asylum in the United States for Chilean political prisoners and took the matter up on the floor of the Congress.

Teddy's program got a number of Chilean political prisoners released. He was Pinochet's implacable enemy through the general's long reign, and Pinochet hated him. When Teddy made a brief visit to Chile in 1986, Pinochet supporters pelted his motorcade with eggs. But the great majority of Chileans loved him and came out in throngs to show it. In 2008, the year before Teddy's death, President Michelle Bachelet, Chile's first woman president (elected twice, the daughter of one of the women who met me in the Santiago swimming pool and gave me valuable information on Pinochet's prisoners of conscience), went to Teddy's Hyannis Port home and awarded him the Order to the Merit of Chile, Chile's top civilian honor, for being "such a friend to Chile in our hour of need." Michelle became the UN's High Commissioner for Human Rights.

For my part, getting in touch with Teddy personally the day I returned from Chile was the beginning of our working together on human rights issues for the rest of our lives.

2

Baltimore and Beyond

WHEN I WATCHED Hurricane Sandy break up the Atlantic City Boardwalk piece by piece and carry it out to sea, memories of childhood summer weeks visiting my grandmother floated in on a tide of nostalgia. The first lines of the old song "On the Boardwalk (In Atlantic City)" returned. It was in August 1934, when I was six, that I remember being packed off to join tiny, nearsighted Nanny, Mom's mom, at the Hotel President for the second August when my older siblings and parents traveled out west. The Hotel President was some distance from the elegant Claridge's and Chalfonte hotels, where high tea reigned. After breakfast each morning, Nanny would let me help her arrange the smooth, mysteriously white marked tiles for her daily daylong game of mahjong with her women friends. Then she'd give me a purse full of coins and send me off: "Go have a good time on the boardwalk, dear. Come back for lunch. And don't go near the water!"

I'd immediately buzz the elevator and wait for its handsome dark-haired sixteen-year-old operator, Dick McCormick, to appear. What a crush I had on him! He took me to the basement, where I walked carefully over the slippery white tiles and out the wide opening to the beach, glancing at the forbidden ocean and the handsome lifeguards, then trotting up the wooden steps to paradise.

Money in my pocket, freedom in my heart, maybe devil in my eye, free of Baltimore supervision (protective housekeeper, cook, sister, brother, parents), I'd begin my magic morning. If there were other children on the boardwalk, I was unaware of them. They were down at the beach. First stop: Fralinger's Salt Water Taffy. Second stop: Skee-Ball, the game I thought I excelled at, getting the little ball into the "100" hole over and over. Third: the Steel Pier, a structure containing delicious terror. Heading down a narrow stairway, I'd enter the vast world of Davy Jones's Locker, an underground aquarium with its bold, enormous undersea creatures that seemed to emerge, then sweep suddenly toward me. My nose pressed to the glass tank waterscapes, I'd invariably recoil. Then, climbing to the top of the pier, I'd watch breathlessly as one young woman, then another, snapped her heels and plunged on her steed into the ocean far below.

Afterward I'd walk farther down the boardwalk to the Million Dollar Pier, where I watched ballroom dancing, the waltzers' gowns not nearly as beautiful as my mother's. (I often helped her pack the satin and velvet gowns in her steamer trunk for voyages with Daddy.) Occasionally I'd drop in at an auction house, a bit baffled by the vigorous bidding for carpets, jewelry, and paintings. (Who would want them? I wondered. Were some of them Aunt Sadie's? Years later, I heard that one auctioneer had fleeced her after she gave the auction house all her jewelry to sell. They never paid her.)

Before lunch with Nanny, I was sure to save enough time to climb up into the high Elephant House, imagining I was a conqueror of some far-off continent.

An hour later, more coins in my pocket after lunch, I'd set off again. Nanny apparently had full confidence in my ability to read, write, make change (and have judgment?). Perhaps I'd ride in a scratchy-seated rolling chair pushed by a bending gentleman of color, and attend a movie (no PG-13 or X ratings then) that made little sense to a six-year-old, but had awesome scenes, like Hedy Lamarr rising naked out of a small pond in *Ecstasy*. Or Clark Gable and Claudette Colbert in *It Happened One Night*. I was scared to admit I was frightened by the shadow of the man standing behind the window shade. Perhaps because at three I was certain I'd be kidnapped like the Lindbergh baby. I bought the movie ticket with the cash Nanny had given me to go see Shirley Temple in *Baby Take a Bow*. Shirley Temple, my age exactly, bored me. Luckily, no gambling casinos had opened yet!

My trusting grandmother was never excoriated by my parents. Somehow I knew my screwy adventures should remain my own heady secret as I hoped for another visit with Nanny the following summer.

I was a privileged child. I knew I was loved and protected. In fact overprotected at home in Baltimore following the Lindbergh kidnapping. The search and progress of the case were on the radio day after day, my parents and siblings talking about it often. At three, I pulled the sheet tightly over my head at night, lying flat so the man who'd raise the ladder to my window wouldn't see me.

At six, Atlantic City was my ticket to the circus. I attended alone, safe each day, my confidence in life's adventures to come burgeoning. I decided I wanted to live by the sea, and travel, just like my favorite fictional heroines, Susannah of the Yukon and Beverly Gray, who went to the Orient, far beyond local super-sleuth Nancy Drew. They and Atlantic City surely set me on a path to becoming a peripatetic Pollyanna and nature nut. The Vineyard Sound beyond the windows over my desk as I write this augurs adventures still to come.

Decades later, despite living through and witnessing some shocking and seriously disturbing events, I'm still an optimist. Except when I'm reading that an enormous percentage of Americans oppose gun control, champion restricted voting rights, support racism, encourage violence, pretend lies are as moral as truth.

BALTIMORE

The steep dark stairs to the attic, forbidden
tempted when I was let's say three
my first escape from a mother-perfect order,
silver laid tables and fresh cut vases,
the breakfront glittering with china from England
and always "someone to watch over me . . ."

The door stood open. I made it to the top—
each bare foot on each steep stair—
piled books, peeled suitcase,

gray tinted photographs
corseted fashionplate sterner than Grandmother
Father in knickers, and a child not me
in ruffles, corkscrew curls
forgotten as the world below.

—from "Out of Doors"

I was born Rose Burgunder in Baltimore in 1928, ten years younger than my sister, Ann, and eight years younger than my brother, Bernei, "B," whom I followed everywhere, outdoors and in, even concealing myself on the cellar stairs to watch him play trains and Ping-Pong with the older boys. Because Ann and Bernei were so much older than I, academic stars going off to college early and traveling in the summer with our parents, I was for long stretches of time the only child at home. I had many schoolmates, and a best friend, Amelie, but at home I was left to my own devices.

My parents' bookcases were full of Rabindranath Tagore and Edna St. Vincent Millay, Rudyard Kipling and Robert Louis Stevenson. I read through shelves and shelves. (I saw many of the same books, including contemporary nonfiction, in Hemingway's library at his home outside Havana in 2000.) Weeknights, my father brought home books for me from the book department of the family's department store, Kann's (from which the Kann's Kapital Kandy I loved came as well). He would tell me to read the books carefully with clean hands so he could take them back the following week to sell—it was the entire Nancy Drew series, as I had the Muriel Denison's adventures of *Susannah of the Yukon* and my favorite, the Beverly Gray series. They whetted my appetite for travel early, and for sleuthing. I also devoured all the Hardy Boys books, which I loved. Albert Payson Terhune's wild kingdom was mine. How I longed to meet a grizzly! Earlier still, the book *Bertram and His Funny Animals* captivated me. These fantasy creatures appeared when Bertram's dad went off to Omaha on business. Have Bertram and Beverly disappeared forever? How lucky I was that my big siblings taught me to read at four years old.

As a small child, I took wonderful daily walks with Florence Small, my nanny from the Carolinas who spoke Gullah. She had raised my brother and sister, and following the Lindbergh kidnapping decided to sleep on the carpet outside my bedroom door at night. (My room was too small for an extra bed.) Florence embodied comfort and devotion, and I felt especially safe when she was near me. We'd traverse our Windsor Hills neighborhood past Winnie Buck Clemson's house on our way down to the Mill Race near Gwynns Falls. I loved the rushing water. Along the way, Florence picked dandelions for dandelion wine, and she encouraged me to search for four-leaf clovers. I was jubilant on finding one or two. She made the wine in my small bedroom closet. The floor below a shelf of folded clothing harbored our bounty. Did my little dresses smell of fermenting dandelions? Florence made me promise not to tell Mom, and I never did. My training in secret-keeping stood me in good stead for Atlantic City, and then, far in the future, for human rights work, and it prepared me for my life as a wife and mother, with everyone (husband, children, myself) keeping their own secrets, which was fine with me as long as it didn't endanger the children or our marriage.

Florence was gone before I turned five. I did not understand what it meant when my mother said, "Florence died." I had just seen her. How could someone be here, taking me on an afternoon walk, and then disappear? Death finally made sense when I came home from my first week in kindergarten to find our fluffy dog Tango lying motionless beside the driveway. In that moment, I remembered my bewilderment when another dog, long, sleek, brown, lay by the walkway along Bateman Avenue when Florence had pushed me in my carriage. I was less than two years old. The creature's huge gold eyes were open, like glass marbles sparkling in the sun.

At age four I could read and write and draw with colored crayons. I so wanted to go to school. Mom took me for a brief pre-kindergarten visit. (No preschool existed then.) When the kindergartners were drawing, I was given yellow and purple crayons. Why not green and blue? I drew a land-and-sky scene, but fretted. I had no blue crayon for the sky. I tentatively overlaid the purple with yellow around the cloud rim and was surprised when the teacher praised me for my "originality," which I guessed meant success. I could barely wait for the coming September.

Kindergarten was pure happiness. Months of pleasure, until my April birthday. That day, my teacher taught our class to cut out spoons from folded paper. I was left-handed, but like all kids then, I was being trained to use my right hand for tools like scissors. (I eventually used my right hand for everything except my very favorite activities, such as tennis and writing.) I carefully followed my teacher's directions, folding the paper as she instructed, but I moved my paper into my lap and cut out a spoon shape in the skirt of my special cranberry-colored, white-sprigged birthday dress. Perhaps I was careless or momentarily confused. I had per-suaded my mother to let me wear

Rose at four.

the dress to school that morning. How could I face her? As was her noble tradition, she said no reproving words. The shame still simmers!

My childhood memories appear as a collage that links the past to the present. It feels good. I long for my uncomplicated devotion to romance. (I wondered for half my life what happened to my first kindergarten crush, Russell Hicks. I did meet him again at my fiftieth school reunion. He was definitely still attractive.) One day Russell, age five, was in the midst of a snowball fight with Alfred Schleinus, who I didn't like. I stepped in front of Russell to defend him and was smacked with an ice ball in my left eye. Russell tried to comfort me. Off I went to the hospital. I recovered quickly, but forever after had a weaker left eye and a slightly drooping lid, which I was not aware of until high school. My first sacrifice in the pursuit of love.

Another kindergarten memory is of being asked to sit next to a German refugee girl, Gisela Cloos, for an hour each day to help her learn English. I wasn't entirely happy about that, though I felt I should be. She was tall, thin, pale, blonde, shy. She did not play with the rowdy rest of us, and I never felt close to her. Twelve years later, we both turned up in the freshman class at Wellesley and greeted each other in smiling recognition.

At one hundred years old, my brother, Bernei, confirmed my

Baltimore, Windsor Hills home: sister Ann, brother Bernei, and Rose, 1935.

memory of a spring afternoon when he offered me as a pawn to a magician entertaining at our school. He was a junior or senior and I was in first or second grade. The magician asked for a volunteer and I was it. I was so proud. The magician, who waved his hands over my head, made me invisible. After the claps and my reentry, Bernei said delightedly, "Okay, Rose, tell us where you went." And I replied, to his intense disappointment, "I just disappeared . . ." I knew I'd let him down and was crushed.

During my eleventh summer, my mother decided I was old enough to take a trip with her and my big sister, Ann, and Ann's favorite cousin, Marjorie, from Philadelphia. To wondrous Mexico. I was thrilled. That year I had decided to be an artist, after two winters of weekly classes at the Maryland Institute of Art.

On July 13, I wrote in my travel diary, "Our first stop was Chapulte-pec Castle, which means Grasshopper Hill. We saw beautiful paintings and rooms where Moctezuma had lived. We then drove around the market and residential sections. The tree where Cortes wept is a huge, magnificent thing. Then the Palace of Fine Arts in which we saw some of the finest murals and paintings in Mexico. Orozco and Rivera painted the murals." Little did I know that decades later I would meet Gabriel García Márquez at Chapultepec Castle while attending the Bertrand Russell Tribunal. That was a pivotal experience in my life, following this eye-opening childhood introduction to travel and unfamiliar culture and history and art.

In Mexico City I was lost in the wonder of what I saw. My mother was constantly turning around on the street and saying, "Hurry up, Rose." After visits to silver-shining Taxco and touring in the flower-laden boats of Xochimilco, I said to my mother, "I want more than *anything* to meet Diego Rivera." Publicly, Mom could work magic. We were somehow invited to his studio. (I wonder now, was that Frida Kahlo walking across the courtyard?)

I wrote in my diary on July 22, "Went to San Angel for lunch and then to see famous artist Diego Rivera. We waited for an hour in his room that is full of dolls, skulls, masks, dishes, and a few paintings. He finally came. He was very cordial and showed us his studio. There were beautiful and horrible pictures, big paper firecrackers about ten feet high in the shape of people, and historic pieces of stone and metal dug up in excavations."

My mother purchased a framed drawing for me that lived on the mantel over our Connecticut fireplace for decades and today resides in my Vineyard living room, atop a favorite desk from my mother's house, its value apparently skyrocketing. (Our only other artwork on display is by friends. Bill was adamant about not spending money on visual art. My parents' bronze animal sculptures catch the window light in son Tom's home still, and a few fine paintings by Vineyard artists I quietly bought for presents hang on daughter Alexandra's Brooklyn walls.)

As we were leaving his studio, the very large Mr. Rivera leaned down and shook my hand. "I hope someday you'll be as great a painter as I am," he intoned solemnly. I thought him wonderful, but told my mother I deemed him definitely too self-important.

Two days later, we visited Cholula, the city of 365 churches, one for each day of the year. I did not care for it at all. Too many churches.

Our Baltimore household was, I'm embarrassed to say now, might-

Diego Rivera drawing from studio visit,
Mexico, 1939.

ily enhanced by "the help," not at all like those in the film of that name. Annie Hill, our light-skinned, tall maid, was clearly one of Mother's best friends. Rosie Harris, the marvelous round cook, ruled the kitchen, bringing her quiet, frail daughter Little Rosie to sit from time to time. I wondered, when two or three, if my big sister, Ann, and I had been named for them. (I was actually named for my dad's mother, Rose, who had died before my birth.) Rosie would embrace me often and lovingly except when she was preparing dinner. If I wandered into her kitchen then, she more than once set a live lively lobster on the floor to scare me away. Once a week, Violet, also round and dark, came to wash and iron clothes in the basement. She'd hum as she washed and let me stand by the mangle or ironing board. I felt content, not minding in the least that I was not invited to join my brother, sister, and parents at the dining room dinner table. Every evening I ate with Annie in the pantry at an earlier hour. My father came home from Washington around 7:00 or 7:30 p.m. He and Mom held hands at the table. She was always dressed up. I was allowed twice to crawl under the table and press the carpeted bell, announcing that Annie would clear.

Our icebox was always full. Each night "the help" took home whatever they wanted, and all was replenished the next morning. The big wooden box atop our back steps was filled every few days by the iceman, who came by way of the alley behind our house—a long paved strip from Bateman Avenue, sheltered from sight by our backyard trees. Sometimes the iceman came in and stored pieces of his bounty in our "icebox," the refrigerator. Each month the scissors grinder would appear there, hawking his wares. I never went into the alley (was I forbidden?), but my brother would cross it, jump, and go down to play with a boy named Junior in the Gundlachs' backyard.

Baltimore was a very different city as I knew it then. Poverty, racism, violence must have been kept publicly under wraps, as in other cities in the South we bordered.

I was a child during the Great Depression. My father understood finances exceptionally well and became a successful businessman. We were not rich but lived comfortably. Our neighborhood, Windsor Hills, was lovely with its narrow streets, large wood-shingled houses, and lots of hedges and trees, affording maximum privacy. Our house, at the top of the hill, was white-shingled with green shutters, and a wide front verandah where I played and watched the world go by. I remember coming home from a summer away and being shocked at its new façade: beige stucco, modern, no verandah, but brick steps with an iron railing and protrusions in front that accommodated a foyer with coat closet and powder room, the wide floor beams of the living room now covered in gray poodle-woven carpet, the shaded side porch where Daddy and I sat together and read on weekends gone, replaced by an indoor "sun porch." I remember having a tantrum, lying on the gray carpet, crying and kicking. But I soon came to love the sun porch with its yellow-and-green-flowered cushions and no carpet, because I could close the curtained glass doors that separated it from the dull dark living room, turn on the Victrola, play Glenn Miller or Brahms, and sing and dance to my child-heart's content. Ann played the Steinway in the far bookcased sitting room, and once in a while I'd stand next to her bench and warble "Smoke Gets in Your Eyes" or "Deep Purple" and dream I might one day be a popular singer. I still have stacks of Ann's Hit Parade sheet music, rarely played.

At age twelve, I was enrolled in an elite Jewish ballroom dancing class (jive and jitterbug interspersed with waltzing). My mother thought I should have some kind of social life beyond my Quaker school. All the other kids went to the private Park School or the public Forest Park. They seemed to me really appealing, maybe more worldly, maybe even smarter, more attractive than many of the stu-

Sister Ann, Brother B, and Rose, Baltimore lawn, 1935.

dents at Friends, most of whom I cherished. Especially the flirting boys. Thus I came to have a double social life in my teens in Baltimore, which was really fun. (Though I didn't attend a bar mitzvah until a decade ago when Geraldine Brooks and Tony Horwitz invited me to their son Nathaniel's ceremony at the Martha's Vineyard Hebrew Center. I love Nathaniel and was so impressed.) My parents belonged to the Suburban Club, the elite German Jewish country club on the north edge of town. During World War II, less likely to travel, the grown-ups attended evening events there. That's where I learned to swim and taught myself to play tennis, until a cigar-puffing coach took over.

In the only picture I ever saw of my mother, Selma Kann, as a little girl, she is perched on a wall, her long curls with a big bow on top, white ruffled dress spilling over leather boots, very pretty, very serious. Mom was named for Selma Lagerlöf, the Nobel Prize–winning Swedish novelist who was the first female to win the prize and was popular in 1896. Mom grew up partly on a farm in Catonsville, outside Baltimore, and once she moved into the city for good, she never wanted to see a farm or a farm animal again.

My mother's family were German Jews who'd come to America in the 1820s or '30s, more than half a century before she was born. Her grandfather started Kann's Department Store in Baltimore and her father, Poppy, moved it sometime later to Washington, D.C. It occupied a block of Pennsylvania Avenue at 7th Street. Kann's soda fountain was the first in Washington to integrate racially. I was proud of The Store, as we called it, and remember my feeling of justice done.

When my father returned from work every day, my mother would greet him, dressed for the evening, often wearing her black velvet robe with its white satin collar I particularly loved. They held hands at the end of the table between courses. Annie served them dinner after Mom pressed the bell under the carpet with her foot. In the mornings after my father left for the office (how I cherished our breakfasts together; he gave me sips of his coffee, initiating my lifelong coffee habit), my mother sat up in bed in their bedroom at the far corner of the second floor and was served breakfast on a tray with the *Baltimore Sun* propped behind.

Mom was beautiful, reserved, much loved and admired, but scarcely a hands-on cuddly mother, at least by the time I came along. Like me, my brother had no recollection of sitting on our mother's lap. She had once been a suffragette—on the back of a truck in D.C.—then settled for being a leading member of the board of Goucher College, and the Women's Board of Johns Hopkins Hospital, and she volunteered at Happy Hills, a wonderful facility for sick children. (Ann took a similar civic path.) Mom was clearly not a farm girl. And though she left college following her wedding—so common in her generation and my own—she attended Johns Hopkins to study archaeology when I left Baltimore for Europe in the early '50s.

A memory comes to me about the first time I saw my mother cry. I was a year old or so, in my playpen, and she sat down on the floor outside it—in a white ruffled dress. She said simply, "Poppy is dead." I remember Poppy. He was tall, stately, bald except for a fringe of blondish graying hair as he entered my bedroom while I lay in my crib. His shadow was huge against the sloped ceiling before he leaned down to kiss me. Clearly there was a closeness, with much respect as well as love, between my mother and her parents. Just as there was love, respect, closeness between my parents, between me and my parents, and between my brother and his wife. I'm happy to say that love and respect and intimacy have moved through all the generations of my family.

The *Baltimore Sun* proclaimed my mother one of the five best-dressed women in Baltimore. She picked out all of my clothes and dressed me on weekends and holidays. (During school weeks for twelve years, I wore the Friends School blue uniform with white collar and cuffs.) Every year I went with my aunt and cousin Barbara and my mother to the Baltimore hotel where there was a display of children's clothing. Barbara and I would get the same dresses, maybe in different colors. My mother had wonderful taste. Cotton when I was little and silky when I was older. I loved to have things matching, just as I still love to set my dinner table in matching colors, amusing myself. From a very young age—elementary school—I liked creating and drawing outfits in my notebooks. I was interested in art, linen and fine china, and adult fashion. It just didn't apply to me and what I wore. But from first grade on, I drew girls in outfits. I liked most of the dresses my mother picked out for me. I am definitely not a "clotheshorse" as she was. Comfort is essential.

As a young teenager I was made to have my hair done every week, and I chafed at my mother's insistence that I wear a girdle, garter belt, and stockings. I surely had discarded them before I went to college, where I wore oversize men's shirts and slacks, daily. When I was nineteen and we were traveling together in Paris during a summer break, she wouldn't walk with me because I was wearing flat Capezios, popular for the first time then. I refused heels, though I was attired in a beautiful two-piece green print suit with a flared skirt that she had picked out for me. I was happy walking the streets of Paris behind her.

My mother never talked about her family or the past. I don't think she was hiding anything; she was interested only in the present and future. On her hundredth birthday, spurred on by my daughter Alexandra's curiosity, I said, "I have a photo of you, maybe in Atlantic City, when you were a little girl, and Al found some large, very old portraits in your top closet just now that must be of ancestors. They're the *best* pictures. Would you tell us just a little bit about them?"

"Rose, *knock it off*" was her reply. "You may be interested in my childhood or ancestors, but I'm not." I wasn't surprised. I laughed.

Girls' hockey group shot (Rose second row, third from left), Friends School Yearbook, 1946.

I asked her again when she was 101 and a half. I had her captive because she'd fallen and broken her hip. I had just come back from my third trip to Ireland, where I felt particularly at home. A lot of people there thought I was Irish. So I said, "Mom, I know you don't like to talk about the past, but do I have any Irish forebears?"

She beamed. "Well . . ." was all she said. She just kept smiling. I decided her generation simply wanted to be known as Americans. To my knowledge we had no identifiable relatives abroad, anywhere. Somehow I have never pursued that. My mother's daughter after all.

My father was Benjamin Bernei Burgunder, also from Baltimore. I felt particularly close to him, as well as to my brother. We breakfasted together every morning before his daily commute on the B&O Railroad to Washington, read together on the porch, and when I was in my teens I went into Washington with him during the summer months to help out in the book department at Kann's. Daddy was a brilliant mathematician. He attended public school and the University of Pennsylvania, and was invited to teach a course at the Wharton School when he was in his sophomore year. That summer his father died, and he had to leave Penn to stay home to provide for his mother, little brother, and four sisters. In 1910 he enjoyed at least fifteen minutes of fame: The *Baltimore Sun* (and other papers) sported

such headlines as "Young Man a Surprise: B.B. Burgunder of Baltimore Aroused Commerce Commission," and "Deep in Finance at
19," and then "Burgunder Testifies Today." Apparently, a thesis he'd
written at Wharton had been published in a New England journal,
and he was invited by the B&O Railroad Union to testify against the
railroad's claim that they needed to offset losses by charging higher
rates to passengers and cutting conductors' and porters' salaries.
"Only 19 Years Old, but He Had the Figures at His Finger Ends!"
The union won. I heard this story when I was a teenager. I was always
proud to be his daughter.

BBB Sr. never did finish college. Still nineteen, he was hired by
the prestigious Baltimore investment brokerage firm Mackubin,
Goodrich & Co. (Mackubin Legg when I was growing up, and now
Franklin Templeton Investments). Then, as the army's youngest dis-
bursing officer during World War I, he was stationed in Washington,
D.C. He met my mother, courted and married her before she was
halfway through Goucher. My parents told me nothing whatsoever
about their pasts. I know only what I observed and what my brother
told me. Once he mentioned that my father's family had roots in Bur-
gundy, France. His daughter is now researching family history, I hear!

According to my brother, B, when my mother's father died, her
brother was too young to run the department store. My father was
asked to take what he thought would be a couple of years' leave from
Mackubin, Goodrich to commute to Washington to head the family
business. He agreed, assuming that one day soon my uncle would
grow up and take over the store. (Sol never did, though he came
and worked there for a short time.) Dad hired the unforgettable Ida
"Larry" Larson, as secretary, and two other World War I disburse-
ment office colleagues. He was attentive to his employees and paid
them fairly, and they loved him. Perhaps not so happily, he never went
back to Mackubin, Goodrich.

I remember Daddy lifting me, at four, to the windowsill of his
high office to stand on it and watch Franklin Roosevelt in an open
car, waving to his inauguration fans on the street below. My father,
a Republican, was not a fan of FDR's business programs, I discovered when we'd listen to his Fireside Chats together on our radio on
Sunday evenings. But like all good patriots, he was impressed by the

ceremony and surely by the presidency, even the brave moral president himself.

Though my family was Jewish, we were not observant. As far as I knew my father never darkened the doorstep of any house of worship. His relatives and the cousins I played with went to Unitarian services. Once a year on Yom Kippur, my mother accompanied her mother, my nearsighted grandmother, to the Reform temple. (Now I wonder if my grandmother's neighbors Gertrude Stein and the French art-collecting Cone sisters attended it as well.) Once I asked if I could come too. I was embarrassed because my mother whispered to my grandmother throughout the entire service. I was not entranced. I much preferred the Episcopal church music I could sing to when I occasionally accompanied a Friends School classmate to church on Sundays.

I treasured the Quakers. The one Jewish occasion I enjoyed was a seder at my friend Amelie Moses's house. After dinner, as on other sleepovers, we went upstairs, lay on her twin beds, and listened, rapt, to Frank Sinatra on the radio propped between us. (I could not possibly have imagined Bill's and my friendship with Frank a quarter century later.) After World War II began, my parents tried to make me aware of what being "Jewish" meant. They sponsored a boy from Germany, quite a bit older than I, and sent him to Friends School. I don't know where he lived or what his name was. I never got to know him, but I'd see him—big, puffy-eyed, sad-looking, silent at recess or on the sidelines of a playing field. It struck a disturbing chord in me. Was he a symbol of what being Jewish meant? I assume I knew nothing yet of the concentration camps.

Reform rabbi Morris Lazaron, founder of the first Common Ground organization, was Mom's good friend. When he'd come over I would occasionally listen in on their conversations. Neither believed a Jewish homeland in Israel was a good idea. Did they perhaps, away from Europe, worry about the possible effect on American Jews (or thought actually another place would suit better)? I didn't know about German and Czech Jews going to Shanghai during World War II until recently. A film about Laurence Tribe's family opened my eyes.

.   .   .

There was a code of silence about many things in my parents' house. You didn't talk about problems—behavioral, political, medical, or your own worries. I didn't question this. It was the way things were. This later turned out to be excellent training for my work with Amnesty International, where keeping secrets (and being a trustworthy witness to history) was essential. Similarly, I'm ashamed to admit, my respect for successful southern feminine ways to approach men of authority didn't hurt my later far-flung encounters with bullies and tyrants. Mom always instructed me to let boys and men lead, and never to be first in my class or outspoken critically of men's behavior or political views. Would she have changed, today?

As for the silence, in my teens this meant not learning that a much older cousin I liked was not around anymore because she'd married a well-known Communist. (My parents were staunchly anti-Communist.) Nor was I supposed to wonder why a favorite neighbor had temporarily "disappeared" into a mental hospital. Or that Mom didn't trust her fun cousin's visitor from New Orleans: Lillian Hellman! When I told Mom in the early '60s that I was socializing with Lillian, she warned me to be careful about Lillian's frequent duplicity. She declared that Lil was ten years older than she professed to be. I remember thinking, "Good for you, Lil. You've got away with it!"

My early secret ventures were apparently the reason I was known as "the naughty little Burgunder girl" in Windsor Hills, our neighborhood. I heard this moniker, in a distinct Baltimore accent, for the first time when I was in New York City, almost seventy years old, standing in front of Scully's big glass Park Avenue window. As I was admiring the china, I saw the reflection of a small old man pointing at my back and saying to his tall lady companion, "There's the naughty little Burgunder girl I told you about." I recognized famous scientist Dr. Wolman from Windsor Hills, whom I hadn't encountered since I was seven. I knew he must have told his consort that on one of my pre-breakfast out-the-window neighborhood cruisings, I'd encountered him with my mother's very dear friend (each had a different longtime spouse) walking hand in hand down Queen Anne Road. I had said pertly, "I gotcha!" I was Nancy Drew, but had no idea of the significance of what I'd seen. Clearly he worried I'd tell my mother, since all three families were neighbors and friends. Of course I would not have told! I would not have wanted Mom to discover my secret dawn excursions. If only on Park Avenue I'd had the wit to turn and say again, "Gotcha!" Instead I ducked discreetly into Scully's and bought a small china sugar and cream set I still treasure.

The incident suddenly made me think back to often being naughty: I once convinced my year-older cousin to hide under the chicken coop at the apple farm Nanny took us to. We listened, giggling, as Nanny called and called. I also persuaded cousin Barbara to abandon the Sunday lunch card table she and I (the youngest family members) were assigned to because my father wouldn't sit at a table with thirteen diners (or inhabit a hotel room that added up to thirteen, plus other superstitions that the dear sane smart man perpetuated). I said, "Let's go upstairs and lock Nanny's bedroom doors!" And we *did*. I felt *very* guilty. Barbara, older, was blamed more than I, per usual. I'd dropped the keys down the neck of a black china cat I loved, whose head bobbed and bobbed. The head stopped bobbing. I was horrified. Guilt and sorrow marked me for sure. Whatever my punishment was didn't matter. Somehow the keys were extracted. Enormous guilt lasted, but Nanny left me the cat in her will. It's atop her china-filled breakfront in my Vineyard dining room now, erect, almost purring. Who can forget such moments?

Throughout my childhood, in the early summer mornings I'd climb out of my bedroom window onto a little ledge just below it, then shimmy down the conveniently leaning sycamore to go running around the neighborhood by myself when nobody was paying attention. I'd be sure to turn up for breakfast. I guess that was the beginning of my age-old dawn walks alone, though I abandoned window exits.

In the winter, whenever it was snowy and icy, I would take delight in risking everything on my Flexible Flyer sled. Once I veered off the road at the bottom of our steep hill, Lawina Road, and the sled shot down into a sewer, ruining the steering mechanism. I was catapulted up into the snow and wasn't hurt at all, but my parents were terrified. No more sledding for me. My big brother told me he had at some point been forbidden to sled too.

Much later, as a freshman at Wellesley, I wrote home that I'd been invited to Dartmouth for a winter weekend that included skiing. My mother clipped every major article on ski accidents (some fatal) from the U.S. papers and sent them to me as a warning. Despite my recklessness, the stories stuck in my mind as I careened down Suicide Six. I would never become a good carefree skier, though I really enjoyed the sport, especially its snowy, high landscapes. I often took my children skiing out west and in Europe as well as on closer New England slopes. Susanna skis the U.S. and European slopes magnificently still.

My aunt Eleanor May provided an alternative family environment when she invited me to visit. As a little girl I loved spending the night at her house. Once when I was five, bandleader and musician Eddy Duchin tucked me in and kissed me good night. (His son, pianist Peter Duchin, later became one of my favorite friends, a companion in funny adventures.) I loved to sing Broadway tunes with Aunt Elly at her piano. At the age of twelve, I went to Pimlico racetrack with Aunt Elly, a highlight of my ordinary life, and she invited me to her summer home in Lake Placid. My mother faintly disapproved of glamorous Aunt Elly's ways. She and my uncle traveled with royalty: ex–King Edward and his Baltimore duchess, Wally Simpson.

Dr. Alan Guttmacher, the premier obstetrician of Baltimore and (years later) the founder of Planned Parenthood, lived with his family next door. I spent many afternoons climbing the ancient maple at the Guttmachers', pretending not to hear my mother or a household member calling me to come home. In the summer his family went to Ogunquit, Maine, and he would come to our house for dinner. By the time I was eight, I wanted to read everything, and would go over to his house to pore over his medical books. He wrote volumes about birth. I particularly recall *Life in the Making* and *Into This Universe*. They made a nice counterpoint to weekly sleuth Nancy. Girls' books about heroic nurses were in fashion then, but they didn't grab me. With my father gone all day in Washington, I saw Dr. Guttmacher often and decided (between becoming a singer and an artist) that I wanted to be a doctor.

Sometimes, on my own, filled with anticipation, I'd take the street-

Rose's senior photo,
Friends Yearbook, 1946.

car from Walbrook Junction at the bottom of our steep Lawina Road, and in twenty minutes be walking through the great doors of the Enoch Pratt Library. There I'd march straight to the bank of wooden drawers and rifle through its endless card file to choose the week's coveted books. Sometimes I'd sit for hours at a long table and start one, or on a particularly nice day, perch on an outdoor landing. In my teens, I'd often join favorite classmates like Sue Freeland at the Loew's movie house for a double feature. Or we'd get our kicks in a small, dark upstairs theater called the Valencia on North Avenue, where horror films (tame by current standards) were highlights. The theater always released a bat or two at each Halloween show to audience gasps!

I attended Friends School as did my grandmother and mother, my sister and brother before me, and later my nieces and nephews (except those who were enrolled at Sidwell Friends in D.C.). I've never forgotten climbing out of the rumble seat of the small family car, taking my brother's hand, and walking into the classroom on my first day of school. Low-key by today's standards, Baltimore Friends has always been a fine school and I got a pretty damned good education there. At some point I must have decided I was a Quaker. I confess to enjoying Thursday morning Quaker meetings in which I more than once got up and spoke for the Lower School. (It was so much easier than public speaking, which I disliked later in life.) Though when I wrote an essay at age ten for an English class, the teacher said, "Well, I guess you're a Buddhist." I didn't know what that was, but I looked it up and hoped she was right. I thought about that moment when I attended Buddhist sessions in Peter Matthiessen's Sagaponack Zendo thirty years or so later. Mostly I was attached to nature and to some idea of morality and humanity, and I certainly believed in doing right, and suffered guilt when I failed.

A new world opened for me when my third-grade teacher, Miss Corcoran, encouraged me to write poetry after I completed my flash card math sessions. I read Poe's "Annabelle Lee" and Stevenson's "How do you like to go up in a swing, / Up in the air so blue? / Oh, I do think it the pleasantest thing / Ever a child can do!" The first poems I wrote were about being in Atlantic City on my own. When I wrote my childhood magnum opus in fourth grade, I focused on Africa, which we were studying in our big dark blue geography books. This many-stanzaed rhymed verse about yearning for the jungle, the children, and wildlife there was published in the Friends High School literary magazine.

But when Miss Rowe, the fourth-grade teacher, read my poem, she called me up in front of the class and accused me of plagiarism. "Plagiarism"? I learned it was when one copied words written by someone else and claimed it as one's own. I thought, "Wow, here's a grown-up who believes a much older person wrote my poem. Maybe I will grow up to be a poet!" That thought persisted, and poetry became my major life track.

Today I hope good teachers instruct and inspire their children to write poetry in class. For years I have been on the board of the Academy of American Poets, which encourages teachers to do just that, helping them include poetry in the classroom through their excellent workshops in person and online. It's a special organization I'm proud to be a part of, especially each April (National Poetry Month), during our annual fund-raiser at Lincoln Center, Poetry & the Creative Mind, which I cofounded with Jorie Graham and Meryl Streep eighteen years ago.

Miss Rowe notwithstanding, my lifelong engagement with poetry certainly bloomed at Friends. In my last two years there, Letitia Stockett, everyone's favorite teacher of English and American history and literature, singled me out and encouraged me. Alas, when she addressed my class, offering a long explanation about evocative writing, she suggested, "If you are describing your characters' features in detail, such as the person sitting next to you with a droopy eyelid . . ." Even though I knew I was her favorite student, this made me unhappily aware that my kindergarten ice ball injury was still visible. My heart sank.

Miss Stockett was the author of two fine books, *America, First, Fast and Furious* and *Baltimore: A Not Too Serious History,* that are enshrined in my bookcase still. She enthralled decades of juniors and seniors, my brother and sister included, as she marched into class and climbed on and across our desks, reciting Longfellow's "Paul Revere's Ride." Just after I graduated, Miss Stockett, on a solo tour west, living fast and furious as always, somehow ran her bicycle into a roadside wall and died. I aced a freshman course at Wellesley because I'd been her high school student.

My handsome, adventurous big brother, B, turned one hundred in September 2020. He was a lifeline to me growing up. The only time I saw him really unhappy with the mother he adored was when he returned from the navy, the Pacific 7th Fleet, and discovered that our mother had dispensed with his beloved set of trains. "Why did you give them away?" he asked lamentingly. (B said he didn't remember ever being cross with Mom.) I had watched him with his trains forever. I hadn't realized that when you grew up you still treasured your childhood things. And because of it, I never gave anything of my children's away. Nor did Mom give anything of mine away. She kept all of my childhood notebooks and drawings and sent them to me later in Connecticut, where they were stored for decades in our crowded attic.

Moving to Connecticut after Bill and I married, I took as a favorite souvenir from our Windsor Hills home B's wooden desk chair, still sporting all the marks of B's drumstick-playing after he and a high school chum returned from a Benny Goodman concert in New York City. He'd forgotten how Mom chided him, but I remember. I cherished listening to him tell me all about the concert and other adventures when I was invited to his bedroom, across the hall from mine.

When I was thirteen, my parents and I went to Seattle to see B, who had enlisted in the navy at the age of twenty-one, after graduating from Dartmouth. He was an ensign-in-training on nearby Whidbey Island. As we waited for our room in the hotel, we saw the headlines in the Seattle newspaper: "Robert Burgunder Gets Death Penalty" or something to that effect, with an article on the murderer. I was fascinated. I wondered if we were somehow related. The next day, my brother and I climbed Mount Washington (surely not to the top) and then he took me to his island base. That evening his navy pals asked me to dance, and I twirled, happy—until one started flirting with me, and B pulled him away, saying, "She's only thirteen!" I was disappointed, but grateful for B's caring.

One special week, after he returned home (I excited to be in my brother's company again), B took me to look at New England colleges. I was a junior who'd somehow aced the SATs, even the Math, which I'd disliked and avoided advanced classes in. I guess I inherited Daddy's genes if not his passion. Before visiting Radcliffe and Smith and Wellesley and Holyoke, the standard tour stops, I suggested stopping at Wheaton where Amelie was a freshman. At her dorm entrance, I asked a student to tell Amelie we'd arrived. She returned quickly and said, "Amelie thought you were coming tomorrow, is drying her hair, and will be right down." A wild-haired blonde beauty soon descended the stairs. B was immediately smitten. My dreamed-of days in his company were short. They married after Amelie's freshman year. Not exactly what I had in mind, but I loved them both and feel as blessed as their fine children must that they were in love for well over seventy years. We mourned their deaths, exactly two months apart.

The Quaker ethos led me to activism and service. I was a pacifist even as *Scholastic* magazine's wartime covers made me swell with pride at our heroes' exploits. I wanted to somehow save at least part of the world. I skipped school via bus another afternoon and attended a courtroom for the first Alger Hiss hearing, standing in the back as Richard Nixon accused Hiss of being a Communist. Reading the *Baltimore Sun* obsessively, I was curious to see these two men in person. I decided Alger Hiss was upright and innocent, and that Richard Nixon was a snake who was maligning him. I continued to follow the Hiss case for years, distrusting Hiss's adversary, Whittaker Chambers. Only many years later, after an unexpected dinner with Hiss, could I bring myself to admit I had been mistaken about his innocence.

My parents were Republicans, but I was definitely on the Democratic hustings. By the time I was in high school, my father and I were having lively political debates. They weren't acrimonious. I just spoke up as a teenager, with passion. I never thought my father was necessarily wrong, but I enjoyed debating with him, even about the financial issues I didn't understand at all. Bernei had been on the high school debate team, and because I wanted to do whatever he did, I joined the team at fourteen. In 1943, the Wagner-Murray-Dingell Bill proposing national health care went before Congress. I decided I believed in universal health care and was asked to debate it with older students, and we won. Eons would pass before even a good portion of such a bill would be in place: Obamacare.

On Veterans Day in 1945, it seemed that all the adults in Baltimore headed downtown to celebrate war's end and join the parade. I convinced two kids from my class to go. We took a bus downtown and joined the crowds, cutting afternoon classes again. Somehow, we ended up at the head of the parade, with a great big classmate named Ozzie Hall. A *Baltimore Sun* photographer took our picture and it ran on a prominent page, getting me in deep trouble with our principal once again. I think perhaps only my family's long Friends School history saved me from a fate worse than detention.

BEYOND

When it came time to apply to colleges, my mother, who attended Goucher, and was probably head of the board of directors, wanted me to stay in Baltimore as my sister had. But I had other ideas. The school principal came to our house and said that we should not be disappointed if I did not get into a college of my choice, despite my academic record. She explained that there were small quotas for Jewish students. I applied to seven colleges and was surprisingly accepted by all. (Those were the days! I feel so sorry for today's worthy seniors— waiting, wondering . . .) My parents vetoed both Stanford (because it was too far away) and Radcliffe (because it was "too radical"). After campus visits with B, I chose Wellesley, where two of my close friends were already freshmen. Besides, it had the most beautiful campus and was near Harvard.

Politics in my eye by then, I was curious that most of my freshmen dormmates were disinterested. They were smart and attractive, fun, mostly devoted to learning and dating, but passive regarding world issues. I spent as much time as I could at Harvard and Radcliffe, where I thought the publicly engaged kids were. Wellesley did have a student government—I got elected to it as the freshman representative. I met JFK there as he was planning his first run for Congress in 1946. We were all enchanted. And I joined our branch of Yenching, the Christian university whose beleaguered students were streaming across China then.

My father died unexpectedly of cancer during my freshman year. I was told he'd gone to the hospital, but for a return of shingles. He was fifty-five. I was devastated. I felt particularly sorry that I'd had no chance for a last resolving of our conversations, declarations of our devotion to each other. His death came as a shock. My mother had decided not to tell me he was dying or suggest I come home or visit him in the hospital. I was heartbroken and didn't understand my mother's professed reasoning: "We didn't want to ruin your first year at college." Perhaps she didn't understand what a close relationship my father and I had. She was not a part of our Washington life and adventures together or our quiet afternoons reading in each other's company although she was a loving wife and mother. By the time I arrived home from Wellesley, my father lay in state in our living room in an open coffin. I walked behind his employees from Kann's, too overcome to speak. Our trip to the cemetery to bury him is still a blur.

Returning to Wellesley, processing Dad's death, I had to bury the understanding that my mother had not seen fit to have me come and say goodbye to Dad in time. I wondered if, born late to them, I was an "afterthought" child. While I had a lovely youth, I wondered if I was not to my mother what her first two children were. She made it up to me later, in travels and at home.

John F. Kennedy came to Wellesley to give a talk during his run for Congress. Four girls and I got to interview him and quiz him about what he'd do if elected. I thought he was terrific—dashing, encouraging all of us to get involved in doing something for our country and the world. I wanted Kennedy to win, but I cannot pretend I expected him to become president or, ever, my friend.

My brother took over Kann's, as my father had. He ran it for years, teaching young kids in his spare hours, then sold the department store. Following my father's death, my mother moved from the Windsor Hills house into an apartment building—the first American one, I was told, designed by Mies Van der Rohe. Its address was Charles Street, just blocks down the road from Friends and up from Johns Hopkins. I visited her often, alone and with my classmates and, later, with my Vineyard friends. (Peter Sacks taught in my old creative writing division at Hopkins. He honored me by writing the introduction to my book of poems *By Vineyard Light,* and then married my friend Jorie Graham.)

Mom decided on her 102nd birthday that it was time to cash in. She kissed her three children goodbye one by one that evening, my privilege being the last to leave, holding her right hand as she said, "I think it's time to go to sleep. Will you come with me?" She then gestured, apparently to my father, raised high her left hand, waved, and almost sang, "I'm coming, darling. Just wait for me!" My atheist mother! She had always insisted there was no life after death, and that we must live our lives here well. After my father died she never looked at another man. Many escorted her to Baltimore Orioles baseball games, her sports passion. (At 100, she declined to go to the games anymore, saying all her escorts were gone, and younger companions wouldn't do.) Before she actually said, smiling, "I'm coming, darling," she surprised me by looking out her tall windows and exclaiming, "Look! Do you think that bird is going to heaven? I wish I were . . ." I held her other hand until she went to sleep that final birthday night. I flew home, and soon after I arrived, Mom's temporary caregiver called, distressed: "Your mother just died." I replied, "I know."

Her life almost crossed into a third century.

3

Meeting Bill: Before and After

Anniversary
too many years to remember
I dream
we are in Rome again, studying
the floppy orange guidebook,
lying on the brown bed
in the brown room
five steps down from the street . . .
    —from "Anniversary"

AFTER MY FATHER DIED, my mother and I went traveling for three Wellesley summer breaks. Since my decade-older siblings, Ann and Bernei, were married by then, my mother arranged grand tours for the two of us, to Latin America, Europe, and North Africa. We sailed in style on the original *Queen Mary* to visit England, France, Spain, and Italy. I think it must have been 1949. One of my memories is of visiting poet Federico García Lorca's grave in Spain (my mother indulged my wish). As a teenager, I was in thrall to Lorca, considering him a political hero. On a gray day, I sat alone by his grave, reciting his verses that I had memorized. His murder by Nationalists left many unanswered questions. (In decades to come, the fights and heroism of other poets marched before me.) A couple of hours later, my mother returned by car from a further countryside drive, and we went off to discover nearby Granada.

Soon we journeyed to Rome, where I wandered, entranced, through the Borghese Gardens and the English cemetery where Keats, Wordsworth, and Shelley rested. I had a foretaste of my chosen path by then.

London. Paris. Delight and amazement everywhere. But I promised myself I'd eventually live in Rome. Our first day in Paris, we read in the *Herald Tribune* Art Buchwald's funny column about a restaurant serving pressed duck. Mom and I headed there. What had captivated me was the illustration in his piece of a duck hanging from a guillotine. I wondered if Art was a diner there that night. The duck was delicious. On our return voyage aboard the *Île de France,* I was bemused by movie star Rex Harrison leaning for hours on the top deck's railing, his long, usually slicked-back hair blowing in the wind, revealing a large bald pate on top. What was he thinking or rehearsing? When we landed in New York, a young man I'd been having a brief shipboard flirtation with—later my husband's boss at McGraw-Hill—invited me to the premiere of *Death of a Salesman.* It was surely the best drama I'd seen in my limited Baltimore/New York theater forays. I was usually on an emotional high when a curtain went up. But this *Salesman* was starker than other performances I'd seen, not related to my personal experience. I suffered every emotion with Willy Loman, becoming as anxious as the playwright intended. I cared about his wife, Linda, and his son Biff, even after the play ended. Little did I suspect that six years later, Arthur Miller, Bill, and I would be Roxbury, Connecticut, neighbors and close friends. (I never met Marilyn Monroe, but saw her walking on their roadside lawn, beautiful in a short black dress and black headscarf. Sadly for us, she failed to show up for dinner twice at writer/anthologist Louis Untermeyer's in Roxbury because "Marilyn is nervous about dining with intellectuals, and kept changing her clothes," as Arthur apologetically put it.)

Following graduation from Wellesley, my Baltimore and Wellesley girlfriend Susie Diggs and I rented an apartment on Sparks Street in Cambridge, apparently an unusually independent move for two young women at the time. I enrolled at Harvard and became immersed in poetry courses taught by John Crowe Ransom and Richard Wilbur.

Ransom was a sort of father figure (at sixty or so) of poetry for me.

He introduced me to the New Criticism I pursued the following fall at Johns Hopkins University graduate school. I loved his gentle tone, his way of rhyming, his subtle perceptions and reining in of emotions. "Bells for John Whiteside's Daughter" was an early memorized favorite. In person, he charmed me with his excitement about his new grandchild. He was old-fashioned, but he influenced my belief in the necessity of the intensive-extensive meaning of each word I would use in my future poems.

Richard Wilbur—already a well-known poet in his late twenties, a scholar and translator—was an influence on my life in more than one way. Having graduated from Wellesley as class poet, I thought I needed to learn the history and craft of contemporary poetry, which I did not really know. In those days, Wellesley did not permit an English major to take more than one writing course. I had signed up for the essay freshman year, and was not pleased with the teacher and her dislike of contemporary thought or activism; the eighteenth-century nature essay was her only passion, and I fretted, realizing I would be forbidden to take a poetry course. I signed up for Wilbur's course at Harvard on Modern English and American Poetry. Mr. Wilbur was any student's dream: young, handsome, knowledgeable, a brilliant lecturer and reader of poetry, good-humored and relaxed, open to questioning. The only teacher who surpassed him, with the widest mind I ever encountered, was Peter Sacks (I audited his classes decades later when I was a fellow at Harvard's Kennedy School). Dick Wilbur's lyric rhymed poems became a model for me. When we found ourselves by chance walking through the Villa Sciarra on a hill in Rome perhaps three years later, a long, casual friendship ensued. Aside from a visit with his wife and kids to Roxbury, and poetry gatherings, plus talks I attended when he was poet laureate, our paths crossed again at the Century Association once, and through other close girlfriends before he died.

After Harvard, I honored my promise to move back to Baltimore and live with my mother for a year or so. Although, as I've said, she was never a hands-on mother, she was kind, warm, and concerned that I have a good, successful year. She was unfailingly welcoming to my old Baltimore friends and new Johns Hopkins classmates, who enjoyed her mutually. She seemed obviously interested in each of their lives. Because Mom never criticized my friends, I thought she approved of each of my potential beaux. Not true, I learned later when I introduced her to Bill. And Dylan Thomas before him.

I enrolled in the Johns Hopkins University graduate school, earning a master's in creative writing, with a bit of philosophy, courtesy of George Boas, and prose classes seated next to wisecracking John (then Jack) Barth. My two years were serendipitous. During my second day on campus, crossing the grass near Charles Street, I was approached by a TV crew who asked if they could interview me on camera. Flattered, I asked why, and the response was "We're doing a series on regional American accents and you have the best Baltimore ['Ballimer'] accent we've heard." I was momentarily demoralized, remembering I'd spent four years in Massachusetts trying to lose that rather nasal, hard-to-describe accent. (As a kid, I had listened to my mother and her girlfriends taking weekly French lessons at our house with Mademoiselle La Rue. Their strong Baltimore accents made French unappealing or amusing, and I promised myself I would shed mine.) But the succeeding classes and fellow students—many guys my senior who had returned from World War II service and benefited from the GI Bill for education—made for a lively, varied group of companions. There was only one other girl, Julie, a serious, accomplished thirty-year-old I aspired to be like.

Two meetings with outside speakers at JHU—extraordinary Dylan Thomas and ordinary-seeming William Styron—played interesting roles in my on- and off-campus life. I first met Dylan Thomas one sunny mild afternoon in 1951 on the green-lawned Johns Hopkins University campus. As a poet, I'd been asked to be his guide and keep him company on his first American visit, and to make sure he got to his 6:00 p.m. reading and talk in the auditorium.

Thomas, whose poetry I admired greatly and memorized sporadically, was more charming than I'd anticipated—funny, observant, easygoing, flirtatious, unassuming, curious, and wicked. I say wicked because my strict instructions were not to let him drink before his evening performance. At about 3:00 p.m. he rolled up his left pants leg and took out a bottle of booze, downing it all. At about 5:00 p.m., ditto on the right leg.

At just before 6:00 p.m., upstairs in the office of program director

Elliott Coleman (which fortuitously had stairs leading from his door directly down to the auditorium), Dylan was standing over Elliott's large, beautifully appointed mahogany desk looking at the professor's papers atop an elegant leather desk set, when I announced that it was time to go out and down the stairs. "Oh," Dylan said amicably, and proceeded to throw up all over the desk and its contents. Disbelieving, I watched him wipe his mouth, smile at me, and walk out the door. Needless to say, I had to do my best to clean up pronto, so I missed at least half of his applause-punctuated delivery. I managed to sit down in the auditorium in time to hear him recite insouciantly, "When I was a windy boy and a bit . . ." How winningly he performed.

About a year later, the poet returned to the United States for an appearance in Washington, D.C. I received a call from Richmond Lattimore, his host, saying Dylan had prompted him to ask if it was okay for the two of them to visit me at my house in Baltimore where I was living with my mother. I was delighted. Mother was not. She had read in the *Baltimore Sun* that Dylan had drunkenly knocked over and destroyed a big valuable ("Grecian"?) urn in some fancy lady's apartment in New York City. "But, Mom," I protested, "we don't have any urns. And your china is all locked in the glass breakfront."

Richmond and Dylan were fine guests. We found lots to talk and laugh about. My elegant mother's rare scowl appeared only when, late in the evening, Dylan took his last drink(s) seated somehow under our grand piano, and had to be coaxed and cajoled to leave—with kisses and promises to meet next in Wales.

I still wake up once in a while reciting "When I was a windy boy and a bit . . ." and I occasionally enter the dark, which I never want to face, saying to myself, "Do not go gentle into that good night."

With two tentative contracts in my suitcase—one for a book of poems (the *Hopkins Review* had featured a number of individual pieces) and one for an expansion of my master's thesis on how the New Critics influenced Wallace Stevens—I set off for Rome via London on a much less grand ship than the *Queen Mary,* traveling third-class and easy.

In London I spent many long hours reading in the British Museum, near the Elgin Marbles. There I met an American woman with a big laugh that woke solemn scholars from their desks. She was tall, blonde, broad-shouldered, exuding confidence. She had been a British WAC and married an Englishman. I was impressed, amused, and we began to converse. Her name was Mary Lee Settle, and it turned out we were traveling to Italy the same day, for an extended stay. Mary Lee was soon to be an established novelist (in 1978 she won the National Book Award for *Blood Tie,* returned to the United States, and founded the PEN/Faulkner Awards).

We decided, traveling together, to visit Pompeii on the way to Rome, where we spent our first night in the Hotel d'Inghilterra. No second night for me (Mary Lee stayed on). The bed was the hardest I'd ever slept on and my small room did not let in enough Italian sunlight. I found an agreeable apartment through an ad in the *Rome Daily American* and moved in with two American girls who had jobs at the American embassy.

Back to meeting Bill: A letter arrived postmarked Baltimore, from Professor Louis Rubin, whose friendship with fellow southerner Bill Styron had led to the author's first public lecture, at Hopkins, when his debut novel, *Lie Down in Darkness,* had soared to the top of the 1951 best seller list. Bill, Louis told me, had just arrived at the American Academy in Rome to secure his Rome Prize, the first novelist to receive one. He knew no one in Italy, so if I found myself at the academy, I should look him up. I barely recalled Bill, who had spoken shyly and surely not profoundly, still in marine khakis a year before. All writing students had been commanded to attend his talk because our total graduate body was so small. We poets and critics had bonded, and did not consider fiction writers necessarily our intellectual equals. I don't recall even shaking hands with William Styron before we went off to carouse.

As it turned out, I had a blind date with a fellow at the academy, a classicist, that very week. He was extremely boring. Ready to leave the spectacular premises, thinking I might never get a chance to explore its studios and villa and grounds, I passed the fellows' mailboxes. I chanced on the label "Bill Styron," stopped, wrote him a note saying Louis had written me, that I'd attended his Hopkins reading, and if he needed company to phone me. Stashing the note into the cubby, I left, expecting nothing.

Bill called the very next day and invited me to meet him for drinks

Bill as a young marine, World War II.

at the little basement bar of the grand Excelsior Hotel on the Via Veneto, close by the American embassy. As I descended the narrow steps, wet from the rain, wearing my new black velvet red-satin-lined raincoat (Bill forever described me in it at that moment), I worried that I might not even recognize him. No problem. There was only one occupied table. A dark, curly-haired guy surely not Bill sat on the left. Truman Capote, his blond bangs and boyish look recognizable from the cover of his recent famous book, *Other Voices, Other Rooms,* sat on the right. Apparently, Bennett Cerf, Truman's publisher, but not yet Bill's, had written him suggesting he look Bill up, and he did. Bill played it safe, I guess, inviting a fellow fellow from the academy in case I was uninteresting, or Truman too challenging. Tall, slim, sandy-haired Bill Styron was in the middle, fidgeting. All three stood gentleman-like to welcome me.

My first thought was that Bill might be gay, like Truman. That thought went away progressively in the next few hours, as I sat quite close to him. His knees shook under the table. He described climbing to the top of St. Peter's that day with an old girlfriend, Wanda Malinowski, who had turned up in Rome from Bolzano, where her famous archaeologist father lived. Always afraid of heights, Bill had had to climb down and was, for perhaps an hour, still shaking. By dawn, as we were leaving after an evening special for each of us, Truman piped up in his high-pitched southern voice, "Bill, you ought to marry that girl!" Our instant three-way friendship (Bill, Truman, and me) led to a number of wonderful walks and meals and conversations throughout the fall of 1952.

Bill appealed to me immediately, particularly because he seemed sensitive, was humorous, with great timing and an offbeat imagination. He told me that he got by on humor as the youngest and smallest in his class at Christchurch prep school on the Rappahannock River in Virginia, where he'd been sent when his mother died. I found him sexy and in command, although more than a bit vulnerable. Was I?

The one moment that night I continued to feel guilty about was my echoing Truman's praise, and painter Al Green's, for *Lie Down in Darkness*. They had read the best seller, his debut novel. I had not, but pretended I had, and echoed their approval. The next day, Bill called for a date, twenty-four hours hence. I thought, "I'd better read that book, fast." I went to every bookstore in Rome. Some carried books in English but not a copy of Bill's. Desperate, I went just before closing time to the American Library. "Have you a copy of *Lie Down in Darkness*?" I asked. "Yes," the librarian said after consulting her file. "Here, take out a library card for yourself and bring it back next week."

I agreed, gratefully made my way to my new pad, got into bed, opened *Lie Down in Darkness* to chapter one, and chapter two. "Oh dear," I mused after an hour or so. "He's cute but he can't write." The prose was flat, the protagonist quite uninteresting. Disappointed, I turned out the lights, worrying about what I'd say when we met again.

Next morning, rising, I picked up the book with its opaque tan cover (all American libraries around the world probably used such covers, only the book's title visible through the clear plastic spine). This time I opened to the title page: "*Lie Down in Darkness* by Harold L. Hayes." Publication date decidedly earlier. Sigh of relief. I didn't know one couldn't copyright a title. I hoped Bill would forgive my lie and think it was funny. He did. We went up to his academy room and he gave me a real copy. Devouring it over the next couple of days (I'm a slow reader), I knew that the critics—who deemed it brilliant— were right. The long adjective-rich sentences pulled me in. I loved it and wept for Peyton Loftis throughout her long, moving, stream-of-consciousness monologue. I had not experienced suicide in real life.

In Rome, Bill and I were soon spending exhilarating evenings with artists from the academy or with Truman. I remember Truman waving at us whenever we walked past the balcony of his apartment on the Via Margutta. He most often wore a sailor suit, and Lola, his mynah bird, would be perched on his shoulder, muttering, "So's your old man." The Irish poet Desmond O'Grady, Ezra Pound's amanuensis in Italy, was around the academy that year, and became a pal. Blond and lithe and full of smiles, he would on occasion prance up and down the academy's wide marble staircase, swishing a fake sword like Scaramouche and reciting whatever. Bill soon introduced me to his favorite friends, Bobby and Claire White. Bobby was a sculptor and a fellow at the academy, which had been designed by his grandfather Stanford White at the turn of the century.

Some of us found the academy a rather stuffy place, an outpost of conservative 1950s American culture in Rome. The first time Bill took me to eat there, I was baffled. All the food was tasteless white Middle American cuisine, while the fare in Rome was colorful, exceptionally delicious. Bill was a gourmet, so we ate out or cooked ourselves. The academy's director, Lawrence Roberts, disapproved of the fellows' carousing and forming romantic liaisons and locked the academy's high iron gate every night about 10:00 p.m. I think I recall that Bobby White became a master of tossing his bicycle over, then climbing the gate to get in and out after curfew.

On our second night together, I had been caught in Bill's room. Chastised by Roberts, Bill decided to rent a small basement flat—actually next door to the academy—for him and me. Surely living together was forbidden. I was not concerned about my reputation. Bill continued to work by day in his academy rooms. I would walk uphill to the scenic Garibaldi Park and write. When Roberts found out that Bill was spending nights with me at our Via Angelo Masina 5B apartment, he barred him from events, mostly social, at the academy's beautiful Villa Aurelia across the street. Fifty-odd years later, when I was traveling in Italy with some of my children and grandchildren, I ran into Roberts on a street in Florence. He greeted me by my maiden name, looked at me surrounded by my brood, who I introduced by name, and commented, "So you married Bill Styron after all!"

While Bill and I were courting, my mother came to Rome, not only because I was there but also because she was dear friends with our ambassador to Italy, James Zellerbach, from San Francisco, and his wife, Hannah. They were all Eisenhower Republicans. She stayed with them at the embassy and invited me to bring my boyfriend to dinner there. Obviously, she wanted to meet Bill. Mom was usually very good about boyfriends I brought home, even when the rest of my family thought one or another was a loser.

Bill had never been to an embassy, nor had I. He knew he had to dress up for this, but the only suit he had was a light blue sharkskin one bought somewhere in the bowels of Manhattan for his award ceremony at the uptown American Academy of Arts and Letters. He bragged that it came with two pairs of pants, too wide-bottomed to be stylish. Normally he just wore khakis and sweaters. He bought new shoes for the embassy dinner, sensing his daily worn espadrilles—Rome fashion then—would not do. He had no necktie, and asked Truman if he could borrow one. A mauve-gray, fringed burlap tie, a red heart in the center, stitched through with a white arrow, thus enhancing the sharkskin suit, was donned. I flinched, but said nothing. I suspect Truman chose it as a prank, knowing his friend's indifference to matters sartorial. I can only guess what my mother's thoughts were, fashion and otherwise. The evening seemed to go quite well. Bill, quiet unless questioned, spoke beautifully of his work. He was amusing, deferential to my mother.

Shortly after that, Bill was going with a group of academy fellows down to Ravello, on the Amalfi Coast south of Naples, to spend a weekend at an archaeological dig. The fellows—artists, archaeologists, classicists, and Bill—were invited. Bill asked me to come along. When I told my mother I was going, she said, "Oh, I'd like to go too. I'll treat us to a room at the Hotel Palumbo." I could scarcely believe it, but then I didn't have the nerve to say "no way," as my kids would have.

I wasn't happy about it, but I couldn't figure a way out. In those days, a young unmarried woman did not travel with her beau unchaperoned if her mother could help it. We went to Ravello and Mother and I stayed at the Palumbo, the academy members quartered elsewhere. Midnights, when I thought Mom was asleep, I'd sneak out to be with Bill. Of course, she figured that out, but said nothing. Her generation enfolded ours in silent discretion, not labeled deceptive then.

Back in Rome, Bill and I grew closer, and by the first of December he'd asked me to marry him. Surprised, hesitant, questioning, totally in love for the first time, I accepted. The bar we sat in at the Hotel

Flora, on the Via Veneto up from the Excelsior, is visually imprinted still: small, curved, ill-lit, with simple wood seats—unlike the fancy Excelsior bar.

By then my mother had left for England and then France, phoning from Cherbourg, where she was boarding an ocean liner. "I'm just calling to say goodbye and what a wonderful time I've had, especially with you in Rome, dear."

My heart tripping, I replied, "Oh, Mom, I have the best news. I'm engaged to marry Bill Styron."

There was a long silence, and then I heard a click as my mother hung up.

I was shocked. She had always cheered me on. I laughingly told Bill it might have been a response to the burlap tie.

When I still lived in Parioli, before moving in with Bill that October, he had bought a little Austin. He apparently told Peter Matthiessen a fellow couldn't properly court a girl way across town without a car. For Christmas, we drove in it with an academy musician/painter couple, Frank Wigglesworth and Anne Parker, from Rome to Paris. Peter and his stunning pregnant wife, Patsy Southgate, got us a room in a little pensione a block from their Montparnasse apartment. When we checked in, the proprietor handed me a letter from Bill's father, which Peter had left there for us. We went up to our room, which was just big enough for its two pieces of furniture—a bed and the mirrored chiffonier at its foot, very French. Bill sat on the bed and opened the envelope postmarked Virginia.

"This is the strangest letter," he said. He began reading aloud: "'Dear Son, what kind of trouble are you in? A gumshoe from Washington came down on the ferry and has been questioning everybody in the neighborhood about our family and me and you. Whatever the trouble is, Son, you can tell me, I'm with you, and I just need to know what this is all about.'"

"Oh my God," I interrupted, mortified. "I think I know that gumshoe. He must be from our store in Washington." When I was thirteen and worked in the book department, he had befriended me. Also, I suddenly remembered when my brother, still a navy ensign, had been going with a girl named Ruth and my mother sicced the store detective on them. Ruth, like Bill, was not from Baltimore; my mother didn't know her family. She wanted to figure out who this girl was and what she and Bernei were up to.

"She put a detective on your family just the way she did to my brother's girlfriend," I told Bill. It wasn't until some forty years later that Bernei told me it wasn't the Kann's store detective but a professional private investigator my mother had hired to look into the Styrons.

Bill and I sat in stunned silence. I couldn't believe my mother had investigated the Styrons. I was upset and said, "Look, I can't let you marry into a family that would do this."

He said, "I agree with you."

Bill wrote his dad to explain. Soon Bill's wicked stepmother, Elizabeth, who'd always been jealous of Bill's father's commitment to him, wrote me, warning me that he'd make a terrible husband. Elizabeth declared that Bill was lazy and shiftless, and even after the success of his first novel she seemed to think he'd never make it as a writer or an upstanding citizen. I tore the letter up. I did not tell Bill about it. Mary Lee Settle was against us too. And Tom Guinzburg, the *Paris Review*'s first managing editor, who was sojourning in Rome and with whom I'd sat on a grassy knoll by the academy each Sunday doing the *New York Times* crossword puzzle. Tom discouraged me, suggesting I stick with him. But love had triumphed. Until now.

Bill and I concluded we should have a good time in Paris and then go back to Rome and break up. We did both. Bill's new friends Peter Matthiessen, George Plimpton, John Marquand, Harold "Doc" Humes, Billy Pène du Bois, and Tom Guinzburg, whom he'd met the previous spring as they were putting together the first issues of the *Paris Review*, showed us a grand time, eventually becoming my friends too. Peter and I clicked instantly. I understood in the ensuing years why every woman he met must have thought him the most attractive guy ever. He was between Bill and me in age. Our friendship continued for sixty years. Literature, birding, island vacations on Salt Cay, trips to Thailand, Antarctica, Chile, Panama, India, and more. We enjoyed family and pals' birthday trips to Italy and Russia, fine quiet evenings on Long Island and in Connecticut with Bill, and my visits to his Zendo on his property, near his house. Then there was humor writer Terry Southern, who'd tried to make Bill smoke pot with him,

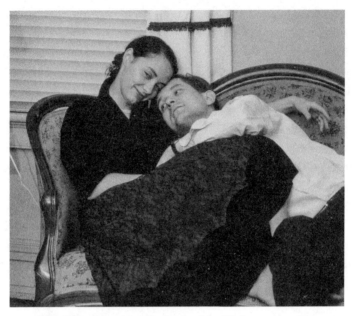

With Bill post-honeymoon in our first New York apartment, 1953.

and popular, older novelist Irwin Shaw, there to celebrate the New Year 1953. Irwin had introduced the guys to the Hollywood crowd who favored Paris then. We were in our twenties—literary, irreverent, energetic, able to drink and stay up all night singing hymns or lieder or classical rounds or country-and-western numbers. Bill had the best voice—perfect pitch, resonant and low, though not bass.

Early in January we drove back to Rome. As we headed into the Italian Alps, west of Turin, the weather turned crazily snowy. We were in a caravan of cars that was stuck in an avalanche and had to be dragged out by cart horses. Slowly. But each car made it out safely, and we eventually got "home."

Soon after we arrived back in Rome, I packed and moved to Florence. We were both convinced our romance had ended. I was quite sad about it, but not so broken up that I couldn't try to figure out how to get on with my new life. I settled down to work on my two books in a room leased by an American artist who'd advertised to share her apartment, a lovely little place overlooking the Arno. I succeeded for the moment in putting Rome and Bill out of my mind.

One day just before Easter, Bobby White, the sculptor at the academy, showed up.

"Why don't you come back to visit Claire and me for Easter in Rome?" he said. "Bill's much too shy to call you himself, but he really misses you. We all think you were such a good pair. Just come stay with me and Claire for a weekend, and see Bill or not, as you choose," he suggested.

Bill with favorite Duke professor Bill Blackburn, late '40s.

I thought, well, why not? The wonderful Whites and their children didn't live at the academy. I might not see Bill at all, but then I had not had a decent date in Florence. I went, and of course they asked Bill over immediately. Somehow I did not go back to Florence except to retrieve my belongings. Within a month Bill and I were planning our wedding. We decided to do it as soon as possible and not invite my mother or his dad and Elizabeth, and tell them later. We wanted no possible emotional complications on the wedding day. I spent more than a month running up and down endless marble stairs because every office where one had to get a stamp or signature in Rome if one was a foreigner was on the top floor of a different palazzo. I was happy but exhausted by the time all the paperwork was in hand.

We set the date for May 4, because I had learned that my brother and Amelie were coming to Europe for the first time, arriving that day. A couple of months earlier, we had driven to Ravello with the Whites to scout out places to rent for our honeymoon. When we drove into the high little town's main square, we were greeted by a parade of nuns in black habits coming down the adjacent mountainside, their starched white wimples flapping like gulls' wings. As they stepped into the doorway of the square's gleaming church, one after another tripped and fell forward with the laughable precision of a slapstick routine. Somebody said it was for a movie. I wondered what kind of movie would include a scene like that.

It turned out that John Huston was there filming *Beat the Devil* with Humphrey Bogart, Jennifer Jones, Peter Lorre, and Gina Lol-

Truman Capote and John Huston, Beat the Devil, *1953.*

lobrigida, and that Truman was writing the script, apparently on the fly, creating new scenes each night to be filmed the next day. The film crew was shooting the church when we arrived, and the nuns were entering for some feast day celebration, and one by one they were accidentally tripping over a fat cable the crew had laid in front of the door! It wasn't a scene recorded in the movie. That evening the crew welcomed us. We were happy to see Truman. John Huston, as I was told, was a great raconteur, although I cannot recall a specific story. Jennifer Jones captivated Bill. I approved of her offscreen simple dark-colored dress, lack of makeup, and easy laugh.

We went up that same hill the nuns had come down and stayed at La Rondinaia, the Swallow's Nest, a dilapidated, old shingled villa owned by an elderly Englishman whom Bobby White's father had known. Gore Vidal would later buy it, restore it to its former glory and more, and live there for thirty years. We scrounged for firewood to cook by and to heat water for washing the diapers of the Whites' third baby, Christian (sixty years later, a fine sculptor himself, he designed Bill's fantastic Vineyard gravestone). Sebastian and Stephanie, several years older, hung the diapers around the living room to dry. From the edge of that property we looked straight down the cliff at Ravello, a view that exacerbated Bill's acrophobia. He went to the edge just once and said he was never taking in that view again.

May 4 arrived. John Marquand and Peter Matthiessen went to the airport to meet clueless Amelie and Bernei. Irwin Shaw had convinced John and Peter to come down from Paris because, he explained to them in a telegram, "a man only gets married two or three times in

John Marquand and Rose and Bernei and Tom Guinzburg, Campidoglio wedding, 1953.

his life." We were married at the Piazza del Campidoglio in Rome. Bronze statues of Romulus and Remus gleamed near the stairs. The ceremony took place in a hall filled with gorgeous white lilies from a funeral that had just ended. Outside the entry stood the grand statue of Marcus Aurelius on his horse. Officiating was a senior Roman judge (I understood he was the mayor), who wore a wide satin shoulder sash in the red, white, and green stripes of the Italian flag. After the ceremony, he went around and shook our party's hands, each time saying, "I hope you will come to my movie theaters." Evidently he owned a chain. Possibly it was his only English. I had been instructed to have a native Italian who could translate for us during the ceremony to make sure I understood I must follow my husband everywhere, forever. Princess Rospigliosi, the academy's person-in-charge, obliged. We all smiled and said in effect, "You bet!"

After the ceremony, everyone went up to Parioli, the international neighborhood north of the Villa Borghese, for a reception at the penthouse that Irwin and Marian had rented. Bill and I were the last of the wedding party to arrive because we had to stay at the Campidoglio and sign more papers. When we got in the tiny elevator of Irwin's new building, there was an older woman with us wearing a wide-skirted brown taffeta dress and brown velvet shoes and white gloves, her marcelled blonde hair half-concealed under a small hat with a veil that had little black birds all over it. I thought briefly of my Baltimore grandmother's hat with a bird veil I'd fancied as a child. May 4 was a hot spring day. I wore a thin blue silk dress, believing (oh, how this dates me) I could not wear white because I was not a virgin.

Irwin met us at the fourth floor and said, "Oh, I'm so glad you all have met."

We looked at one another. He identified the woman with us. "This is Lillian Hellman. Lillian, this is Bill and Rose Styron." It was our first introduction as a married couple.

I was astonished. I had seen *The Children's Hour* and assumed that Lillian Hellman was a tall, steely, gray-haired type, an older version of her main character. Our meeting was momentary, but we would get to know her quite well as neighbors on Martha's Vineyard in the coming years.

After the reception, we went out for dinner and dancing at a restaurant called Ceccarelli's on the Gianicolo, with lit arbors and sweeping views of the city. We danced under the trees and drank wine till dawn, Italian-style. Soon we left for Ravello. The hotel owner had indeed fixed up a fine honeymoon pad for us with a canopied bed, a large round table for Bill to work at: perfection. It had been the town jail, empty for years. He'd covered the concrete floor with turquoise tiles on which I practiced rolling pasta with his old cook whom he sent to give me lessons. Glass doors replaced the prison ones. They looked out onto a lemon grove, the view almost to Naples.

Our honeymoon in Ravello turned into an extended holiday, from early May to late December. Peter and Patsy Matthiessen and their first baby, Luke, who arrived in his basket, came to live with us for a while. Bobby and Claire White and their children took a house down the hill. Very quickly that summer other friends and literary mentors arrived for short visits from Rome, Paris, London, and New York.

"We had a nice routine," Peter recalled in an interview years later. "We'd go down to the sea every day and have lunch and wine and sport about. Bill and I had an ongoing chess game, which was marred by drunkenness. We had a ground rule, no vomiting on the board. And if you overturned the board you were docked two games." From time to time, Patsy and I coaxed Peter and Bill onto the tennis court with us.

Bill had trouble making headway on his planned big second novel, to be called *Blankenship*. "I can't work here," he said. "It's too beautiful. All I want to do is look at the view and take walks down the mountain to the sea."

As fall came on, the Matthiessens decided to return to the States, and they settled on the tip of Long Island in a cottage with a guesthouse ideal for Peter's work. George Plimpton returned to New York, as did Tom Guinzburg. By December, Bill decided he had to get back to America, to the New York he claimed to hate. I reluctantly acquiesced, reminding myself that during our Italian wedding ceremony I had agreed to follow my husband everywhere. It was time to return to the States, where as a married couple, we would first see our parents, who had missed out on the wedding. (My brother refused to forgive me for not inviting Mom.) Then we'd find an apartment.

In mid-December, we sailed from Naples third-class on a ship so tossed by the high winter waves we passengers were all nauseated and leaning over the deck rails, except Bill, who sat in the upper bunk, legs dangling, writing unperturbed. I was not happy. We docked in New York City just before Christmas. As a married couple, we went to Baltimore to spend the holidays with my family, and my mother really connected with Bill. Then we went to Newport News to get his family's approval. We were doing our duty. I loved his dad, "Pop," from the moment we met (as had my mother when he took the ferry to Baltimore to meet her after our wedding). Bill's stepmother, Elizabeth, was cool toward Bill, but nice to me. Pop, when I met him, fulfilled my expectations. He was courtly, gentle, fulsome with the history of his beloved son. He acknowledged that he had wanted to be a writer himself before he became one of the financial directors at the Newport News Steamship Authority. Next, Bill and I headed for Manhattan to rent a flat and start our new life together.

A jamming reunion—Bill and James Jones, Paris, mid-'60s.

I think it took me until we got to New York—Bill's territory, not mine—to understand that we were a really good pair who could have a wonderful life together, not just a fling in that romantic fantasyland: Italy. In our tiny new apartment, I diligently began painting the walls outrageous bright orange and deep teal blue with white trim— tackling whichever room Bill wasn't sleeping or writing in. I savored our satisfying sex life, intimate meals, separate writing areas. At night, I'd fix his favorite mixed grill dinner or spaghetti carbonara, and we'd stay up late, listening to music, singing along now and then. Bill's mother had been a classical soprano trained in Vienna and a church pianist. Surely she inspired his love of music. I had warbled the leads of several high school Gilbert and Sullivan productions and joined Wellesley's Glee Club, so duetting with Bill was easy. I found him intellectually curious, with wide-ranging tastes in music and literature, but little interest in art. In politics, we had joined together in Italy, opposing America's death penalty and intolerable acts of racism.

Bill cherished and was in constant touch with his doting father, who had left the Presbyterian Church he decided was racist, and later became an elder in the Episcopal Church. Bill talked at length about his former roommate and marine buddies, one a prominent sheriff in Florida then. He still contacted each of them by letter. His sense of humor unfailingly surfaced to save a difficult social situation or a less-than-promising writing day for either of us. Our social life surprised me. There were evening visits or excursions in downtown New York with his old Village pals James Jones and Norman Mailer, or transplanted *Paris Review* colleagues George Plimpton and Tom Guinzburg and their current girlfriends and spouses. One evening Jimmy Dean appeared at our door (I can't recall why) and, entering, picked up and turned over a black tin wastebasket to drum on. I was charmed.

Then, very soon, the building across the street began to be torn down. Incredible wrecking balls and jackhammers created a deafening, distracting noise. Bill couldn't think. The bulldozers and cranes arrived as they started to rebuild. More distracting noise. Elizabeth McKee, Bill's agent, was so distressed by his new writing block that she invited us to spend a weekend at her modest house overlooking a quiet stream in Roxbury, Connecticut. Before we accepted (which led to our settling in her town for a half century), Peter Matthiessen convinced us to take a small summer rental near him and Patsy, in Springs, at the tip of Long Island. We relaxed. I got pregnant. New York, revisited in September, was abandoned.

4

Settling in Roxbury

ELIZABETH McKEE AND HER HUSBAND, Ted Purdy, in September 1954, insisted we stay on past the weekend we had agreed to visit while they went to New York City for literary business. They would return the next weekend, but meanwhile, unasked, she sent Roxbury's one real estate agent to show us houses we had no idea we might want to see, including one we bought at the end of that improbably bright Sunday. At 10:00 a.m., the officious real estate agent Malcolm Bray rang the Purdy doorbell. He said the Purdys had paid him to come and show us houses. I woke Bill and said we were obligated to go and maybe it would be okay. The first house Mr. Bray took us to was owned, he told us, by the Styrons. "We're the Styrons," Bill said, amused.

"No, no, *they* are," Bray insisted. Ringing the doorbell of a little white clapboard southern-style house—time-slanted white pillars flocked by hollyhocks—we got no answer. But refrains of *Lohengrin* were blaring from inside. Bray asked if he might boost me to a side window to see if there was a person within. Peering down, I could see an elderly couple, martini glasses beside them, stretched out on the floor near their record player. Bray brought me down, and knocked again, repeatedly. The music stopped. A slight, dapper Reverend Arthur Styron (recently defrocked by his Roxbury Episcopal church for drunken behavior) opened the door. We introduced ourselves as the William Styrons, and he exclaimed, "Oh, Cousin Bill's son! Welcome! I'm the only Styron north of the Mason-Dixon line. You know, I'm a writer too. My recent book was *The Last of the Cocked Hats*. Presidential history, you know."

We digested that, chatted, agreed to keep in touch, moved on, to unpaved uphill Rucum Road. An old, empty white clapboard house in need of repair, with a crumbling white picket fence, full grape arbor, fragrant pink-rose-covered trellis, and

Bill's mother on the left—while studying in Vienna at the turn of the twentieth century.

unkempt lawn caught our eyes. A sturdy barn at the upper end sported smoke from a large stone chimney. We opened its gate, knocked on its red Dutch door, the top half of which opened slowly. We were greeted by a scantily clad middle-aged, curly-haired blond figure who disappeared, reappeared, opened the bottom half of the door, and let us in. He said he was the lone member of his Russian family still residing in Connecticut—his uncle, a famous St. Petersburg doctor, had been head of the Russian Red Cross. Sensing ongoing disaster in his country, he had bought the house in 1916, and hosted countless artists and diplomats fleeing the 1917 Russian Revolution. They had all left Roxbury—for New York, California, or France—several years or decades earlier. He cited among his guests Alexander Kerensky and a Tolstoy, a well-known dancer, and more. We bought the property and moved in as soon as he departed, leaving behind a closet full of unseemly sex toys, shelves sporting peeling nineteenth-century Russian medical books and dictionaries, and anthologies, and a marvelous photograph album featuring early multigenerational tea drinkers and long-trousered, large-hatted, white-clad male and female tennis players in action with their small wooden racquets.

This became home for me and Bill for fifty-plus years. Bill and I were cozy there, and happy. We stayed in the "Little House" (as we later called the converted barn) for three years, while fixing up the long-unoccupied "Big House" one room at a time. It was a shambles. Nobody had lived in it for decades. A sweet stray hound adopted us. Bill abandoned *Blankenship* and started *Set This House on Fire,* its setting inspired by the town of Ravello, which he named Sambuco. We were eagerly looking forward to the birth of our first child in February— the delivery was planned at New York's Mount Sinai Hospital by the beloved next-door neighbor of my childhood, Dr. Alan Guttmacher (who I think had delivered me as well).

Susanna was born on schedule. Bill was crazy about her (as was I!), and he got me to put her on his wake/sleep schedule, more or less late night to bed and late rising. My mother, soon visiting, objected to my picking Susanna up from her crib when she cried. Mom firmly followed the instructions of early-twentieth-century guru John Dewey, and she never endorsed being soft on babies or indulgent with children. We adopted her strict rules briefly, and when she returned to Baltimore we resumed our established schedule.

Bill kept his writer's hours, often sleeping till noon, joining Susanna and me for brunch, and taking long solitary walks with our big new beloved Newfoundland puppy that Bill named Tugwell. Then he would settle in upstairs at a long desk facing a wall (no Italian or Connecticut views) until evening. Around 7:00 p.m. he'd descend for a drink (Jack Daniel's, later Dewar's), put Mozart or Bach or Beethoven on the record player, review his day's work (a page or two or three), and await dinner. After dinner we would put Susanna to bed and return to the living room, where Bill would read to me his new pages and we'd talk about them and possibly what was on the creative horizon.

Those were our closest and cherished moments. Later, Bill would make notes for the next day, probably have a last drink or two, then hand me clean yellow-lined pages filled with his beautiful slanted script. I'd take them upstairs, and the next morning while he was asleep, I'd type up the pages with my two-finger typing. Occasionally I'd make a note to myself, though I didn't always follow through with making suggestions to Bill. This ritual went on for many years, even when the children were in school. By the time he got to the second

Rose with Bill and firstborn Susanna, 1955, Roxbury, Connecticut.

half of *Nat Turner*, I found somebody to do the typing better and faster. But we continued our evening ritual of Bill reading his new pages to me for the next thirty years, until his depression in 1985, when he preferred his solitude.

From the start, Susanna and I would awake early, but not *too* early. She was the easiest baby, the sunniest, most articulate and sociable child. We'd go out to greet the neighbors' cows who lumbered down the hill as soon as we emerged from the red door, arraying themselves just beyond the stone wall at the rim of our little lawn. They must have known I was a fellow lactator. They'd blink their great brown eyes and watch me nurse Susanna. Some days I'd put her in the car for a drive or a trip to the Roxbury Market. Late afternoons found us with books or balls or rolling down our own hilly lawn awaiting Bill.

Occasionally, we'd go to nearby Northville (twenty-five minutes away) to visit Al and Sesyle Joslin Hine and their daughters Alexandra (Andy) and Victoria. Sesyle wrote the children's etiquette books *What Do You Say, Dear?* and *What Do You Do, Dear?* with illustrations by Maurice Sendak. Al was the editor in chief of *Holiday* magazine, and wrote novels and books on Americana. Mary Ann Carlson, eight years old when we moved in, would often take us downhill to her dad Carl Carlson's farm stand or paddock or fishing hole. Carl, a.k.a. "Pinky," brought me the first trout he caught at that fishing hole every

spring until he died. When our son, Tommy, born in 1959, was growing up, he helped out at the farm stand after school. It was a popular
meeting place for all of Roxbury, and I made neighborhood friends
there early.

During our first summer in Roxbury there was a catastrophic
flood that knocked out all the bridges on the Housatonic River. With
Susanna on his shoulders and me trailing, Bill walked down to the
river to watch furniture and actual pieces of houses rushing on the
current down from Washington Depot. We were alerted to this event's
beginning by Mary Ann, padding up the hill in big boots and knock-
ing on our red door early in the morning while we were abed. Used to
her coming to play with little Susanna, I called out, "Oh, Mary Ann,
please go away and come back later." I heard her starting to trudge
away when in a small, tearful voice she said, "Okay. I just came to tell
you there's a flood and Roxbury's cut off from the world!" I hastened
down to hug her, and woke Bill, and we went to meet the Carlsons by
the river. It was an awesome sight.

Our second New Year's Eve in the Little House, we invited the
Paris Review crowd up from New York City and Long Island—the
Matthiessens, the John Marquands, Tom Guinzburg and Rita Gam,
Doc Humes and his wife, Anna Lou, Bob and Gloria Loomis, and

Breaking in the new swing set—Susanna, Bill, Paola, Rose, Roxbury, Connecticut, 1959.

George Plimpton—to celebrate. They slept on couches, in lounge chairs, on the mattressed floors, wherever. We were all so young!

Because it was bucolic and peaceful, yet just two hours' drive from New York City, Litchfield County attracted writers, graphic artists, theater and film people in the 1950s, '60s, and '70s. Arthur Miller had moved up when he and Marilyn Monroe were married. (One of the paparazzi who were trailing them, a French photographer trying to get pictures of their rural wedding, tragically ran his car into a tree at the top of the hill and was killed.)

Whenever the poet and anthologist Louis Untermeyer invited the Styrons and Millers to dinner, the Millers failed to show. Twice Arthur phoned to say that Marilyn had spent so long changing her clothes that it was too late for them to come. She may have been one of the most celebrated beauties in the land, Arthur said later, but she was dreadfully insecure and nervous about meeting "intellectuals."

Alexander Calder lived up the hill. Joey Tillinger, who was one of Arthur Miller's directors, moved nearby. Then there were Lewis and Jay Presson Allen. Lew and Bill, Virginia expatriates, had been friends for years. The Allens got married in New York around the same time Bill and I did in Rome. Lew had an earlier moment of fame as the escort of America's first successful female bullfighter, in Mexico. He started out as a writer and became a creative theatrical producer. He and Mike Nichols produced *Annie* (the first production was in Connecticut). Jay wrote several plays, including *The Prime of Miss Jean Brodie,* and *Tru* (about Truman Capote), and screenplays, including *Cabaret.* Their only child, Brooke, between our first two in age, became like a fourth daughter to us—and still visits with her husband, Peter Aaron, and daughters between sessions teaching at Bennington and at Connecticut's maximum-security prison and writing for various journals.

Bill was a great lover and I got pregnant again quite soon. By the late '50s, after a miscarriage, we had two more children, Polly (Paola) and Tom. We then planned to go back to Rome, perhaps to live there for a year after New Year's Day. But when Tommy was two months old and Polly was seventeen months, I somehow got pregnant again, though that wasn't supposed to happen in the first weeks after giving birth. I couldn't imagine how we could manage four children. Tommy wasn't weaned. Polly declined to walk much on our planned journey abroad. I talked it over with Dr. Guttmacher and he recommended and arranged an abortion for me. Three children was enough at that time. Alexandra surprised and delighted us almost eight years later.

Once we'd moved into the Big House, the Little House remained Bill's studio, except when he lent it to a friend or colleague. Only Bill extended the invitations. The Little House was his domain.

In the fall of 1960, just back from our months in Rome, Bill heard that James Baldwin,

James Baldwin in Bill's Roxbury studio contemplating Another Country, *early '60s.*

who'd been living in France, whom we'd met a few times and whose writing we admired, needed a place in the United States to stay and work. Bill offered him the Little House for as long as he needed it. He stayed through that fall, winter, and spring. He and Bill worked by day (Jimmy had quite a number of guests that winter), and they had memorable evenings by our fire discussing race, American history, and writing. Jimmy encouraged Bill to write *The Confessions of Nat Turner* in the first person (Bill tried the beginning of the novel in both first and third persons), apparently neither foreseeing the controversy that would spark, while Bill applauded Jimmy's working on (the incendiary) *Another Country*. Writing separately by daylight, Bill and Jimmy would meet over drinks, and once I'd fed the kids and possibly helped with homework, I'd serve supper and listen to their conversations.

A following summer while we were on Martha's Vineyard, Philip Roth stayed in the Little House to work on a novel, nearly burning the whole place down. One night he called us in a panic. He'd been cooking and started a fire in the kitchen and wanted to know if there was a fire extinguisher. I said, "Don't call us, call the fire department, but there's surely an extinguisher on the kitchen wall in the Big House." He dropped the phone and ran off. Somehow the guesthouse was saved, but Philip was a wreck. He never stayed there again, buying his own home in nearby Cornwall Bridge.

In the 1980s, our friend Reverend William Sloane Coffin, who had christened all of our children at our home while he'd been the Episcopal chaplain at Yale and was now the senior minister at Riverside Church in Manhattan, was a leading figure in the sanctuary movement for refugees who'd fled Central American tyrannies like El Salvador and Guatemala. Our government, which supported their regimes, still refused them asylum, calling them economic refugees. Bill Coffin arranged with me to use the Little House as a kind of Underground Railroad stop where refugees traveling north to asylum in Canada could stay for a few days. I believe this was the only time I asked my husband if he might give up his privileged space. He was not exactly happy about the arrangement, but graciously moved his work (again) to the main house to accommodate them.

Our longest and dearest tenant in the Little House was Gray Beverley, who rented it every summer from 1970 to 2008. Gray was Lew Allen's friend from Winchester, Virginia, horse and hunt country. He was in advertising in Manhattan and then investment banking. Gray was a tall, dashing, fair-haired southerner. At first he, his wife, Rosie, and their kids rented each summer. Then he and Rosie split, but Gray continued to come up alone every June through October after Bill died. I gather he became the favorite bachelor in Litchfield County. New York editor and publisher Joan Bingham was perhaps his last liaison.

Gray used to love to take a plunge in our ice-cold pond on warm days after tennis, and then lie out on the grass beside it. That's probably how, in August 2008, he caught the tick-borne disease ehrlichiosis. It's rarely fatal if treated immediately, but apparently Gray failed to seek help in time, and, one shocking weekend, he died in our local hospital.

It was incredibly sad. About 150 people from all over Connecticut and New York came to a memorial on our lawn that September. Ellen McCourt had a small plaque secured to the bench on our

*Jay Presson and Lew Allen
in Roxbury, Connecticut, early '70s.*

tennis court dedicating it to Gray, "Master of the Games," and a memorial game ensued that very afternoon. When I sold the house, that bench was taken to another player's court. Memories!

Through the 1960s, Bill and I were both involved in public political campaigns—local, national, and international— always in sync. I was more strident. Along with our political engagement, our local social life definitely expanded as well. The *Paris Review* gang came up often. One spring, several of them decided to practice parachuting from the skies at a farmer's field atop Rucum Hill. Bob Silvers, who graduated from the *Paris Review* to head the *New York Review of Books,* was the most comic, quite plump in those days, landing somehow amid cows and rolling downhill. The cows seemed so alarmed that their farmer refused to allow any more parachuting. Peter's current girlfriend was scared for him. She sat on our doorstep and cried, not watching. I think the guys' next try was in Orange, Connecticut. Wish I'd been there.

Lewis and Jay Allen and Richard and Jeannie Widmark soon settled in the neighborhood, and we became close. Dick and Bill were hilarious together, commenting on famous personages like Ronald Reagan, whom Dick remembered Hollywood pals calling Chester Chatterbox, avoiding sitting with him at lunch in the Hollywood commissary. Dick was nothing remotely like the twisted gangsters he played in his early films. He was intelligent, handsome, witty, principled, and very private. Jeannie, a screenwriter, was funny as well. We were constant companions for years, and actually bought land together in Kent, but after one grand picnic, sold it. If Bob and Norma Brustein came over from Yale, Bill might be sure to play tennis with us, but Jay and Bill would soon bow out. Lew also loved the Brusteins, whom he'd met on the Vineyard, as all Styrons did.

Richard Widmark with Polly's cat in our Roxbury living room, late '60s.

Basically, we artists (writers, actors, musicians, painters) enjoyed a close, pretty quiet, multigenerational community life. Arthur Miller, divorced from Marilyn, married Inge Morath, a talented Austrian photographer whom he met when she was shooting stills during the filming of Marilyn's 1961 movie *The Misfits,* which Arthur wrote. Arthur regularly played tennis on our resurrected court, with me and Dick Widmark and a fourth who later might have been Frank McCourt's wife, Ellen, or Arthur's son-in-law Daniel Day-Lewis. The Millers soon moved from the house Arthur lived in with Marilyn to another one around the bend from it. Our family became good friends with Arthur and Inge and their daughter, Rebecca.

When Rebecca was four or five, Arthur and Inge had a baby, Danny, who was born with Down syndrome. Alexandra was born a week or so earlier, and when she was a few weeks old, I went up to visit Inge and her infant son. Inge was holding him and crying, saying, "Arthur is making me send him away." Arthur had said he would ruin their family life. Danny was taken to a nearby place that was renowned for excellent care, fifteen minutes away, where Inge would visit him every Sunday. When he was two years old, Inge brought him home, hoping to persuade Arthur to let him live with them. He was so cute. He periodically pulled treats out of Inge's pocket, a game that he was accustomed to when she visited him. Arthur said no, that Danny was like a little animal. Inge, sad, took him back and Arthur never saw him again until the year before Arthur died. Danny, then a high-functioning Down syndromer, learned from the couple who had adopted him in Waterbury (where he was employed too) that Arthur was coming to speak nearby and he went to the auditorium to listen to his father. After Arthur spoke, Danny went up and said, "Dad, I'm your son Danny." That was their only meeting. Arthur did not even invite him to his mother's funeral. Rebecca, who used to go with her mom to visit Danny, still sees him regularly when she is in the United States. I've always respected the privacy of my friends' and their families' lives, but the pain of this situation surely distressed me for a long time. I so love and admire Rebecca.

The Allens, Widmarks, and Styrons bought a huge property together up and over the hill from us, where the Widmarks and the Allens occupied their houses. We had the big field across from them. We thought we might build houses up there, but since each of us was settled and happy where we were, we Styrons never did. Bill told our youngest daughter, Alexandra, that he'd save a piece of that land for her, but unbeknownst to me he sold it a number of years before he died to pay some taxes. Alexandra was quite disappointed about that, as was I. She wanted to move back from New York with her husband, Ed Beason, and their two little children, Huck and Sky. I would have loved that, and of course I tried to help promote it. Al had building plans all set. But it was still too expensive, and Bill made the financial decisions for the family as was common in those days. Another regret.

After our beloved, fun-loving pal Jeannie Widmark died and Dick remarried and moved to his wife Susan Blanchard's house in Roxbury Center, he offered to lower the price of his property by half for his goddaughter, Al, and Ed. I was elated. Then the price of building a wing for the growing kids (Dick's house was a one-bedroom) turned out to be even more prohibitive. They couldn't afford it, nor could we help enough. Our finances were unusually tight at the time. Al and Ed relocated in Brooklyn. I knew on my visits to their two successive homes—digs just large enough, beautifully arranged and decorated— that after a disappointing situation they'd made perfect choices for themselves and their two children, now teenagers: sweet, amazingly talented, Huck a musician and Sky an artist.

Soon after we had moved to Roxbury, through introductions by Bill's agent, we felt adopted by our community of artists. Ten minutes west of us, over in Bridgewater, lived the literary historian and critic Van Wyck Brooks and his still beautiful, charming wife, Gladys, who I was told had been a model for Charles Dana Gibson's "Gibson Girl" drawings around the turn of the twentieth century. Just beyond them, in Sherman, were other members of the older generation who would invite us over: the Malcolm Cowleys and the John Cheevers, and the painter Peter Blume and his wife, Evie. Peter Blume bought the farm where the artist Arshile Gorky had hanged himself in 1948, after years of pain and torment (cancer, a broken neck from an auto accident, his studio barn burning down, his wife and children leaving him). Later the choreographer Martha Clarke bought the house. My daughter Polly, a lead dancer with Martha for more than twenty years, moved to her home, Sherman, famous for its wide gardens of spring daffodils and irises, and both live there still.

Christmases always seemed magical to me. We went to the Van Wyck Brookses' two early Christmas Eves. The first time we carried baby Susanna in a little basket. Gladys Brooks ceremoniously lit candles on the big tree, one by one, to a hushed audience. I realized I'd stashed Susanna's basket directly under a spreading branch. She was wide-eyed under it, and I, panicked, not knowing what to expect from a wildly glowing candlelit tree, quickly moved her and the basket, to guest laughter.

Twice, on later Christmas Eve afternoons, we drove to the Leonard Bernsteins' in Fairfield, a forty-five-minute drive southeast. When we got back home those nights, Bill always read *The Night Before Christmas* to me and the kids by the fire in the old living room. We hung stockings, joined in the recitation we all soon knew by heart (Polly and I recited it to each other on Christmas Eve 2021), wrote notes to Santa Claus and his reindeer to leave on the china plate with cookies and milk, and the kids climbed the stairs to bed before midnight. Then I stayed up wrapping presents and putting them all around the room for a morning surprise. I had never experienced much of a Christmas as a child, and I happily overdid it.

On one of the drives home from Fairfield, we were pursued, then headed off, by an angry man in a pickup truck. Bill stopped the car, ordered us all to run up a steep green hillside right there. Al was in my arms again, no longer a baby, and we hunkered down. Bill thought the man was brandishing a gun. When he finally left, Bill called us down

Tommy's second Christmas, 1961.

to our car, and we sped up the road to Styrons' Acres, as James Jones called it, and to *The Night Before Christmas,* as if nothing had happened.

For years after the Fairfield jaunts ended, we turned our own Christmas nights into memorable gatherings, with the Bernsteins, adding Roxbury neighbors. I was never happier or more excited than on Christmas morning as I watched the children (and later grandchildren) embrace their new stuffed animal or admire a shiny car or clasp a new book or play with the trains I'd set in motion under the lit tree we'd trimmed the afternoon before, with shimmering, special ornaments saved year after year. Could the children have been half as happy as I? Bill, of course, wouldn't wake up until nearly noon. He'd appear in a short plaid robe, bare-legged (he had beautiful slim legs), feigning horror and refusing to open his presents before the front room mess was cleared, all the wrapping paper burned in the roaring fireplace, the kids' presents stacked in neat individual piles or stashed upstairs or, if new skis or little sleds had arrived, propped outside on the often-snowy porch.

We'd eat a helter-skelter lunch and play with the new toys, then prepare for the evening party in the larger back room we built to my design (stolen from the barn structure of the cottage but with huge windows, high ceiling, sliding doors, a big bar under the balcony). Arthur Miller, an accomplished carpenter as well as playwright, built the wooden staircase that led up to the balcony. We moved my parents' Steinway from Baltimore into this room, and it became a center of the evening's festivities, year after year, long after Bridgewater and Fairfield destinations.

Friends and neighbors filled that room with mirth and music. Some were regulars, others came and went over the years. The Bernsteins always joined us. The Millers, the Allens, the Widmarks, and later the Bill Luers, the Frank McCourts, Mia Farrow and André Previn, and once Jerzy Kosiński seeking Lenny for a favor. Lenny played Christmas carols on the piano as we stood and sang, always ending with a rousing rendition of "The Twelve Days of Christmas." Each of us sang the same part every year. Our son, Tom, and Lenny's son, Alexander, who was a couple of years older, did the "five go-old rings" as a duet. Neither of them apparently could carry a tune, and year after year they delighted in belting it out off-key, to our laughter. Bill chose ever to be the soloist of the tenth verse, deliberately getting the lords a-leaping and maids a-milking all mixed up. Lenny at the piano then sang mock Christmas carols in a variety of accents and languages for the grand finale.

After Arthur cast Dustin Hoffman in the 1984 revival of *Death of*

With Mother, holding baby Polly, and Susanna, Roxbury guesthouse, 1958.

a Salesman, Dustin bought a house just over the hill from us, where he and his family lived for a few years. His kids and ours would write and rehearse wonderful little plays they performed for us up on the balcony before the Christmas music even began.

From time to time, we would be joined by Bill's mentor Hiram Haydn, under whom he'd studied creative writing at the New School, and who was his editor on *Lie Down in Darkness.* Hiram and I disagreed strongly over Vladimir Nabokov's novel *Lolita,* which Lew Allen had just smuggled into the country from France. I engaged in close conversation with Hiram, saying how terrific Bill and I thought the book to be, and urging Hiram, who was now Bennett Cerf's senior editor at Random House, to publish it. But Hiram declared *Lolita* disgusting, not funny. Bennett loved the book but did not want to contradict his senior editor, so Random House passed on it, as Bill's former publisher/employer had passed on *Kon-Tiki* at Bill's determination—before Bill was fired.

Our home was the scene of many birthday celebrations, especially Bill's every June 11. I remember Vladimir Horowitz sitting down at the Steinway once when I'd neglected to have it tuned, playing "Happy Birthday" to Bill and groaning at the sound. And Tom Brokaw starting to toast Bill one birthday in the front room crammed with festive tables when a French film crew barged in, unsettling him.

Bill and Rose in France filming the documentary on Bill, 1996.

The director, who has the unforgettable name Variety Moszynski, was shooting a documentary, *William Styron: The Way of the Writer,* and had not mentioned her planned visit with crew. I can't remember if what they filmed, post-toasts, made it into the French-sponsored movie. I wonder if it's still available.

Norman Mailer and his wife, Adele, moved up to Connecticut in 1956, because Norman, Bill, and Jim Jones had been friends in Greenwich Village before I knew any of them. Norman was struggling with his writing and his fast New York City lifestyle, and believed, as Bill and so many others did, that a quiet rural setting might help him get back on track. Norman bought a quaint saltbox in nearby New Milford with some of the money he made selling the film rights to his novel *The Naked and the Dead.*

One of the first things Norman did when they moved in was to build an "orgone box" in the barn behind the house. The orgone-accumulating box was invented by the psychoanalyst Wilhelm Reich, whose theories about the mental and emotional damage caused by sexual repression were controversial in the repressed America of the 1950s. The press had a field day writing about "sex boxes," which eventually led to Reich's being arrested. The poor man became a cause célèbre among intellectuals and died in prison in 1957.

The other thing Norman built in the barn was a boxing ring. He'd taken up boxing when he quit smoking. Maybe it was another way for him to feel properly manly. Norman was always competitive with other writers, including his friends. He closely watched every development in Bill's and Jim's careers. Temperamentally, Bill and Jim were more alike, more laid-back, than stormy, pugnacious Norman. As Bill and Jim drew closer, Norman felt jealous. Perhaps one of his reasons to move near us was to become closer to Bill.

Norman thought his second wife, Adele, wasn't interesting enough compared to the other women in our circle. He enrolled her in Hans Hoffmann's art classes and displayed her large, bright abstract paintings on every wall in the house. Saltboxes had never before been so startlingly decorated! For our fifth anniversary party, a low-key home celebration to which our parents and Bill's publisher, Bennett Cerf, were invited (Bennett and my mother had danced together at cotillions thirty or forty years earlier and had a sweet reunion), Norman sat crouched outside our front door, challenging each male guest to arm wrestle in the cluster of blossoming andromeda before they entered the house. He convinced Adele that she should pretend to be bisexual and come on to all the women.

I was never quite sure why Norman decided on that fiasco. He always liked to stir things up, to make an impression everywhere he went. So Adele got dressed up like Goya's *maja*, with a long black lace dress, heels, and a black mantilla. She looked glorious. The rest of us were in casual country attire. Norman coached her to try (to no avail) ridiculous tricks she should play upstairs in our bedroom where several female guests wandered to leave their coats. Jay and I were in the hallway then, and watched, amused. Another night at his pal's house, once inhabited by Arthur Miller and Marilyn Monroe, Norman tried to get six of us to tell personal stories, then sleep together after recording salacious tapes. Suspicious, I found the tapes under a couch while the others were spouting tales. Primmer Bill and I left in disgust. No bedtime for us!

Soon afterward, I was in Mount Sinai having our second daughter. She arrived two weeks late, early one afternoon. We named her Paola, in honor of both Bill's mother, Pauline, and our beloved Italy, though we knew we'd call her Polly. Following her birth, Bill said, "I'll see you tonight," and went home. Around 6:00 p.m. Jim and Gloria Jones surprised me by appearing in my room. It was the eve of their leaving for Paris, where they would live for the next seventeen years, Styrons visiting every spring. They opened a bottle of champagne. Polly at my breast soon was sound asleep, and she slept most of the next two days as I swelled uncomfortably. When Bill returned that evening, he had the longest face I'd ever seen. The Joneses were obviously concerned too.

"What's the matter?" I asked him.

"I just got a terrible letter from Norman," he said. It was a single typewritten sheet. There's a photocopy of it in James West's biography of Bill. Bill read it aloud to us:

Bill,

I've been told by a reliable source—closer to you than you might expect—that you have been passing a few atrocious remarks about

Adele. Normally, I would hesitate to believe the story, but my memory of slanderous remarks you've made about other women leaves me not at all in doubt. So I tell you this, Billy-boy. You have got to learn to keep your mouth shut about my wife, for if you do not, and I hear of it again, I will invite you to a fight in which I expect to stomp out of you a fat amount of your yellow and treacherous shit.

Bill was dumbfounded and crushed. He and Norman had been friends for years. He wrote a brief reply on the bottom of the letter saying he had no idea what Norman was going on about. Norman responded that Bill's note was "a crock of shit" and dared Bill to meet him face-to-face and repeat it. I had just had a baby. I kept my speculations to myself.

The Mailers moved back to New York not long after this. We all celebrated. In 1960, Norman came home to their Upper West Side apartment, drunk and in a rage, and stabbed Adele under the heart with a penknife he'd picked up on the street. She was hospitalized but soon recovered. She adored him, so she didn't press charges. They did divorce. Years later I saw Adele once, working as a salesclerk behind Henri Bendel's glove counter. I was surprised and pleased to see her, but after a few pleasant words together decided not to pursue more contact. When Norman died in 2007, a *New York Times* reporter looked her up and found her living in a squalid tenement apartment. She had been an artist. Norman denied her any support. Looking back, I wondered how many women ended up in similar circumstances.

For almost a quarter of a century Norman harbored his grudge against Bill. He trashed him in print every chance he could get, including writing scurrilous things about him in his book *Advertisements for Myself*, where at least Bill was in good company, since Norman wrote awful things about almost all of the contemporary writers with whom he felt himself in competition. Bill declined to respond to Norman privately or publicly, though James West notes in his biography of Bill that Bill did weave some of Norman's less appealing characteristics into the character of Mason Flagg, the brilliant, madly egotistical rapist in *Set This House on Fire*. Strangers probably wouldn't have noticed, but friends did.

Bill and Norman did eventually reconcile, more or less. Two convicted murderers brought them back together. Over the years, Bill and I had become increasingly concerned about our country's prison system and the death penalty. Amnesty International made me a continuing activist for that cause. In 1962, *Esquire* printed two articles Bill wrote about Ben Reid, a young Black man on death row in Hartford, Connecticut. (They are included in Bill's collected essays, *This Quiet Dust*.) Bill didn't dispute what Ben had done that resulted in the death penalty: At nineteen, he had slammed an older woman on the head with her purse, which he was stealing, and she died. Bill argued that Ben's background as a poor Black youth made him "a kind of wretched archetype: the Totally Damned American." Largely as a result of Bill's involvement (although others got involved in the case), Ben's sentence was commuted to life in prison with the possibility of parole.

In 1970, he earned that parole, and as part of the process of his reentering the world, Bill agreed to let him stay in our guesthouse for a couple of weeks, until we found him a place to live. I was entirely sympathetic with what Bill was doing for Ben, but I did not really want him near our children.

Just a few days before his release, Ben escaped. He abducted a woman and raped her. He was soon caught and got a new sentence of ten to fifteen years behind bars. We never saw him again, but I read up on his complicated life in and out of prison afterward. Very, very disturbing.

Norman later sponsored Jack Henry Abbott. Abbott, who'd knifed another inmate to death in prison, was a gifted writer. In the late '70s, Norman helped him to get his book *In the Belly of the Beast* published. Norman was instrumental in his getting paroled in 1981. Abbott moved to a halfway house near the Mailers, and Norman squired him around his literary circle. Six weeks later, when Abbott stabbed a young man to death—a waiter, also a struggling writer—Mailer was widely reviled in the press. Bill came to his defense. He wrote a wonderful piece, also in *This Quiet Dust*, saying he understood what Norman had tried to do. Norman wrote him a letter thanking him, and they tentatively renewed their friendship. I wondered how it would develop.

· · ·

I put the publication of my adult poetry on hold while raising Susanna, Polly, and Tommy, born the year after Polly. (Alexandra arrived more than seven years later.) I slid the poems I still wrote regularly into a drawer, and there they sat. I didn't read those poems to Bill. He was happy that I was writing, but he wasn't involved in my work. It hurt my feelings a lot at first, but I put it down to his writer's natural narcissism. I didn't know how to have a good marriage and an independent, time-consuming literary career. I had been taught by my mother, as I've said before, to always let the man lead, to accommodate his needs and promote him. Her words were in my head, even much later when I didn't always act on them.

I did write for and about my children when they were young. I conceived all the poems outdoors while enjoying being with the kids, climbing trees, tumbling down the lawn, sledding, hiding Easter eggs, watching Tom in his go-cart and all their drama with each other. When I was young I'd been pretty solitary at home in Baltimore. This was my new childhood. The poetry about Alexandra came a decade later. The early poems were in the children's voices. The simplest among them were little summer ditties. Some were more meditative, tinged with a bit of melancholy, because, after all, children know that summers end and they will grow up. On one of Tom's young birthdays, as I watched him walk an island beach, I wrote:

> *I'm older than these spiky cliffs*
> *and older than the sea,*
> *walking the silent sunrise beach*
> *there's no one old as me;*
>
> *no one to think of deaths to come*
> *nor watch our footsteps fading*
> *fast in the sands of morningtide*
> *where the wind and I go wading.*

A collection of these poems became the book *From Summer to Summer,* which Viking published in 1965, with charming illustrations done by an Italian artist named Rita Fava.

The one time Bill actively discouraged my writing involved Robert Penn Warren, one of the American writers Bill most admired.

Although Bill and Red, as he was known, were a generation apart, they had bonded as southern writers (Red was from Kentucky), and they respected each other greatly. Bill read *All the King's Men* in New York City in 1947 and would say it was his chief inspiration for writing *Lie Down in Darkness*. They met at Van Wyck Brooks's home in Bridgewater in the late '50s and became instant friends. Red understood Bill's writing and was always encouraging to him. When Black intellectuals attacked *The Confession of Nat Turner* as inappropriate (cultural appropriation) of a Black "hero" never written about before 1968, Red participated in a literary panel at the annual meeting of the Southern Historical Association in New Orleans to discuss it. He invited Bill to participate along with Ralph Ellison and C. Vann Woodward, who also supported Bill's decision to write the novel in first person, Nat's voice.

Red's wife, Eleanor Clark, was a tall beauty everybody admired. She grew up in Roxbury. After graduating from Vassar in the 1930s she went to Mexico, worked as a translator for Leon Trotsky, and was married for a few years to one of his secretaries, Jan Frankel. She wrote novels and travel books, most notably *Rome and a Villa*. It came out in 1952 and we read it in Rome. We first met her with the composer Alexei Haieff at the American Academy, and later met her again as Red's wife in Connecticut. They lived in a large converted barn in Fairfield and had two great kids, Rosanna, who started as a painter and became a respected poet (still my friend and colleague), and Gabriel, who became a sculptor. They used to invite our family up to their place in Vermont to go skiing in the '60s. Eleanor was a crack skier, swift and aggressive and beautiful. Red and Bill, cautious southerners, weren't much for skiing. Bill never put on a pair, and Red only tried it at Eleanor's urging. He was on the ski lift, probably daydreaming, and fell off from such a high point that he broke both legs. He never put on skis again. Instead, he used snowshoes to trudge around. Bill loved that idea, and while the rest of us skied, the two of them would snowshoe, then sit by the fire and talk literature.

Eleanor liked me (especially after I wrote a laudatory article about her for the Book of the Month Club magazine). But she wanted nothing to do with Bill after an annual black-tie December dinner in their home in the late 1970s. The table was magnificently set and lovely classical music was performed by special guests, followed by a sump-tuous dinner. At one moment during the first course the literary critic Harold Bloom declared that Red, who had just published a new novel, should stop writing fiction and stick to poetry. Bill found this rude and angrily defended his friend. Eleanor evidently felt that Bill went too far in attacking Bloom, and from then on we didn't see much of the Warrens. When Red was dying in 1989, Eleanor wouldn't let Bill come visit him, which Bill took very hard. I stopped visiting on my own. I had regrets about the decision, but at that time maintaining a peaceful marriage with Bill was uppermost in my plan.

In addition to being a great novelist and essayist, Red was our poet laureate, the Consultant in Poetry to the Library of Congress, and an excellent teacher. He cowrote the enormously influential New Criticism textbook *Understanding Poetry* with Cleanth Brooks. New Criticism was very much in vogue when I was at Johns Hopkins, and I was a great admirer. After *From Summer to Summer* came out, Red asked if he could read some of my unpublished adult poems. He invited me over to Fairfield to bring the poems and talk with him about them. I was flattered and delighted.

When I arrived, Eleanor fixed us tea. Red and I were sitting with my poems, he giving me much-needed good advice on cutting, and on endings, when Bill stormed in and had a fit that I was there. Robert Penn Warren was *his* admired friend, and Bill didn't want to share him with me intellectually.

"We're leaving," he said. "Let's go."

I was shocked that he was so angry and putting on such a display in front of Red and Eleanor, who were equally startled.

"You don't have to go if you don't want to," Red told me. But Bill was in such a state. I didn't want our marriage or our friendship with the Warrens to be ruined over my poetry, so I left with him. It was an embarrassing and uncomfortable moment for all of us. I never again talked to Red about my poetry. I did, however, take the advice he gave me that afternoon about cutting "To Samarkand," and potentially reconsidered the last lines of other poems that were soon published. Interestingly, my younger admired poet friend Jorie Graham offered similar advice on a later poem or two. I am still learning.

I might never have published a second book of poems, for adults, if it hadn't been for Jerzy Kosiński, who found all the ones I'd stashed in a drawer in my office. He was teaching at Yale and occasionally came over to Roxbury. One day in the early '70s I came home from delivering the kids to school and Jerzy was at my desk, rooting through the drawers. He was a real snoop and I protested.

"Whose poems are these?" he asked.

"Mine," I said.

"Why haven't you published them?"

I told him I didn't know and asked him to put them away.

"Well," he said, "if you're not going to take them to your publisher, I'm going take them to mine. I'll ask my girlfriend, Kiki von Fraunhofer, to type them all up at our New Haven apartment."

I guess I was pleased, and must have replied, "Thanks, I'd love to have her type them. Then I think I should take them first to Viking." Viking soon published the collection as *Thieves' Afternoon* in 1973.

Aside from our forays to Fairfield County and the Westport area to visit friends, we went most frequently to New Haven to visit with our friends Bob and Norma Brustein. Bob founded the Yale Repertory Theatre in 1966, and we'd go see all the plays. Meryl Streep was a star performer in its early decade. We saw her in several productions and became friends long before she auditioned for *Sophie's Choice*. Philip Roth and others of our writer friends tried out their plays under Bob's auspices in New Haven, as did Bill with his humorous *In the Clap Shack* in 1972. That season Bob had accepted a post in London, and the production (in New Haven) never got a second chance, to Bill's disappointment.

Bob decided to stage a production of Chekhov's *The Seagull* outdoors on our lawn in Roxbury after the close of his final semester at Yale in 1979. It was an experiment in what he called location theater. Chairs were set up on the lawn, with the idea that we'd shift them around to watch scenes performed at spaced sites, concluding under our flowering cherry tree. Bob and his wife, Norma, took small parts, she as Polina and he as Shamrayev, with students in several of the other roles. I asked our farmer neighbors, the Carlsons, if Yale could transport a white horse to their farm to stay for the day, until the young blonde actress could ride him uphill onto the set. In further preparation, we thought it best to separate our randy Newfoundland, Beauregard, from Tommy's pretty young goat Heather, with whom Beauregard was clearly in love. We tethered them on separate ropes to the opposite doors of our toolshed, down the walk behind the house.

Bob was pleased with the crowd the production attracted, especially the appearance of Arthur Miller, even though he, Bob, had not responded kindly to Arthur's plays and Arthur wasn't speaking to him at the time.

The performance had been going along beautifully when we all turned our chairs to face the flowering cherry tree for the last scenes. A breeze came up on cue, perfectly rustling the blossoms for the last scene. But nobody was watching it. They were watching Heather the goat, who had chewed through her rope, and was being humped by Beauregard in front of the toolshed, down beyond the cherry tree.

Bob was furious at the animals for "ruining" his production. That June, after the kids and I left for the Vineyard, Bill shipped off our dear Heather to a distant farm. Tommy and I were distressed, but Bill couldn't stand any more problems. We used to get calls from neighbors, like the one at 6:00 a.m.: "Your dog and your goat have burst through our porch screen and are in our bed. Come get them immediately!" When I arrived, I surprised a local workman, our good pal, who was having an affair with a local wife, the one who'd called. I blew his cover. I was sorry!

Bob had directed a new full production of *The Seagull* before leaving the Yale Rep to start the American Repertory Theater at Harvard. While preparing for that production, he and Norma spent two weeks with Bill and me on Salt Cay. Norma, oddly it seemed then, kept walking the beach, talking to a baby in her empty arms. Barely months before, the Styrons and Brusteins had chartered a big sailboat and had a joyous week with our children circling the Caribbean. Bill had just finished *Sophie's Choice* then, and Norma, who loved his writing, grabbed the manuscript, reading it first before passing the pages along to the rest of us.

Norma was the first woman I knew to have a face-lift. She invited all her girlfriends to come visit when she was in bed to view her "transformation" as she healed. I wondered how she could be more beautiful. She was preparing for a role or two in Bob's plays. Her regular job was teaching theater at Yale.

Norma was one of the most fun of my mid-twentieth-century

gang of girlfriends. We met on the Vineyard when she was very pregnant with her son Danny, between Tom and Al in age. He and Al,
as they grew up, became pals, playing at the Brustein home in New
Haven (Katie Feiffer, Jules and Judy's daughter, was their third play-
mate) and sailing the Caribbean with us all on spring vacations.

The *New York Times* critic Richard Gilman slammed Norma's performance in *The Seagull,* which sent her into a depression. As I mentioned, I was baffled by her walking the beach at Salt Cay with us,
scant weeks before, as if she had a baby in her arms, perhaps talking
to it. I put it down to her being an actress. But apparently she was on a
strong antidepressant (possibly an MAO inhibitor as Bill was soon to
be), which forbade drinking alcohol and eating organ meat. Following the performance on our lawn with its comic side scene (Norma
laughing at Bob for his fury), Norma went home. She returned for
lunch at Mendy Wager's in Roxbury the next noon for a celebratory
cast party. Mendy was an actor, famous for his TV voice-overs, and
a close friend of the Leonard Bernstein family, especially Felicia.
Norma, carefree after the play, drank a lot and ate forbidden foods.
She went home. Bob was being feted at his farewell dinner since they
were heading for their new apartment in Cambridge the next day.
Norma dropped dead. Danny, a teenager, found her on the floor.

I was devastated. Bill and I adored her. Bob was of course in
despair. He grieved deeply for the next seventeen years, appearing
like a sad Chekhovian character, until he met and married the lovely,
smart, extraordinary Doreen Beinart. They are still happily married.
She has saved his life and sanity more than once. Each of us wants
her as a close pal.

Immediately after Norma was buried, before Bob and Danny
moved, Bob asked me to come to their New Haven house to pick
out a favorite piece of Norma's clothing to keep. Norma and I used
to shop together, in the days when I still enjoyed it. I chose a white
lace-trimmed skirt that she bought on one of our outings. I still wear
it on special occasions every summer.

5

Roxbury Years

BILL AND I had a deep and satisfying marriage for almost fifty-four years—in quiet rural Roxbury, Connecticut, for most of it. We were close, sharing pleasure in the property we planted and rebuilt, good sex, and wonderful children who arrived and grew up together, with us, outdoors and in. We treasured our many evenings together after the kids were in bed or, soon enough, engaged in their own personal lives. At night, after dinner, Bill would read me his afternoon writing, which I unfailingly admired, occasionally made a suggestion for. We watched the news, rarely a movie, and if we had not had company for dinner or gone to another couple's house, would say good night by 11:00 p.m.—I needed only six hours of sleep, never much liked getting up in the dark. I often wrote my poems before arising. In old age, I stay in bed longer (doctors' orders), scribbling whatever.

Bill would stay up way past midnight, probably have another drink, planning the next day's writing. He'd come to bed then for cozy hours. After dawn, I'd tiptoe out, have my own cherished morning hours with our children, take them to school or playdates or not, and, returning to myself, type Bill's yellow-lined pages filled with his beautiful slanted script, a teacher's dream. Or I might go shopping (Bill loved to do the food shopping on his daily trip to the post office, surprising me before it was time to cook dinner). Or I might garden or write—a poem, an article—until he arose, near noon. Then brunch. Walks: Bill's with his dog or dogs, me joining some afternoons. Afterward, Bill would settle in his office (no longer our bedroom once we'd moved to our remodeled "Big House" (definitely not a jail!). I'd resume life with our kids—mostly separated from Bill (who, as I've said, required absolute quiet for writing hours, full attention concentrated on his inner self . . .). Only after Bill died did I discover how many of those hours must have been spent writing letters to friends. I collected the best of them for a volume, *Selected Letters of William Styron,* published by Random House in 2012. He wrote long, beautiful letters to pals and, the best, to sixteen-year-old daughter Susanna whom we sent off for a post-graduation gap year at Franklin University in Switzerland. What adventures Susanna promoted in Switzerland and Italy! "Number One," as he always called her. He permitted her to buy a car, specifying which not to consider. He filled her in on what her parents were up to, described our trips and daily sentiments (he always included me in his letters to everyone, knowing I was not a letter writer). I'm grateful still. And that encouraged me to go check up on her, which I did, delightedly, twice. I found copies he'd saved, written to most valued compatriots from Professor William Blackburn to Robert Penn Warren, Willie Morris, Jim and Gloria Jones, Peter Matthiessen, and to literary cousins such as John Updike and Philip Roth. He never promoted himself, his stature as an American writer. In one missive he described himself as "a mass of insecurity." Correctly, I thought.

Those were years of deepening love between Bill and me. My understanding of his personal fragility—that accompanied (day-to-day) his extraordinary talent and total devotion to his writing, which the literary world so promoted—was revealed by his pretense that he didn't read reviews and was voiced whenever a poor one appeared.

As to my poetry: As I've written, I was quite surprised and disappointed at first that Bill did not want to listen to what I was writing—needing creative thoughts for himself, really rarely appreciating his younger kids' ideas and activities and achievements either, it seemed too often. I'm certain they felt neglected.

Bill and Rose, 1960s tennis game, Martha's Vineyard, before retiring from tennis.

I asked each of our kids if they remembered special moments with Dad. I won't record them here, except to indicate his lack of attending their school events that I so looked forward to personally and always attended when home.

Polly says her dad was too scared she'd get injured (as she did once when thrown off onto a paved Vineyard road, on her head, by her beloved steed). She says he did come to her performances onstage, especially her dancing in Martha Clarke's spectacular events. Nor did he ever attend Tom's expert playing in ice hockey games at Taft. Alexandra, however, says he did cheer her on at her pony riding events—perhaps because he was older and calmer? Closer to Al when I was away? Psychologist Tom commented recently that he had warm feelings for Daddy despite his "grossly egregious parenting." Surely he attended Susanna's film premieres, also the in-progress days of "her" *Shadrach,* based on one of his short stories.

But my life was so full—so rewarding with Bill's and my time together personally, socially, intellectually, politically—that when I wrote my poems (frequently in my car while awaiting kids' exits at school) I was content to just tuck them in drawers, assuming I would

Bill contemplating his future pages, 1970s, Connecticut.

finish each, enhance and type them sometime in the future. I did
not have time or need for meeting with other poets often, but treasured invitations I accepted occasionally for literary excursions on my
own—for instance, to Ireland.

As you might guess, being our opinionated selves, we argued frequently, often too loudly. Did that scare our kids?

An observer once commented that I must compartmentalize my
brain. Another suggested I did that with success, between public
and private life. I never planned it, but human rights missions surely
required new personal programming.

I trust Bill enjoyed our trips together with our growing children
each winter as much as I did, especially around the Caribbean, on
hired boats or in island hideaways, always with friends like the Brusteins or Joneses. We brought the kids sporadically to France, Italy, or
once Egypt. What a peripatetic family we turned out to be, in contrast to the settled at-home one in Roxbury. Then and now we call
home Martha's Vineyard as we each are for long, varied, comforting
stretches of time here.

6

Buying the Vineyard House

A FEW YEARS AFTER OUR WEDDING, Bill and I and little Susanna visited Michael Carlisle and his Coffin grandmother on Nantucket. Bill's editor Hiram Haydn called to say we should take the ferry to Martha's Vineyard and visit him and his wife, Mary. We agreed to meet at the Vineyard Haven dock. When we arrived on the agreed-on afternoon, there was no Hiram. He'd forgotten our plan. As we stood puzzling, a blonde angry woman swooped past us, chasing the biggest black poodle I'd ever seen. "Gregory Zilborg!" she kept shouting. "Come back here!" In vain. She then spotted an older man (Harry Levin, head of Russian studies at Harvard) on a wobbly bicycle heading down the street. "Harry! Go get Gregory!" the woman shouted, and he dutifully turned in chase.

The woman suddenly turned and spotted us, and we recognized each other. "What are you doing here?" she asked. It was Lillian Hellman, whom we had met at our wedding reception in Parioli. Hearing our plight, she insisted we come to her house, a short walk up the beach, and call Hiram from there.

Through the garden and onto a porch we trooped with Lil, followed by the large, breathless Gregory Zilborg (named for her psychiatrist). Dashiell Hammett was sitting in a rocker and he lifted Susanna onto his lap. By the time the Haydns arrived, we'd had tea and cookies and

Lil had persuaded us "not to go to that vile island Nantucket ever again." She instructed us to book two weeks the next summer at an old white-shingled house near hers, and we did. From 1960 until 1963, we Styrons rented for a summer month on Martha's Vineyard—on the way to West Chop, in Katama (next to Wal-

With Lillian at beach, early '70s.

ter Cronig, whom we did not know then), and in Vineyard Haven. Vineyard Haven was our favorite spot, even though we were teased about being centered on Murderers' Row, as the strip of Vineyard Sound land was known, where Lillian Hellman, Philip Rahv, Mary McCarthy, John Hersey, and Diana and Lionel Trilling spent social but often spiteful summers.

Around Labor Day 1963, after sending our three kids home to Connecticut with Bill while I closed down the house we had rented from the Philip Rahvs, I walked to town. My mission was to go to Carly Cronig's real estate office to rent for the next summer. I arrived five or ten minutes before six o'clock closing time. The phone rang as I stood before Carly's desk. He answered it, saying, "Oh, Mrs. Eels, I'm so sorry. Your husband died this morning? Of course you want to go back to Cleveland right away. Yes, I'll be glad to see to it for you, yes, completely furnished," or words to that effect.

Bill and I had never thought of buying a summer place on the Vineyard, but I heard myself say brightly, "Mr. Cronig, what will the price of the house be?" He replied on the spot: "Seventy-five thousand dollars." Bill and I didn't have that much in the bank, but I knew his new novel would be ready soon, and I decided I could

Bill with Lillian Hellman on Lil's porch for afternoon cocktails, '70s.

call my mother in Baltimore and my brother in Bethesda to see if they would put the amount in the Styron account, to be reimbursed within a year or so. I told Carly we wanted to buy it, immediately! I had not consulted Bill. Carly replied, "If you can have the check ready at 9:00 a.m. tomorrow, it's yours."

By 10:30 p.m., I was squared away with Bill and with my family. I reported to Carly, who reported to Agnes Eels, and I prepared a check—thrilled.

But at 8:00 a.m. the next day I received a phone call from the real estate broker, saying, "Oh, Mrs. Styron, I'm *so* sorry you didn't get the house. My other client will pay twice as much, and of course, I have to get that for Mrs. Eels."

Confused and saddened, I hung up. I called Agnes Eels to, again, express my condolences about her husband. And to say how sorry I was not to get the house. Silence for a moment on the other end. Then: "What do you mean you didn't get it? We agreed last night!" Then, "This isn't Agnes, it's her sister-in-law. You better get over here with your check right away. Agnes has gone to the hairdresser to look proper for you at 9:00 a.m. Hurry!"

I went, pronto, check in hand. Both Mrs. Eelses greeted me, put my check on the mantelpiece, gave me two hugs and a glass of tomato juice.

"I'm so glad to have someone with young children buy our house," Agnes Eels began. "Three generations of us have been happy here. You probably don't know it, but your daughter Susanna [eight then] tried to ride her bike across our narrow seawall and fell off, down into the sand. We rescued her and she and my granddaughter Marianne are now playmates at the Yacht Club." I had apparently walked on the little beach past her property to the club almost daily with our three kids. I realized I'd never even *seen* this house I was buying: A row of trees blocked it from beach sighting, but the lawn before them was wide and inviting, as was the raspberry patch at the seawall's edge. Those trees soon blew down, in Hurricane Bob, and our view from the slightly sloping old lawn to the Sound is endlessly life-enhancing.

At about 9:15 that morning, as we three women were sitting contentedly, Carly entered behind us and, seeing me, said, "Oh, Mrs. Styron, I'm so sorry you didn't get the house."

Agnes stood and said, "What do you *mean*, Carly? We settled this last night. Of course Mrs. Styron got the house."

Carly dug in his heels and said, "But, Mrs. Eels, I'm your agent and I've got twice as much for you—$150,000."

Agnes didn't believe him and asked how he managed to up the price after 11:00 p.m. He explained that when he saw last summer that her husband was ill, and heard he was declining during the winter, he brought his client to look in the windows. And then they managed to get in through the back door.

Agnes was furious, and I watched as Carly continued talking, saying that his client insisted that he wanted to buy the property if it ever came up for sale. Carly had called him when Mr. Eels died.

"*Get out,* Carly! No commission for you. The house is Mrs. Styron's," Agnes shouted. Then we learned that Carly's client had hired a private jet from Washington and was on his way to the island. Carly was frantic. Agnes instructed him to use the kitchen phone and call the man and tell him the deal was off.

Carly obeyed. We could hear him whining to his client's wife in D.C. that the sale was off, and yes, he knew how angry her husband would be, and, okay, he'd go to the airport to meet him. Now!

And off he went. His client was so angry that he echoed, "No cut for you, Mr. Cronig," and added, "I'll sue her!" In those days Massachusetts was one of the few states where an owner could be sued for "wrongful sale."

Agnes Eels then said to me, "I know you can't afford it, but I'll block him through every court. You'll probably have to rent our house next summer." And we did, acquiring it in 1965, after the three state courts he petitioned at $25,000 each (lawyers, paperwork filings, whatever) turned him down.

Our fifty-seven years on High Hedge Lane have been incredibly rewarding. The narrow byway was named by me a few seasons ago when the island suddenly required each resident to have an exact address for the fire and ambulance and plane rescue teams we value highly.

We've met wonderful folk on Martha's Vineyard, and entertained a great assortment of pals from the United States and abroad. I've so benefited by introducing a number at our dinner table. Lillian Hellman and I soon became friends when we started summering on the island. She invited me to come down to her house so she could teach me how to play Scrabble, which she played daily with her sweet friend from Chicago, a member of the Marshall Field family whose unique nickname I forget. Lillian taught me so well that soon I was beating her at most games, which she insisted on playing for small amounts of money. By the next season I could see she was cheating, scrutinizing the letters that she picked up each turn, placing them in her lap and exchanging the ones she didn't like. I thought it was funny and never called her on it. Often she invited me to her beach shack in outer Chilmark, and we would play in the sand while munching our sandwiches. I enjoyed those outings a lot. I knew Lillian got cross if I missed a weekly date with her because I was spending time with someone like Virginia Durr, whom she envied and disparaged loudly.

After Lillian died, the heir to her homes, Peter Feibleman, wrote a small book about her. While he was embarking on it, knowing that Bill and I had separate issues with Lillian, he said to me, "Of course you know it was you not Bill she was in love with." I laughed and said, "Don't be absurd." He said, "Didn't you notice that whenever you came down to play Scrabble, she had done her hair and donned her best island clothes? Also that whenever I came into the room with you two, she shooed me out?" I laughed again, and said, "I tried to shoo you out too. You always hovered, trying to advise one or the other of us what moves to make."

Lil was an ace fisherman, and she went out in rented boats and then her own. She persuaded Dick Goodwin to share in buying a boat one summer, which was disastrous as they fought over the payment and who could use it when. The denouement was that Dick went off with the boat and sold it. Lillian didn't speak to him again. Just as Bill and Dick didn't speak after Dick stole Bill's Cuban cigars. But I loved his second long-term wife, writer Doris Kearns, and still do. Usually Lillian is the bad guy in the stories, but this time it was Dick. I hear a fine marriage reformed him.

Lillian was always trying to separate Bill and me, except during her dinner parties. She disinvited us once after inviting us in early

June for a July dinner. The morning of the party, her secretary called to say that Lillian Hellman was so sorry that Bill and I had declined the invitation to the party. I said we had accepted weeks earlier. Of course, we didn't go. John Marquand said the reason we were dissed was because Jackie Kennedy was coming and Lillian didn't want to share Jackie with us. Jackie was *our* friend, and she was Lil's star for the evening.

Bill always ordered Smithfield hams from Virginia. He would soak them and get me to help him make the glaze and put in the cloves. (When Al was around four, he decided to soak the ham in her bathtub, instead of the laundry tub he usually used. She went into her bathroom and saw it and came running downstairs crying, "Daddy, there's a dead man in my bathtub." Because of course Smithfield hams bleed. It's why you have to soak them.)

Bill prepared the hams and sliced them paper thin, often serving them in biscuits. Lillian said to him one day, "Bill, you serve these wonderful Smithfield hams. Why can't you give me one for my dinner?" He did. When he and I arrived for the meal she prepared, he saw that Lillian had cut deep into the ham and was serving inedible thick chunks. He was so angry with her. There were times, like that one, when the two of them didn't speak for months. In the end they always made up. He took her out to a last dinner before she died. Her eyesight diminishing, she dropped all the ashes from the cigarettes she kept smoking during dinner into her food and seemed not to mind the taste.

I never got into it with Lil. My mother had warned me about her. I kept my personal, my interior, distance from Lillian. When I read her story "Pentimento," I knew who she'd gotten it from. I thought it was one more way in which Lillian, who was brilliant and charming, got away with it, pretending to be who she wasn't. Though in the end she didn't, when research connected to the Mary McCarthy lawsuit revealed the real "Julia"—Muriel Gardiner. I'd met Muriel Gardiner once through Amnesty. I don't know if Lillian ever met her, or if she adopted the story and made it her own, but Lil and I had lots of good times together. Among them were catching crabs up-island, covering her porch table with paper, and cracking them open southern-style with Bill and others. Bill often made us all delicious crab cakes (at least as good as those I remembered from my childhood cook, Rosie) from the leftover crabmeat for our shared dinner.

When I attended Arnie Reisman's funeral recently at the Abel's Hill Cemetery, a grassy, hilly, sprawling expanse up-island, one of the speakers mentioned that he'd seen Bill and me there at Lil's burial thirty-seven years earlier (with Warren Beatty famously popping up). Fonder thoughts of Lil surfaced again.

7

Friendships

MY LONG FRIENDSHIP with actress and fellow activist Mia Farrow began on the Vineyard, in the summer of 1965, when she (all of nineteen or twenty) and Frank Sinatra were courting. They sailed into Vineyard Haven on his chartered yacht, the *Southern Breeze,* and anchored in the middle of the harbor across from our dock. Rosalind Russell and husband Freddy Brisson were with them, and another couple who were screenwriters, the Goetzes, and Claudette Colbert.

Susanna, a fearless, strong swimmer at ten, convinced the current family babysitter to let her swim out to the *Southern Breeze* from the Yacht Club dock. She swam to the boat, circling it. Frank's weather report apparently indicated a storm was brewing, and when he saw Susanna, he worried about choppy waters. He later told me that he leaned over the railing and said, "Little girl, do you want to come up on the boat?" Susanna apparently said no thank you.

Susanna's memory is that "they all came out. They were waving, and then Claudette was yelling, 'Wait! Don't swim back. We'll take you!' Or something like that." Frank then commanded Mia to get Susanna into their little launch and accompany her home, which she did.

Salt Cay, the Bahamas, with Carol Southern, Lillian,
John Marquand, Sue Marquand, Bill, our kids.

I had been downtown, oblivious. Bill was extremely cross with me for "allowing" her to go, but I was home waiting when Mia shepherded our adventurous daughter back to shore, and Mia and I met for the first time.

After Mia's delivery of Susanna to our door, we became good friends, and she fell in love with the Vineyard immediately. Following her marriage and breakup with Frank but before marrying André Previn, she bought a charming little house on Lake Tashmoo.

"I determined that I would have a house that I would never give up, no matter what," Mia said. "Because I left Frank without taking a thing. I loved the Tashmoo house so much that when I did marry André, I would call the house even though I knew no one was in it. I figured the mice would hear it, that sound of the phone ringing against my books."

Bill and Mia and I had a long, remarkable friendship. Soon after Mia and I met on the Vineyard and she bought the house on Tashmoo Pond, she and Bill became close friends. That persisted until Bill died. Mia came for dinners with just the two of us or multiple guests. During both of Bill's depressions, Mia was always on hand to be with him and talk. He loved her. She would stay with him if I had to go to town to get meds for Bill, or when I had a special hour or two with the kids and he needed company. I loved their closeness and relied on Mia. She and I connected with each over motherhood and activism. She and Bill had their own private conversation.

By 1981, getting back and forth to the Vineyard with all her children was becoming difficult. And the mosquitoes were multiplying insanely on Tashmoo Pond. That winter, when Mia was visiting us in Roxbury, a real estate friend of mine showed her (me tagging along) a property for sale in Bridgewater, fifteen minutes from ours. The place looked rather barren the day we went, though the setting was promising, with woods and open snowy fields.

The house only had a few bedrooms and Mia had nine children, so she assumed it couldn't possibly be suitable. Plus, everything was falling apart, obviously. Then one day that spring, Bill and I invited Mia to lunch. Bill brought out a bottle of wine, which we polished off before going over to see the Bridgewater dwelling again. That's when she saw its myriad possibilities, and decided it was the *perfect* house. It turned out that the big space covered with snow that we'd seen earlier wasn't a field, it was a gorgeous lake, and the trees that were gray in winter were exploding with leaves and blossoms. Mia turned the house and surrounding property into a wonderful lakeside home that she and her ever-burgeoning family have enjoyed ever since.

I met Frank Sinatra the day after Susanna's swimming adventure. That night, Frank's first and second mates had gone into Vineyard Haven by launch and picked up two girls in town. It was already after midnight when they wanted to come back to the boat with the girls, and there were no launches, so they walked up and got a rowboat off the Yacht Club beach, adjacent to ours. (Luckily it wasn't our boat, a stone's throw away . . .) There were only two life jackets since there were supposed to be only two people in the rowboat. But there were four passengers. The girls were given the protective gear. As they rowed out toward the *Southern Breeze,* the water became super choppy and the boat turned over. One of the mates didn't know how to swim, and he drowned. We woke up early in the morning with helicopters flying overhead and boats looking for the young man, whose body was found near the harbor entrance. Frank's craft was impounded. He and the crew had to stay. I can't recall exactly how we all met.

Frank and Mia got married soon after that. Then they got divorced because she insisted on leaving California to star in *Rosemary's Baby* and Frank threatened that if she did he'd divorce her. And he did, quickly, to Mia's distress. Later, Frank would come to visit, usually when Bill's publisher, Bennett Cerf, and his wife, Phyllis, would charter a boat to sail up from their home in Mount Kisco.

Frank lived in the Cerfs' guesthouse in the summers. Bennett's wife was crazy about him. They sailed up to Martha's Vineyard for three summers. For the first sail, we hosted a dinner and invited Lillian Hellman, who behaved badly, not being the center of attention. She got up and left. The next summer, I told Lil I was having Frank for dinner, and she said, "How could you invite Frank Sinatra again?," adding something quite disparaging about him and about my upbringing. Hours before the dinner, she pretended that she was meeting another famous person and asked if I would like to join them in the Edgartown Harbor on his boat. Naturally, I declined. John Marquand, my perpetual spy, assured me later there was no famous person or boat. I was amused, as always.

On one occasion, Bill and I were off to Nantucket with Bennett on his boat, and Frank arrived at the Vineyard airport too late to join us, so he went to our house to wait for our return. A new sitter, an islander, was keeping baby Alexandra occupied until we returned. The sitter was so startled to see Frank strolling up to our door that she fell apart, handed eight-month-old Alexandra to him, and fled. When we docked a little later, we saw Frank sitting cross-legged on the lawn with our baby safe in his lap.

Another memorable evening with Frank occurred one summer in the late '60s and involved our new friends and neighbors Sheldon and Lucy Hackney. Sheldon was from Alabama, a historian of the South, and over the decades had been the provost of Yale and Princeton, president of both Tulane and the University of Pennsylvania, and chairman of the National Endowment for the Humanities, never abandoning his teaching of southern history. Lawyer Lucy was a major champion of civil rights and children's defense. She grew up mostly in Virginia, the product of generations of Alabamans, the daughter of Clifford and Virginia Foster Durr.

Virginia was the granddaughter of a slave owner. At Wellesley, after being chastised for declining to dine at a table with the only Black student there, she began to reevaluate her southern upbringing, recognizing and regretting her unwittingly racist response. She found her voice and became a major champion of civil rights in the South. Clifford had been in FDR's cabinet, and his uncle Hugo Black on the Supreme Court. Their house outside of Montgomery was a famous hangout for civil rights leaders and for students and Freedom Riders during the "Mississippi Burning" years. Once she ran for Congress in Virginia but was not successful. She and Clifford moved back to Alabama permanently when he left FDR's government post, spending much time also in their famous country home that is still called P Level. Granddaughter Elizabeth, writing a historical novel about it, recently speculated that it was actually called that because they grew peas there. (In the late 1980s, *Esquire* asked various famous men to write about the woman of their dreams. They all seemed to write about nubile young actresses and models—except Bill. He wrote about Virginia, who was in her eighties at that point.)

Back to the late '60s. Lucy and Sheldon rented a cheap apartment for several weeks in the ramshackle Bayside Inn, just through our hedge in Vineyard Haven. One night they invited us to supper. Noth-

Family on Martha's Vineyard lawn with babysitter Christine, 1967.

ing fancy, Lucy assured us, just spaghetti and salad. About an hour before we were to arrive, Frank called us from his boat, which had just pulled into the harbor. I phoned Lucy and asked if we could bring a guest.

"Sure," she said. "Who is it?"

"Frank Sinatra," I replied.

"Frank Sinatra!" Lucy cried, dismayed. "Are you sure you want to come here? It's just spaghetti."

I assured her that spaghetti was Frank's favorite dish. Lucy often recounted the evening, highlighting the humble meal they served the star, with beer "and probably really bad wine." She remembered Frank taking one look at the drinks and getting on the phone to his yacht. Mates soon arrived and hauled cartons of liquor up the stairs to the apartment. Next, Frank and Bill decided to phone Cuba, trying to order the good cigars they both treasured, from Castro himself. Frank had a very young woman with him who made Lucy cross by flirting outrageously with Sheldon. Frank never seemed to be aware of her presence. Lucy and I laughed forever reminiscing about that— our first evening together. We became each other's very best friend.

I loved Frank. He was great fun. I looked forward to greeting him on the Vineyard and attending his spaghetti dinners at different restaurants in New York. I had a hard time forgiving Bill for turning down Frank's spontaneous invitation to join his cruise to London and events there, even though he offered a side trip to Paris, which Bill always told him was his favorite place. I of course would have accepted. Bill rarely did anything spontaneously, while I latched on to any promised adventure. Sometimes I wonder how we lasted together for more than half a century. I guess love beats all differences.

Among the special friends I've spent time with on the Vineyard are members of the Kennedy family. I first met Jackie in April 1962 when Bill and I were invited to the White House for a state dinner honoring all forty-nine Nobel laureates then living in the West, along with various notable writers and artists. It was probably Dick Goodwin, a big fan of Bill's writing, who arranged our invitation. Jimmy Baldwin— living with us in Connecticut the winter before—was also invited, and we went together. I sat between two Nobel Prize–winning scientists, one of whom was the tall, impressive Linus Pauling. Kennedy had recently announced that the United States would restart atmospheric testing of nuclear devices, which had been suspended a few years earlier. Pauling was a leader among the thousands of peaceful protesters who picketed outside the White House the morning of the dinner. Hours after the demonstration, he changed into a tux and came back for the evening event. On my other side sat Albert Szent-Györgyi, a short, gently spoken, gray-haired twinkly Hungarian who was obviously a great scientist. I knew what Linus Pauling had done to win his Nobel Prize, but I didn't know about Albert Szent-Györgyi. I asked Pauling, quietly, what Szent-Györgyi's Nobel was for. Someone had mentioned that he worked in Woods Hole, Massachusetts. Pauling said simply, "Mussels." I assumed he was an oceanographer or marine biologist. Then, as I was talking to Szent-Györgyi, he smilingly informed me that it was not mussels, but *muscles*—he was a biochemist working on the chemicals that give muscles their energy. He'd won his Nobel back in 1937 for extracting vitamin C from—naturally, being Hungarian—the paprika plant. He graciously laughed at my misconception.

Soon the White House military band started playing in the hallway to signal we should move for the postprandial musical gathering across the way. Pauling got up and asked the woman on his right to

Ready to sail with Teddy Kennedy and friends, '70s.

dance, and Szent-Györgyi asked me. Apparently, no one had ever danced to the announcing band at White House dinners before. But after we took the floor, several couples got up and danced away too. Years later, at the John F. Kennedy Library, I saw a photograph on the wall of Pauling and his dance partner. I think I spotted a more distant one of Szent-Györgyi and me.

When the president stood to address us, mid-dinner, he made his famous remark, "I think this is the most extraordinary collection of talent, of human knowledge, that has ever been gathered together at the White House, with the possible exception of when Thomas Jefferson dined alone." Much later, when the affair broke up and Bill and I were heading for the exit, an officer in dress uniform suddenly stopped us and said we were invited upstairs to the Kennedys' private quarters. Never having met them privately, we were surprised, but of course, most pleased. We went up to their drawing room and joined a small gathering that included Bobby and Ethel and other Kennedys, Arthur Schlesinger, Robert Frost, and Lionel and Diana Trilling.

By this point in the evening, Bill was, as he later wrote in *Vanity Fair,* "plastered." The liquor and wine had flowed freely, as they did on such occasions in the '60s. Bill had just rushed home by plane from France, where the French edition of *Set This House on Fire* had been published to rave reviews. (Its reception in the United States had been decidedly more muted.) In Paris, Bill had caught the flu and this night he was drinking on top of his flu medicine. So when he saw JFK's famous rocking chair, which Kennedy favored because of his bad back, Bill plopped himself down in it. The president came in and gave him a genial look. Several other people shot him sterner ones. But Bill was in deep conversation with Trilling, and the president was too much the gentleman to shoo him out of the chair. To my relief and delight, the president sat on the couch next to Robert Frost, who was next to me. It was only when Arthur Schlesinger leaned down and suggested that Bill get up and give the president his seat that Bill realized his faux pas. He got up. Kennedy laughed, and, as I remember, the two discussed literature at length.

Jackie was lovely and gracious. Bill described her as "shimmering." She and I talked about Martha's Vineyard, and she said they would sail over from Hyannis that coming summer.

And they did, inviting us to meet them in Edgartown as they sailed from Hyannis on the cabin cruiser *Patrick J.* They picked us up at the public dock, along with their old friends John and Sue Marquand. John told us he had dated Jackie in their younger days. This windy, sunny afternoon we went on a cruise around the harbor, relaxed and chatting, drinking Bloody Marys. Jackie laughing often, her big bare feet propped in Jack's lap at the on-deck massage table that accommodated his bad back and soon, with a tablecloth placed atop it, our lunch. A mate brought us beers in tall, conical glasses. It was a beautiful day, but the water was rough. A wave knocked over the glasses. None of the beer spilled out. It had frozen down below in the boat's fridge. We all laughed, set the glasses upright, and waited for the beer to thaw. Then the same mate brought lunch, oeufs en gelée. The eggs had frozen too, but jolly conversations resumed.

As we came back in, we headed straight for the Edgartown Yacht Club. A crowd had lined up along the dock. The captain assumed that people were waiting to greet the president, but when we had drawn quite near, Kennedy blurted, "Oh no, they don't want to greet us. There's not a Democrat on that platform. Turn around and go back to the town dock." We did, hating to have the afternoon end.

The last time we saw President Kennedy was in the fall of 1963, at a party at Steve and Jean Kennedy Smith's comfortable two-story town house in Manhattan. We left our coats on the second floor, and as we descended the wide stairs, we came upon the president, standing alone, "looking momentarily lost and abandoned," Bill later wrote. He threw his arms around each of us and said to Bill, "How did they get *you* to come here? They had a hard enough time getting me." The president was utterly charming. He asked Bill how *Nat Turner* was coming along—they had talked about it months earlier—and the president requested advice on which Black writers and leaders he should be consulting on the civil rights issues he was determined to deal with, inviting Bill to come down to Washington before Christmas to consult.

Two weeks later he was killed in Dallas. Bill and I sat with his visiting father, Pop, who cried as we watched the Arlington ceremony on our small TV in Connecticut.

·　·　·

The following August, Jackie brought Caroline and John-John for a weekend visit with us on the Vineyard. John-John was going on four and Caroline was six. Jackie stayed in the back guest room. The kids slept in twin beds in the middle room. Bill and I were in our front bedroom. John-John had brought his new pet rabbit along and in the morning turned him loose in the middle room. The rabbit disappeared "down the rabbit hole," a roundish break in the floorboards between the beds, which we had never noticed. Cries erupted. I walked into the room and saw Jackie on her hands and knees between the beds, reaching down into the hole, determined to pull the rabbit out. But she was unsuccessful and the creature went all through the house. The Secret Service men were stationed at every possible exit, some on their bellies, and finally the bunny was caught by afternoon.

The sun was descending. A relieved Jackie suddenly turned to me and said, "Where's John-John?"

"Oh, probably playing with the other kids," I ventured.

"Well, I see all the other kids out on the lawn," she replied, "and I don't see him."

Two Secret Service men were posted on the dock at all times, and two more on the seawall, but none had noticed that their small charge had disappeared. (Each August, a few years later, an amiable pair of Secret Service men who guarded our next-door August neighbor, Mrs. Lyndon Johnson, would sit similarly on our dock. I asked Lady Bird's nephew Phil Bobbitt, who joined us frequently, why they would

With Jean Kennedy Smith at an event.

never lift a finger to help her around the place or carry her things, especially the load of pots and pans she would cross our lawn with at the end of each visit to store with her friends the Hackneys, across our hedge. He said the men believed they had to keep their hands free for their guns and walkie-talkies to protect her!)

In this moment the Secret Service panicked. Luckily, James Terry, a Black southerner who had moved us to Connecticut and became our beloved caretaker there with his half–Native American wife, Ettie, whom we adored, was visiting from Roxbury, and helping to cook for us and our guests. He went alone to look for John-John and found him up the beach toward West Chop. It appeared that John-John had seen people roasting marshmallows on the sand and wandered up there to join them. The picnickers welcomed and fed the little boy. He was fearless, repeatedly jumping off the Yacht Club dock into the sea, to the consternation and envy of our son, Tommy, who was a year older. Over the years all our children, it seems, were later struck by the many Kennedy cousins' daring.

Fifteen years after our weekend with the rabbit and John-John wandering off, Jackie bought Red Gate Farm in Aquinnah. Almost four hundred acres, secluded and largely undeveloped, with freshwater ponds, untouched dunes, scores of birds, and an endless long, gorgeous beach, it became her perfect summer refuge. She was very, very private, and only her closest friends and family were invited to visit. I considered myself lucky to dine there at lunch twice. And once a year, every Labor Day, Jackie would host a large beach picnic and invite the rest of the Kennedy family from Hyannis or wherever they were at the time, with all their children and grandchildren: a lively reunion. We were always invited to swim and lunch too, along with the Buchwalds, the Wallaces, Carly Simon, and Jackie's other island friends. It may have been the only time she saw that huge Kennedy clan, though she and Teddy were close. Caroline and John looked up to Uncle Teddy with special love and admiration. When Teddy and Caroline suddenly spoke out so effectively to support Barack Obama's presidential candidacy in 2008, I was reminded of that bond, and silently applauded.

Bill and I once went cruising on Maurice Tempelsman's boat with Jackie. Maurice had become her companion after she split with Onas-

Summer of 1993 on Jackie's beach (Red Gate Farm, Aquinnah),
with Caroline holding daughter Tatiana, and Jackie.

sis. Maurice struck me as a slightly older, plump Buck Mulligan who
was courtly and always nice to us. Low-key Maurice let Jackie carry
the ball conversationally. Our paths still cross from time to time at
the Council on Foreign Relations or the Academy of American Poets
board meetings. He always greets me warmly.

I remember coming upon Jackie once in our kitchen, sneaking a
piece of Bill's famous fried chicken. (That was before he taught me
and then Daphne, our summer cook, how to make it and gave the recipe to Tamara Weiss's Vineyard cookbook, *Potluck at Midnight Farm*.)

Her last summer on the Vineyard, there was a quiet lunch on
her terrace for her old pal George Plimpton and his mother. That
day Jackie gave me a recipe I had requested for her wondrous dessert, "summer pudding." Following Jackie's death, Caroline and Ed
Schlossberg had taken over the house, and they invited me for lunch.
I went into the kitchen after dessert to see Marta, the splendid cook
and housekeeper, whom we'd all known for a long time. When I told
her I never got Jackie's summer pudding recipe quite straight, she
said, amused, "Oh, Mrs. Styron, Jackie didn't know how to make summer pudding. She asked me for the recipe that day and wrote it down
for you. I guess she left something out." Marta and I laughed as I told
her I'd inflicted an unsuccessful version of it on guests. "You know
you have to get good currants, *off*-island," she told me. For years I had
the recipe posted, faded, on our pantry bulletin board.

At Jackie's Labor Day party on the beach that year, she giggled

Ted Danson, Bill Styron, and Bill Clinton, mid-1980s, Martha's Vineyard.

as little Jack, her grandson, squealed to Carly Simon's rendition of "Eensy Weensy Spider," with tickles. Then, emerging from a swim, Jackie's laughter rang out as she and I tried in vain to stop our family dogs' tug-of-war over the blue shorts I'd shed on the sand.

I first met Ted Kennedy at Art and Ann Buchwald's rented house next door to our new home in Vineyard Haven in 1965. A score of Kennedys had appeared for a party on Art and Ann's sloping seaside lawn. (We had actually rented that property before we bought our own. Browsing in its adjacent music house, I had found in the piano bench an opera score written by the wife of the owner with opening instructions for the cast to run down to the water and plunge in, singing. The lyrics began, "See our naked bodies! Here we come!" Lawn scenes there must have always been classic.)

The next summer the Kennedy-Buchwald-Styron reunion was on *our* lawn. It is memorable for more than one reason: Ted, Bobby, Ethel, Sarge and Eunice Shriver, and a boatload of younger family members had anchored at the public dock in Owen Little Park, visible from our seawall, and everyone had walked from the beach up to our porch. I recall being taken at the sight of Teddy in coral linen beach pajamas, curly hair protruding from his half-open shirt. I welcomed the family and entourage. Moments later, Art Buchwald, who

With Obama at The Granary, Chilmark, Massachusetts, August 2007.

had taken his first series of driving lessons ever, was heading his car down our lane and directly over Bill's treasured new vegetable garden, flattening his young cornstalks and burgeoning produce. Bill could be heard loudly cursing his friend. I saw Kay Graham hurrying up to the house as far from the driveway as she could, looking panicked.

Once Bill had calmed down and we convened in the living room, it was Ted who laughed loudest and put everyone at ease. Bobby, too, soon implored me to drive him and the crew from Hyannis not only down to the Owen Park dock but onto the walkway dock boards all the way to their boat tie-up for a quick getaway. I was severely reprimanded by the police as I backed cautiously all the way down the dock to park safely.

Next morning, Art appeared before 7:00 a.m. as I was retrieving the *Boston Globe* and the *New York Times* from the driveway. He staked a cord fence around the ruined garden and attached a sign saying, "Corn killers will be shot on sight." Friendship resumed.

That was in the mid-'60s. Teddy made many trips to the Vineyard, sailing over from Hyannis in various Kennedy crafts, swimming or rowing in from the Harbor or Sound where he'd parked securely, climbing our dock, or, if he had tethered at the Vineyard Haven Yacht Club, scaling our seawall onto the lawn. He was always merry, and we were overjoyed to have him appear. Bill's mood inevitably soared.

After the assassinations of his brothers, it became an annual ritual for Teddy, paterfamilias, to sail from Hyannis to our house midsum-

mer, bringing his children and a slew of nieces and nephews, a babysitter, sometimes Ethel, sometimes a sibling of Teddy's, Eunice or
Jean. The children brought sleeping bags, which they deposited on
the lawn. We would try to find beds or couches for Eunice or Jean
or Ethel. Teddy, and often little Patrick, who had asthma, slept in
Bill's studio (the only individuals who did then). Twice we had to
take Patrick to the Martha's Vineyard Hospital at night. Years later,
when my granddaughters decided to bunk there and Emma got sick,
we discovered that the unheated, uninsulated little shack was full of
mold, which we then had removed. I wished I'd known about it years
earlier. Today it's the teenage boys' exclusive hangout.

Once, Eunice was in the only available guest bed, and Ethel gamely
found space under the dining room table when it started to rain on
her porch couch. I found her asleep there in the morning. Her lack of
comfort may have been what prompted her to throw a glass of milk
in Bill's face later that day when she took offense at some remark he
made. Both referred to it, teasingly, for years.

The Styrons and the Kennedys would have grand times on those
visits. Ted would always help fix supper, grilled on the lawn, and get
the children to spread their sleeping bags across the grass. In the
morning, Ted would cook a mountain of scrambled eggs, I his crisper
assistant for pounds of bacon. Then we'd all repair to an ocean
beach—different each year as we famously wore out our welcome.

Teddy was an exceptional father. He organized football games and
flashlight tag, which they called Farmer Brown, on our late afternoon
lawn. One time Teddy was Farmer Brown and disappeared. Nobody
could find him, which seemed a great coup on Teddy's part—he
was found hidden at the bottom of the shallow cellar stairs, cushioned and half covered by wind-deposited leaves. Triumphant, he fell
asleep. The champion, he awoke and entertained us at dinner with his
great laugh when we finally found him.

Often, after breakfast, we would pack up the Styrons and the whole
Kennedy clan and head for a beach, with the Buchwalds usually in the
lead. Once, we were unceremoniously ordered off a beach we thought
public just as we sat down to an elaborate lunch table we'd laboriously
set up. Art Buchwald presented me with a painting he'd bought on
Cape Cod of crowds pressed together, titled *Rose Styron and Friends*

Jackie's picnic with Carly Simon, 1990s.

at a Private Beach. It still hangs above our stairway.

Another adventure was in a three-vehicle caravan down the steep and rocky road to Jackie's unpeopled stretch of sand. She was not in residence, the family knew. There we had a splendid picnic and long swims. When it was time to head back, Teddy and I left first with some of the kids. Then Ethel rounded up the remaining crew and picked up whatever she saw on the beach, including Eunice's clothes and bathing suit. Then she drove up the hill and back to Vineyard Haven.

As it turned out, Eunice had gone to hide behind a secluded dune to pee, and Ethel had left her stranded, naked, except for a not very large white towel. She was forced to climb the rock road barefoot and walk the long driveway out toward the road, Moshup Trail, to hitchhike back, wearing only that towel. And it began to rain.

Meanwhile, the rest of us were back home, Teddy starting to fix supper, I counting noses before setting places in the dining room and on the porch.

"Where's Eunice?" I asked.

We all looked around. And then the Kennedys whooped. They realized we'd left her behind.

It took Eunice three rides to get back across the island to our house. By the second one it was raining hard. She finally appeared on the porch, totally wet and bedraggled in her towel, caught between fury and tears. The other Kennedys all laughed. Eunice smiled gamely. You had to be able to in that family. I took her upstairs to shower and gave her some of my clothes. She came down to supper and never said another word about it. How I admired her!

One morning, possibly the next summer, we all headed to Windy Gates and its endless steps to the beach below. Teddy Jr., twelve, had just lost one of his legs from bone cancer. His dad seated him in our car, pointing out Vineyard sights and history all the way to Chilmark. There was no way his son could maneuver the 132 wooden steps (I counted) down to the beach and back up, but Little Teddy, as he was known, gamely agreed to wait on a bench at the top landing. I had called the Baldwin family house early to ask if we might come and swim for an hour, promising to leave before the owners and guests descended, before 10:00 a.m. A cheery female voice had responded, "Of course! Come!" But when we ascended on time and collected Little Teddy, a man and a woman were pressed against the rail behind him. We smiled, nodded, left. An hour after we returned to Vineyard Haven, the phone rang. An angry man's voice shouted at me, "Don't *ever* come to our beach again! How dare you?! I don't care how many poems you've written about Windy Gates." (I'd recently published one in the *Vineyard Gazette*.) Taken aback, I sort of apologized, saying I'd called first and got permission. "That was our babysitter you talked with, not us," he shouted. We both hung up. I was soon told their beef was that I had not introduced them to Senator Kennedy.

Despite the fact that Roger Baldwin, then ninety or more, my mentor at Amnesty International and the founder of the ACLU, had invited my children, Bill, and me to come anytime—and we did, the kids and I climbing and then sliding down the golden dunes, dunking in the deep clay pits before refreshing swims—we were now informed that Roger's late wife had owned Windy Gates and willed it to her children. They wanted no intruders. Roger, a staunch Democrat, was disapproved of by his right-wing stepchildren, who immediately installed guards on the edge of their section of beach property, turning away trespassers. Someone told me Roger was not welcome there anymore, either.

Vineyard events were, of course, soon truly tragic for Ted, though not as tragic as for Mary Jo Kopechne—the Chappaquiddick bridge incident, the drowning, the accusations and unanswered questions. Our babysitter Polly Busselle (whom Teddy had hired to work in his office after meeting her with us the summer before) was called at our home the next morning to identify the body of Mary Jo, her Washington colleague.

That week, Ted, returning to the Vineyard for court matters, appeared on our back lawn—tentatively, as if not sure of our welcome. The Styron family fixed that.

A few years later, Teddy phoned and asked if I would invite Jerome Wiesner, Jack's science advisor, who was currently the president of MIT, to lunch at our house with him. I did, of course, pleased, no questions asked. And of course, Ted came. He wanted advice on an important matter—whether or not he, Teddy, should run for president of the United States. As he talked to the three of us, it became obvious that he wanted to fulfill his obligation to his family, especially to the memories of his two assassinated brothers and to his oldest brother, a pilot, killed in a World War II plane crash. And to his ever-ambitious father. He wondered, at length, if we thought the Chappaquiddick incident would scotch his chances. I privately thought it would, but was silent. The men, especially Jerry Wiesner, encouraged him, saying the incident was past history and his record as a senator would be foremost in voters' minds.

When he did declare his run for president, Teddy invited Doris Kearns Goodwin and me to join Bob Shrum in Washington as his potential speechwriters. During our first planned session there, after a poor performance on TV the night before, not answering Roger Mudd's question "Why do you want to run?," Ted withdrew. Doris and I went home. I reflected that he was deeply divided about running in the first place. Instead he became the best senator of the century.

One of the few times I enjoyed Teddy in Boston was in the early twenty-first century, when he was the invited conductor of the Boston Pops. In a huge shoulder-stiff white jacket (I was sure he didn't own it), he arm-waved the orchestra through rousing music, much of it popular, fun for us all in the audience. We even joined in, singing.

In 2009, at his moving, crowded memorial service at Our Lady of Perpetual Help, also in Boston, I found myself seated between Gerry Adams and Martin McGuinness, who I first knew in Ireland from my Amnesty missions and legal meetings during and after the Troubles.

Even now I smile to remember seeing Teddy swimming from his parked craft, in what seemed to me rough seas, with a rope over his

Patriarch Teddy retrieving sleepover provisions.

shoulders, bottles of wine for us, his hosts, tied to each end. How we all looked forward to his annual anniversary trips in June with his spectacular wife, Vicki. Vicki's father had been a supporter of Teddy's, which was how they first met. Dark-haired, tall, beautiful, she understood Teddy better than any other woman had, and made him supremely happy. Bill and I were always delighted when the two would sail over to spend their anniversary evenings with us. After Ted's death, Vicki founded and built the Edward M. Kennedy Institute near the JFK Library. One large room replicates the Senate floor and encourages students and the public to come and discuss issues as they might if they were senators. I was more than pleased to be invited to the groundbreaking ceremony and a subsequent celebration. The institute is a great contribution to the American Senate and the ideal way to honor Teddy, by educating the public about democracy, the workings of the government. It should encourage new generations to become civically involved, securing our democracy. I'm so pleased now that Vicki has been appointed our ambassador to Austria.

Ted was, in my opinion, the best senator of our lifetime, surely the last to cross the aisle and—through sheer force of thoughtful, moral, personally involved performance—unite Republicans and Democrats, at least for a time. Now I worry that will not happen again while I am alive.

Teddy Kennedy, George Plimpton, and Rose at a New York party, '80s.

My year-round political friendships were often sparked in the summer when they deepened socially with those of my other friends who were more centrally connected to the arts, education, and leadership. All in all, Martha's Vineyard has enhanced the intellectual, creative, and activist richness of my life immensely, though anxieties plague us as the pandemic has.

8

Roman Holiday with Family

IN 1967, BILL AND I WENT TO EGYPT for Easter with the Robert Penn Warrens. We brought along Susanna and Polly, and the Warrens brought Rosanna and Gabriel. We left Tom and six-month-old Alexandra with my mother, who had hired a nurse for her, a tall lady from Washington named Christine. I wish I could find the funny photographs of Bill and Red Warren looking very uncomfortable on their camels in the Egyptian desert. The one picture that I have is of Polly, always the most graceful of our family members, wearing a gorgeous large sun hat and flowing dress on the desert sand. The four children loved climbing in and out of the pyramids, daredevil Gabriel scaring his mom by skipping ledges as he leaped down the pyramid sides.

We Styrons went from Egypt to Rome, and were so happy to be there again that we decided to spend the rest of the spring and summer in Italy. We sent for Tommy and Alexandra. Christine brought them by plane to Rome. The idea was that she would stay for a couple of days, helping us get settled in an apartment. We were staying at the Hotel de la Ville, right at the top of the Spanish Steps, next door and down from the much bigger and fancier Hotel Hassler. We had a suite on the top floor.

The day after Christine arrived with the children, I asked her if there was anything special she'd like to do while she was in Rome. She, a Catholic, replied that more than anything she wanted to see St. Peter's. We made a plan to get up early the next day and go before the crowds.

At ten to seven that morning, I stepped out of the hotel, carrying Alexandra. She was wearing a little thick white sunbonnet. Rome was quiet at that early hour. No tourists on the Spanish Steps, just a few taxis parked in front of the Hassler and a Vespa coming up the steep street two blocks away. I paid no attention to it as I hailed one of the cabs. As the taxi was coming down to me I stepped off the curb to meet it—and the man on the Vespa ran me down. Like a good Italian, he'd been staring at me and lost control of the motor scooter he was riding.

I landed flat on my face in the street, knocked out cold. Little Al flew out of my arms and, I was told later, landed on her head, right in front of the oncoming taxi. He screeched to a halt, thank God. When I came to minutes later I was lying in the street. The man and his Vespa were lying on top of me.

"O Dio mio!" he kept moaning in terror.

"Get off me! Get off me right now!" I shouted.

I got up. Nothing felt broken. I looked around at the crowd that had gathered and spotted Alexandra in Christine's arms.

"Is the baby okay?" I asked. She assured me Alexandra was fine. The puffy sunbonnet had cushioned her fall.

I found Susanna and Tommy rooted to the sidewalk, their eyes wide with fear.

"Everything's all right," I told them. I looked around and asked, "Where's Polly?"

"She went up to get her father," Christine told me.

People helped me walk into the hotel. I sat on one of what were actual thrones decorating the lobby near the front door, with Alexandra on my lap. We were like figures in a Renaissance painting, especially with the Vespa driver on his knees beyond my feet. I learned Polly had taken the elevator upstairs and awakened Bill, crying, "Daddy, you have to come downstairs right away, Mommy and the baby are dead!"

Bill later described how he got up and stood in front of the full-length mirror to get dressed. Dazed, he watched himself pulling on his pants, and the only thing going through his mind, he said, was the thought, "How do I ship two bodies back to the United States?"

When he got down to the lobby, he saw me on my throne with a crowd around me and the unfortunate Italian kneeling before me babbling, "O Dio mio! Oh, lady, don't sue, don't sue!" Continuing in Italian, he explained that he was a postman who usually delivered the mail on foot, but because he had been running late he'd borrowed a friend's Vespa. He didn't know how to use the brakes.

By this point I was tired of all the commotion. I said, "Look, I'm fine. Let's put all this behind us. Everybody go away. Christine, let's take the kids to St. Peter's as planned."

Bill returned to the hotel room and off I went with Polly, Susanna, Tom, Alexandra, and Christine. We took a taxi across the Tiber to the Vatican. I had no trouble crossing St. Peter's Square, but when we started to climb the steps up into the basilica, I finally began to feel the pain in my legs. I couldn't make it up the marble steps. We turned around and went back down to get another taxi.

I told Christine that I needed to go to the hospital. My legs were swelling. "I'll call Bill from there and tell him to come," I assured her.

The driver took us to the hospital Salvator Mundi, which was not far from the Vatican, on the Gianicolo near the American Academy. Bill came to meet us there.

He immediately said, "Let's get you out of here." He dreaded hospitals and anything medical.

But the doctor was adamant: "No no no. We have to operate. A blood clot will go to her brain."

Bill interjected, "Couldn't we just get on a plane and go home?"

"She'll never be able to sit on a plane in this condition," the doctor argued. "Let me do it right here."

I said no to that. I explained that I always bruised easily, then recovered well. But Bill panicked and told the doctor to go ahead. Trying to compromise, I agreed to surgery on one thigh only.

He operated, cutting open my right thigh, but when the bloodletting procedure was done, he left some gauze inside. Two days later he had to go back and remove it. Which meant almost a week in the hospital.

As I sat up in my room with its fine view of Rome, I was amused to watch through my open door troupes of visitors go into the room across the hall. They were wearing a variety of odd costumes and weeping and wailing. It was histrionic even by Italian standards. As I learned from a nurse, filmmaker Federico Fellini was in that room with a terrible case of pleurisy. The late afternoon visits were from the cast and crew of the movie he was currently working on. They feared he might die.

On the second morning I heard a lot of animal noises down the hall. Barnyard animals, jungle animals. I asked the nurse what was going on. She told me there was a special clinic at the end of the hallway for fat people who needed to reduce. A woman was making the noises. She was a movie actress and animal voice dubber who fell off a horse while filming in Israel. She had damaged her thyroid gland and as a result became very, very fat. She was entertaining the other reducers. Further personal amusement for me, who was already feeling like I was in a Fellini movie.

On the third morning, a crazy-looking bearded man with graying hair, wearing a long old coat, appeared at the foot of my bed.

"I read in the *Rome Daily American* that you had this accident," he began.

I queried, uncertainly, "Doc?"

It was Doc Humes, whom I'd met with the *Paris Review* crowd back in 1953. Bill had told me he and Doc had made a not-too-happy trip across Europe the summer before. I'd gotten to know him better later. He had married a girl named Anna Lou, who also went to Wellesley. (All the girls in that circle were Wellesley or Smith, it seemed, and had married these guys who together started the *Paris Review*.) He and Anna Lou had three little girls who were my children's ages, and they visited us in Roxbury once. But I hadn't seen him in several years. Anna Lou had left him for another writer, Nelson Aldrich, and we'd lost touch. I almost didn't recognize him.

"What are you doing in Rome?" I asked.

"Oh, I just came from London," he explained. "I hung on to the wing of a British Airways flight all the way here."

I asked him to explain.

"Well, Interpol has been following me. They put a little radio in the filling of a back tooth so they can hear what I'm doing. Talking to subversive people. They think I'm a spy of some kind. They locked me up inside a place that they made look like an insane asylum. I got out and went to Heathrow. Saw a plane leaving for Rome, so I hung on to the wing and here I am."

I recalled how unpredictable he'd been, brain-strained by intense drug-taking with Timothy Leary in his Harvard days. I needed amusement and he provided it, daily!

"So, Doc, what will you be doing here in Rome?" I pressed.

"I'm digging under the Vatican, because Christ told me that I should come to Rome, and on the day the world ends, I should dig under the Vatican and I'll find all the important artwork he brought with him when he came from Tibet. As you know, the world ended yesterday."

I had read in the paper that morning that archaeologists had indeed started excavating under the Vatican for some advertised remains. I figured he'd read that too.

Every morning that week Doc came to see me and fill the room with wild stories. On the morning of my last day in the hospital, he asked me when Bill was coming to collect me. They had not run into each other, as Bill came in the afternoons.

I told him Bill would be working for a while. That I didn't think he'd arrive before four o'clock.

"I'll come back at four," Doc said. "I need to ask him a favor." (I was suspicious.) "I need to borrow money from him so I can book passage back to the United States on a ship this week. Because, as you know, Nelson Aldrich stole my wife, and I'm going back to kill him."

"Oh," I said, my eyebrows descending. "Come back at four."

When he left, I called the doctor and said, "I'm out of here at noon, okay?"

"Fine," he said. "You can leave anytime."

I called Bill and asked him to arrive at noon, and he did. We did not meet Doc. But should I have warned the Aldriches?

I didn't see Doc again for many years. One day he suddenly showed up on our doorstep in Roxbury.

"I've come to warn you," he said when I answered the door. "Come outside."

I stepped out. He pointed to the sky.

"See that lenticular cloud?"

I didn't know what a lenticular cloud was, but there was indeed a very strange cloud overhead, curved like the lens of an eye or like the top sliced off a mushroom cloud, and ominously dark.

Doc pronounced it a symbol of doom. "They're watching you." He went on and on about Doomsday, and what an ill portent that cloud was for Bill and me. It was a bit unsettling. Bill was nowhere around. The cloud and Doc disappeared.

The last picture I saw of Doc, still with long beard and long overcoat, was on the front page of one of the New York rags. He had just received an inheritance and was throwing hundred-dollar bills into the air as grateful bystanders gathered at his feet. He died in 1992. In September 2001, I suddenly thought of Doc when I saw on TV a dark lenticular cloud form over the destroyed World Trade Center towers. It was surely a day of doom.

After George Plimpton died, his widow, Sarah, invited Peter Matthiessen and me up to their apartment to look at the first version of Doc's daughter Immy's film about her father. Peter and I went upstairs and sat with Sarah and Immy Humes, watching the beginning of *Doc,* which in its first moments outed Peter as being co-opted by the CIA as he graduated from Yale and paid to start the *Paris Review.* Peter stood up and said to me, "Rose, we have to leave." We did.

It turned out that Peter was about to be married and he and Patsy really wanted to move to Paris. The CIA had asked him to start a literary magazine there, one featuring American voices that, if needed, might succeed in countering the Communist propaganda spreading across Europe. That became the *Paris Review.* Peter had told no one, not even George, until shortly before George died. George was apparently startled and displeased. Peter said the CIA gave him initial funds but never interfered at all. (It turns out they also funded a more famous literary magazine in London, *Encounter,* founded by Stephen Spender, whom I encountered as a fellow poet.) Peter, outed, soon regained his good humor and wrote trenchantly about it in more than one publication. I did not see the rest of the film, even when it was premiered at the Museum of Modern Art. I watched it on my computer recently, interested to behold Doc again.

9

Nat Turner, Frankfurt, Moscow, Uzbekistan

M Y TRANSITION from a person who was prey to strong
political opinions to being an engaged activist began
pretty late, well into my thirties. During the Vietnam War,
I marched on Washington, arm in arm with Tom Hayden. Alexandra
was born in late 1966, and I was still primarily a poet/housewife/
mom in 1967. But the United States was in such political turmoil and
social upheaval that one couldn't be alive then and not be aware. Bill
and I became—both as a couple and individually—publicly involved.

In the late fall of 1967, Senator Eugene McCarthy announced that
he would run for the 1968 Democratic nomination against President
Lyndon Johnson. He was a progressive, a poet, and an opponent of
the Vietnam War. Resigned to the fact that Robert F. Kennedy was
not running, Bill and I decided to campaign for Gene. I persuaded our
friend and neighbor Arthur Miller to join us. Arthur had been more
politically involved than we, before this. In 1965 he'd been elected
president of International PEN. In 1966, when Olga Carlisle and I
conducted an interview with him for the *Paris Review,* Arthur had said,
"I always drew a lot of inspiration from politics, from one or another
kind of national struggle. You live in the world even though you only
vote once in a while."

Many other prominent people in the arts participated in the McCarthy campaign. Gene was the only viable counter to the rather hawkish Hubert Humphrey and the Republican front-runner, Richard Nixon, whom I had long disliked.

I traveled across the country with McCarthy and, among journalists, Seymour Hersh. (I did not begin to think of myself seriously as a journalist until 1974, after my first mission for Amnesty, when I began publishing in *Ramparts*, the *New York Review of Books*, the *New Republic, Ms.*, and newspapers nationwide.) By the time I got to Milwaukee with the McCarthy campaign, I realized that though I liked McCarthy, I wasn't sure I wanted him to gain the supreme office. I thought perhaps even he was not keen to embrace winning, possibly preferring to become a well-known poet. Bill and Robert Lowell had joined him in Chicago earlier, and Gene had seemed happier talking poetry with Lowell than politics with anyone else.

From Milwaukee we went to San Francisco, where I was to speak with Gene on a platform at the Cow Palace. I hated public speaking but had agreed to do it for the campaign. (In later political campaigns and war protests my companions onstage were most often writers, and I think I was less uptight about speaking then.) By San Francisco, I'd already decided I was leaving the McCarthy campaign and had bought my ticket back east on the next day's plane when two of the staff approached me.

"Please, would you go to Portland, Oregon, tomorrow and speak for Gene? His wife, Abigail, was supposed to give a major talk and she's bugged out." I declined and headed back to Connecticut. Bobby Kennedy had just (finally!) declared his candidacy after all. I wanted to work for him. Alas, his assassination was imminent. Our friend and eyewitness to the murder, George Plimpton, gave us the awful, vivid details: how it had only been a last-minute decision to go through the kitchen, and how there had been an intense struggle for the assassin's gun, with Plimpton and Rosey Grier pinning him down. George seemed to harbor a deep, lasting sadness, something I'd never seen in him before.

Coming just months after Martin Luther King's murder, Bobby's death seemed further proof that America was tearing itself apart. The Democratic Party reeled into its tumultuous national convention in Chicago that August. Bill, Arthur Miller, and not-as-close-but-wonderful near resident Paul Newman attended as McCarthy delegates for Connecticut. Though invited by the Women's Group, and initially agreeing to join them there, I decided not to go to Chicago. Bill had declared it would ruin his time there because he would always be worrying about me. I'd had much experience with that, even in Roxbury—his total distraction and distress when he feared need-lessly about my safety. If I stayed too long away on daytime errands, he would be frantic. I didn't want to compromise his current writing time. My respect and love for him was foremost, still foremost, fifteen years into our marriage, so I stayed in Connecticut. Fretting, ultimately disgusted with myself for acquiescing, I vowed not to let such considerations curtail my activism in the future.

That violent Chicago time, which Bill succeeded in writing about movingly, is well known. After Bobby's assassination, Ethel Kennedy and her family offered McCarthy their full backing, but he turned them down. I reflected I'd been right in assessing his reluctance to be president. Humphrey won the nomination, only to be defeated in November by Nixon.

The social turmoil in America came home for Bill and me in another way. Random House had published *The Confessions of Nat Turner* in the fall of 1967. It sold very well, won the Pulitzer. Scores of review-ers hailed it as a great literary achievement. Hollywood producer David Wolper bought the film rights for an adaptation that would be directed by Norman Jewison, whose *In the Heat of the Night* had just won the Academy Award for best picture of 1967. Bill was on a high. Jewison subsequently dropped out of the project because of a sched-uling conflict, and Sidney Lumet (*12 Angry Men, Dog Day Afternoon*), the current husband of my good friend Piedy Gimbel, took over. But because Bill was a white man who'd written in the voice of a Black slave, *Nat Turner* also became embroiled in the racial fear and animosi-ties of the times. Bill was denounced because he dared inhabit the mind of an African American. There had been no published record of Nat's life. Did they consider him a heroic ancestor? The authors of *Ten Black Writers Respond* declared that Nat could not have, as the leader of a revolution, killed only one person, a young white woman he was described as feeling tenderly toward. They suggested he must have been married to a Black woman and killed countless whites.

Several well-known Black writers, including James Baldwin, Skip Gates, and the prominent historian John Hope Franklin, defended Bill handsomely, but the reaction hurt and depressed him. Bill protested in vain that he'd written a novel, just "a meditation on history." Sets for the film adaptation had already been built in Virginia when the project came to a halt, the studio fearing bad press. We had both looked forward to Sidney's talented hand, and James Earl Jones's extraordinary acting. Bill was beyond disappointed.

Bill had been fascinated with Nat Turner since his teenage years in Virginia. A sign marking the spot of the revolution stood where he sometimes walked. He had labored on the book for a decade. I'd found the only treatise on Nat, his actual confession published in the nineteenth century, in Bill's room at the American Academy in Rome back in 1952. I knew he and Jimmy Baldwin had had long discussions about Bill's writing *Nat Turner* early on and Jimmy had encouraged him to go ahead with it, and to write it in Nat's voice. Neither of them anticipated the reaction evident in *Ten Black Writers Respond*. Jimmy was quoted in a 2016 article in *Vanity Fair* saying, after publication, "Bill's going to catch it from black and white. Styron is probing something very dangerous, deep and painful in the national psyche. I hope it starts a tremendous fight, so that people will learn what they really think about each other." I had never heard Jimmy say that before the novel was published.

We got hate mail at our home in Roxbury, and Bill began to worry (as he did over any imagined possible calamity) about the safety of the family. The children were not to stay outside alone. Whenever I left the house, he wanted to know when I'd be back and insisted I call if I was running late. Once I went to New York to meet some Russian poets whose work I was helping to translate. Bill called my hotel to check on me, and when I wasn't there he began to be concerned. There was no phone where I was and I probably lost track of time, so I didn't call him. Bill went into a full-blown panic and drove to the city to look for me. When I, unaware that any of this was happening, walked into the hotel, his reaction was alternately relief and rage. It was a disturbing pattern I had to deal with again and again, and I often didn't do it very well. Years later, I thought these moments should have been harbingers of his coming full-blown depression, which he labeled "melancholy."

Bill and dogs waiting for his wife or Connecticut mail, mid-'80s.

In the midst of the late summer of 1968 strife, Bill and I were invited to be observers at the Afro-Asian Writers' Conference to be held "behind the Iron Curtain" (as it was known in those days) in Moscow, then in Tashkent, Uzbekistan. Because *Nat Turner* was about a slave rebellion, the Soviets apparently thought Bill was a good revolutionary. They were about to publish *Nat* in Russian. I was invited because Olga Carlisle and I had translated twentieth-century Russian poetry that had appeared in several magazines, including the *Paris Review*. Olga was the granddaughter of Russian playwright Leonid Andreyev, and her father, Vadim Andreyev, was a well-known poet. She would go to Moscow to visit family and come back with batches of poems by dissidents who'd died under Stalin. Anna Akhmatova and Marina Tsvetaeva were among my favorites, Osip Mandelstam the one I loved most. In the 1960s, little of this poetry had been translated into English. Not a professional translator, I started by enrolling in a Russian language course at Yale, and despite a couple of our uncaught mistakes, we managed to put together a volume for Viking, *Modern Russian Poetry*, in the early '70s, then another, *Poets on Street Corners*, bearing Olga's name as author.

On our way to Moscow in 1968, Bill and I flew first to Frankfurt, to its famous book fair, the huge annual trade event where publishers from around the world show off their new books and buy and sell foreign rights. Select star authors made appearances. In 1968, Bill was one of them.

We were returning to our hotel from the fair when we saw scores of young people protesting on the street outside, waving signs and chanting against Léopold Senghor, who was also staying in our hotel. I had no idea why. Senghor was the first president of Senegal after it gained its independence from France. He was also a poet who wrote a great deal about what he called "negritude," the common Black culture of all Africans. Senghor was in Frankfurt because a new book of his poems had just been published. But as Senegal's leader he was also busy abusing and incarcerating political dissidents. Leading the protesters was Daniel Cohn-Bendit, "Danny the Red," who had become a world-famous figure for us when he demonstrated "at the barricades" in Paris in May. Like most liberals, Bill and I had felt supportive. Jim Jones, who lived in Paris, inspired us with details. I was surprised to see Daniel in Germany. I didn't realize then that he was German as well as French. Thirty years later we met again at a conference in Spain. He was Germany's star representative, stockier, but engaging and as provocative as he seemed in Frankfurt.

When Bill and I went up to our room and I stood at the window, which faced the square, I watched with excitement as the protest swelled, and couldn't resist going down to join it. I abhorred the idea of a poet who would silence the voices of his own people. Soon the shouting crowd surrounded the hotel.

That afternoon, we were scheduled to take an Aeroflot flight—the only one that week—to Moscow. I returned to our room wondering how we would get out of the hotel. I suggested going down to the basement and out the back. Bill agreed. We stole a porter's dolly, piled it with all our bags, and left the hotel, pushing the dolly along the cobblestone streets in the direction of the airport. Luckily a taxi came along.

While waiting for our flight at the Frankfurt airport, Bill and I bought a couple of newspapers, which were full of stories on Czechoslovakia. The Soviet Union had recently invaded the country, bringing a brutal end to the Prague Spring and reforms enacted by

Alexander Dubček's government. Dubček and other high government officials were arrested and taken to Moscow. They were allowed
to return to Prague eventually—now occupied by Soviet troops—but
their reformist movement seemed unrecoverable.

In the United States, we Americans were having our own devastating year: the assassinations of Martin Luther King in April and
Robert Kennedy in June, riots in many cities, and the chaos at the
Democratic National Convention in Chicago that August. Bill and
I should have thought more about Soviet policies, but we hadn't. In
the airport we realized it was too late to back out. Our bags had been
boarded, and Russian writers were meeting the plane.

When we landed in Moscow, we were completely disarmed by our
welcome. Many contemporary novelists and poets wanted to meet
Bill. Yevtushenko (always called Genya by his countrymen, among
others) took us on an exhilarating drive down crisp autumn streets
to the magnificent Kremlin. Multiple conversations went on long
into the night. Certain host writers agreed with us that they should
protest their country's invasion of Czechoslovakia. I guess one or
another did. Our Moscow visit ended abruptly and we were all flown
to Tashkent (where we could not be heard).

I wrote an article for *Vogue* about our time in that seductive city
in Soviet Central Asia. As the plane from Moscow dipped suddenly
and the damp land below slanted up (looking, I thought, like the
brown watered silk my Victorian grandmother wore on Sundays in
Baltimore), then leveled out to reveal long stretches of sand, dusty
tree-lined green fields and vineyards, low precise houses, then marble
towers, painted domes with hints of industry in pockets of squares,
finally the airport drowsing under arches and balustrades seemingly
painted with mud. The faded drooping flowers around them completed the presentation of a rather doleful stage set.

We waited in its hot, dry oasis, recalling our disarming welcome
by literati at the bustling Moscow airport and the reception there
with our new Russian, Eastern European, African, and Asian writer
acquaintances. For me, the Russian poets shone: Yevtushenko,
Voznesensky, Ahkmadulina. But apparently whoever was designated
to meet us here in Tashkent was busy at the session we had specifically been invited to join. Bill and I, invited to attend, not to speak,

were the sole North Americans. We and an Australian and a Chilean comprised the West.

Once remembered and called for, we were deposited in a quiet, obviously Soviet Modern hotel. Huge banners of welcome in four languages were its façade. It faced a charming square graced by high-showering fountains, stern statues, and children running everywhere. The adults clustered at kiosks munching piroshky and drinking vodka or orange juice or whatever.

Bill and I opened the French doors of our stunning room and stood on the balcony. The scene below sported a blue circus tent, where we spied a strongman in red satin trunks hoisting his dumb-bells, and a lone elephant with pink scalloped ears waving his trunk. He (she?) seemed almost to dance to the music of "Some Enchanted Evening" emanating from a transistor radio his trainer was carrying.

Abruptly, we were called downstairs. It was time to drive to a scheduled poetry reading. New Soviet architecture had replaced certain destroyed palaces and villas, but not the feel of the ancient city that had begun as an oasis on the Silk Road connecting China and Europe. It had survived more than one earthquake and other disasters, like being sacked by Genghis Khan and ruled by the Soviets.

It was, for us, a fitting introduction to the variety and difficulty of the conference. The poetry reading began with an Indian poet leaning above baskets of pink and yellow roses that bloomed from the floor, moaning, "Emotions are more important than words." A stocky, gray-haired Russian next beamed poems of love for the ladies. An open scroll behind the platform sported five arms of different colors—brown, black, yellow, white, red—joined in one large hand-clasp. I was to notice this often as the symbol of the symposium joined in literary friendship, as well as opposition to neocolonialism and Western imperialism.

Cameras flashed, TVs whirred, forty poets and twenty translators of Russian, French, Uzbek, English, Japanese, Spanish, Hindi, Arabic, Hebrew, Lithuanian, Bulgarian, Rumanian, Swahili, and Amharic spoke in turn.

Then a handsome dark-eyed poet from Jordan took the stage, his lined face reminding me of Auden's when young, his voice alternately staccato and rolling, rhythmic, resonant. His name was Muin Bseiso.

(He later asked me to translate and publish his poems. I did a few translations separately but did not take on his volume.) Yevtushenko, coming forth from the back row, stood beside him translating his poem "Empty Drums" into Russian. My English translation:

> *The Land is gone and nothing is left,*
> *Not even a rein in a hitching post,*
> *And the sword is gone and the windmill*
> *Gone, and we haven't a single dovecote . . .*

There were brief speeches damning the Vietnam War, damning Israel as the agent of American imperialism, and words of harmony for the writers of the world. The audience, about two thousand strong, was of every age, race, and costume.

Hungry, we left before the end. We missed the climax of the night, Yevtushenko's own poems, which apparently received such stampeding applause, complete with young girls fainting, that even the poet was said to be embarrassed.

We returned to the hotel for the first of many meals there: delicious flatbread, tomatoes, grapes, and ice cream offsetting tasteless fried sturgeon.

Yevtushenko knocked on our door early the next morning smiling, insisting we accompany him to the sprawling Tashkent market for breakfast. He had not slept, he said, because the elephant had wailed all night "like the sick conscience of the world." As we strolled, Genya chose a football-shaped sweet green melon from a huge multicolored melon pile, which he and Bill sliced like competing surgeons in a tiny café we settled in, and we gloried in the fresh bread and strong tea accompanying the sweet melon.

A formal session of the symposium followed, with writers from various countries—Sudan was first—thanking Russia for supporting their independence. One writer quoted Pushkin: "This is not time for sunsets, reality is the true clock."

An elegantly garbed Black delegate from Kenya rose. He began: "When two elephants fight, it is the grass that suffers; when Capitalism and Socialism clash to crush the small countries of Africa and Asia, it is their artists who bleed." This man of dignity and simplicity,

Bill and Rose aboard the SS America *returning from Europe, 1960.*

old enough to have led his people for some years, asked the Russians, "Do you promise to support us in our quests for liberty, for the defeat of poverty?" He was the first delegate to speak English that day.

A lawyer-poet from Senegal rose next and was presented with birthday flowers by Uzbek schoolgirls. A Moscow-based critic praised Norman Mailer as a writer who resisted U.S. politics. Norman was the only American writer whose name we heard from any platform.

JANKEES! HANDS OFF HEROIC VIET NAME, read a banner as we went off to visit a collective farm. There we were met by a gentleman with flashing gold teeth and a great drooping mustache, who wore a bemedaled general's uniform rather like the one in Stalin's Yalta photographs. He talked glowingly of American places he had visited—especially Florida—as he led us to a small gazebo to sample his farm's colorful and delicious bounty.

We walked through endless exquisite vineyards with grape-leaf-covered arbors, sipping cognac, tasting a variety of grapes as we somnolently listened to our guide describe the annual production of eighteen tons of grapes. He was a scholar, an agriculture expert who had been awarded medals for thirty-seven years and was annually reelected by the people.

Bill with Yevgeny Yevtushenko, Roxbury.

The director placed enormous bouquets of the farm's beautiful flowers in my arms later as he bowed and beamed and finally said farewell.

Walking around Tashkent the next morning we passed the spiraling glass Café Pinocchio and a monastery where a worker dangling his legs in an open manhole talked on a polished telephone to someone below.

We arrived at a marble palace with the numbers 5-2-5 on top, to celebrate the 525th anniversary of the birth of the "Shakespeare of Uzbekistan," Alisher Navoi. Who was this poet and patriarch whose image pursued us through speeches and dramatic offerings in the days to come? Long-throated silver *karnay* horns welcomed us from a high parapet as the president of Uzbekistan, a woman recently out of purdah, trilled in Uzbek, and everyone munched pears. Bill's comment: "We've landed in Oz."

At five o'clock we met Yevtushenko and climbed hastily into a car with him. We were almost late for a poetry reading he was giving for the students of Tashkent University. Genya, Russia's fair-haired boy, was tall, slim, with an athletic build, a fine-boned face, straight blond hair, mischievous eyes, and boundless energy and enthusiasm. At times, he could be tiring. (A year later the poet Joseph Brodsky, living in New York, expressed his distrust of Genya, suspecting that he did not defend him when he, Joseph, was being sentenced to exile. Who knows?)

The hall was packed. Kids stood pressed together in the aisle, clapping, cheering, wild with affection. As we sat at the side of the stage, looking down at the mass of eager young smiles, I was reminded of the last time I had sat on a stage—when Senator Eugene McCarthy and I had delivered speeches at the Cow Palace in San Francisco. The students now pressed to the platform, their hands reaching to touch the poet's.

"Execution," a poem about a police chief whom Lermontov accused of killing Pushkin ("God's judgment is more important than the world's . . ."), was Genya's first offering. The hall hushed. Erect, dressed this time in a light blue shirt with a stiff white collar and cuffs, his blue eyes flashing, Yevtushenko could have been part of an honor guard, but as he began to recite in a voice that modulated from crisp announcement to anger to sadness, high right arm and then left arm, moving slowly in arcs of emphasis, he was young Olivier playing Hamlet. A girl fainted. There was a flurry of excitement as her friends carried her out with the poet in concerned attendance.

He returned and began his next poem ("My darling, sleep, don't torture me . . ."). It was delivered like a lullaby. The kids began to write notes, fold them, and throw them onto the platform at his feet. These young people were much better-looking, more stylish than their elders. Their faces seemed not only Russian but Eskimo, Japanese, Indian.

Yevtushenko introduced us to the crowd as his guests. The clapping was loud, and Bill stood to take a bow. They continued to look at us with friendly curiosity as the poet launched into a long new poem. A light "Ode to Mushrooms" came next, and then witty stanzas about Russian soldiers who, to their delight, were taught to read at the end of World War II. "Masha ate a dictionary for beginners like gruel!" Most poems were delivered completely from memory.

A standing ovation, the traditional rhythmic clapping, the presentation of flowers and a cap and teal silk robe that the poet donned onstage marked the end of the evening. Yevtushenko went out the back, squeezing us into a car as fans pressed at the doors. We drove off, with translator Tanya and two young men introduced as leaders of the regional Komsomol, toward the country, an hour's quiet.

Bill said to Genya, "You're just like an American rock star."

Genya looked insulted. "I'm not a rock star, I'm a poet." Was there ever a poet so incredibly feted in the West?

During our stay at the conference, under minimal surveillance, I met many poets and heard their stories. They all wanted to be published in the United States, despite the heightened level of anti-Americanism throughout the Soviet Union then (as now, under Putin). Several of these brilliant men (they were all men) pressed their manuscripts into my hands and said, "Please take these back with you and get them translated." I assured them that I had only a smattering of Russian and knew no Arabic or the Asian languages in which they wrote, but they insisted I take them. Once home, I delivered all to Yale and hoped I'd convinced *them* to translate and perhaps publish them.

We returned to Moscow, where the Soviet Writers' Union gave a luncheon for us. This was the official literary wing of the Communist Party. Over the years it expelled and banned many nonconforming writers, from Isaac Babel to Mayakovsky to Solzhenitsyn. The director, a broad-faced man named Surkhov, gave a speech at the table in which he started denigrating the United States as the country of slavery, going on and on about the evils of contemporary America. Bill, incensed, looked across the table and said, "Well, at least we don't put our writers in prison, the way you do."

Surkhov turned red in the face, got up, and stormed out. The Russian edition of Bill's *Nat Turner* was canceled.

From Moscow, we made a day trip out to Kolomenskoye, its scenes from a beautiful bit of Old Russia (the Orthodox Russia that was so suppressed in Moscow), with onion-domed churches and monks going in and out of a serenely quiet monastery.

We took an overnight train with Yevtushenko to St. Petersburg (then Leningrad), the train rattling through the dark as we talked and sang all night. We arrived to an absolutely gorgeous morning. It was September, and the leaves had just turned gold and snow was falling in soft, white slanted sheets across the Neva River, which wound through the city.

As we penetrated deeper into the heart of the city, we sensed gloom, saw poverty and shabbiness, sunless cobblestone streets with laundry strung across them. I thought of Raskolnikov's alleys. I'll never forget the bizarre sight of so many pale-bodied Leningrad citizens leaning against or lying along the parapets of the Peter and Paul Fortress on the Neva, stripped to their underwear, their arms and chests pale as fish bellies, trying to catch the noon sun. They looked like prisoners on a break from cold, dark jails.

The Hermitage was closed, its light green walls peeling, but if you knew the right people, you could get in, if only to certain rooms. "You could go up these stairs but *not those*. You may look into *that* room but do not enter it." The Impressionist gallery was staggering, as was the room full of Van Eycks and painters of his period. From the third- and fourth-floor windows one looked down on the stunning bronze equestrian statue of Peter the Great out in the square, and at Alexander's Column, topped with an archangel.

While we were in Leningrad, Yevtushenko said, "Let me take you now to Siberia, where I grew up."

"Terrific," I said.

"Nothing doing," Bill countered. He was still upset about the luncheon in Moscow, and by this point he was done with Russia.

"Okay, you go home and I'll go to Siberia," I must have told him. Unlike Bill, I loved travel and adventure, and I saw it as the chance of a lifetime to have a tour of Siberia guided by Yevtushenko.

"If you go off with him," Bill replied, "I won't be home when you come back. It'll be the end of our marriage." I had never told him that in Moscow Genya had implored me to meet him, clandestinely, by a certain monument. I didn't, and Genya said he had waited and waited. Bill may or may not have been suspicious. I surely was not interested in such a romance.

We had a big argument about it, but in the end I gave in. Bill could be adamant, and I, again for a "last time," conceded. By the 1970s, I would be embarking on a lot of travel on my own for Amnesty International, often in places and situations that might have made Bill really worry. I worried about *him,* then, but pursued what I felt I must.

There was no direct way out of Russia in those days. We had to fly from Leningrad to Finland to Frankfurt, and from Frankfurt to the United States. As they were checking our papers and passports at the Russian airport, they told Bill he was lacking some kind of exit stamp and couldn't leave. He was frantic. So was I. Desperate, I went rummaging around in a suitcase and came up with a Russian magazine that contained an article about Bill, with his photograph. That changed everything. Writers are such heroes in Russia. The man was impressed and waved us through. I was relieved and my regrets about missing Siberia ebbed. Bill, after all, was my true love and concern.

10

Amnesty International

TRAVELING BEHIND THE IRON CURTAIN, meeting writers who had suffered under repressive or tyrannical governments, opened my eyes. What little I and most of my friends knew then about tough life in the Soviet Union had come from a book or two, such as Solzhenitsyn's *One Day in the Life of Ivan Denisovich,* which had been published a year or so earlier than my first visit there. I became obsessed with helping to change antihuman policies abroad. I stopped writing poetry. For twenty years.

First, I went to Yale and gave them the manuscripts I'd brought back, asking them to please translate and publish them if possible. Then I went to Washington for a meeting in the State Department, relaying what I'd heard about abuses and repression in the Soviet Union, in Egypt, in Turkey, and more. No interest. I got nowhere.

I went home, despairing, wondering how to meaningfully parlay my new knowledge of the physical and emotional plights of so many moral citizens abroad. (I had not yet concentrated on America.) Discouraged, I experienced a new sharp lack of self-regard until I recounted my experiences to our neighbor Philip Roth and his spectacular girlfriend, Barbara Sproul. They listened, and Barbara gave me hope. She had just joined the New York chapter of Amnesty International, the first (we believed then) in the United States. (Barbara is

Philip on our Roxbury terrace, mid-'70s.

still a leader in AIUSA groups.) She asked me to come to a meeting
with her in the city and tell the group what I'd learned. That broke
the loneliness.

I knew nothing about Amnesty. Few people in the United States
did. "Amnesty" was for conscientious objectors in world wars. In
1961, a London lawyer named Peter Benenson and a small group
of others had organized the Appeal for Amnesty, taking space in
the *London Observer* to publicize the cases of six "prisoners of conscience" in various countries who'd been jailed for expressing their
beliefs. The appeal was carefully crafted to be international in scope
and politically nonpartisan. It was a plea for human rights in all countries, under all forms of government. The prisoners whose stories
were told included the archbishop of Prague, jailed for opposing the
Communist Czechoslovakian government, a Greek Communist jailed
for his union-organizing activities, and a white clergyman who'd been
jailed in Atlanta for helping Black people try to desegregate a Baptist
church. The appeal ended with a list of goals:

> To work impartially for the release of those imprisoned for
>   their opinions.
> To seek for them a fair and public trial.

To enlarge the Right of Asylum and help political refugees to
find work.

To urge effective international machinery to guarantee freedom
of opinion.

The response was immediate. Newspapers around the world
reprinted the appeal. Benenson organized an international meeting,
which led to the founding of a permanent organization, Amnesty
International, with the Irish activist (and later Nobel Peace Prize laureate) Sean McBride as its first chairman. Soon Amnesty International (AI) groups were starting up in many countries. Within two
years there were several hundred.

Amnesty's methods were simple but effective. It identified and
"adopted" certain "prisoners of conscience" around the world, gathered information on them, then directed public appeals at their jailors
on their behalf. This was done through organized letter campaigns to
the top officials in that government, also to lesser officials and even
the chiefs and guards at the prison, as well as reassuring correspondence with the prisoner if allowed, and with the prisoner's own family. Also, letters were written to officials in governments that had trade
or other relations with the prisoner's government, and to relevant
professional associations. For example, if the prisoner was a dissident Soviet scientist, international associations of scientists would be
informed of the case and asked to help.

Knowing that Amnesty was monitoring a prisoner's status, governments and guards might be less likely to mistreat them, even persuaded to release them one by one. By 1963, more than 700 prisoners
around the world had been adopted. Amnesty had so far been instrumental in getting 140 of them released. Cases in which a prisoner
was at risk of being tortured or his immediate safety was endangered
in other ways required swifter action than a letter campaign. In 1972,
Amnesty would begin the Urgent Action Network, in which Amnesty
members stood by ready to send faxes, telegrams, and, later, emails to
authorities. The Urgent Action program passed its first test that year,
when a Brazilian history professor was seized and subjected to torture
by the government. His wife appealed to Amnesty, and our campaign
secured his release. "When the piled letters you wrote me got a foot
high, the guards decided to release me," he said.

To be effective around the world, AI maintained a policy of strict political neutrality, as well as not aligning itself with any corporate or business interests. That way it could never be credibly claimed that AI was biased in any of its campaigns. The organization also followed principles of total nonviolence. It refused to adopt any political prisoner who had taken up arms.

The New York group, called the Riverside Group because it met on Riverside Drive in Manhattan, had begun shortly before Barbara told me about it. It was run by a professor named Ivan Morris, an English writer and expert on Asian languages and cultures, who was teaching at Columbia. They met at his apartment, which Ivan's mother owned. There weren't a dozen people in the room that first night Barbara took me. I sat on a hassock in the corner while they all sat around Ivan's mother's four-poster elegantly draped bed (their ad hoc table), pen and paper in hand. I sat and listened until I was asked to detail my experience in the Soviet Union. After I spoke, I was invited to join, and did. For the first time in my marriage, I found myself leaving home and family and driving back and forth to New York monthly and sometimes weekly. In the beginning, we had only one staff person, a Greek woman named Amy Augustus, who took notes and kept a desk in a small office.

We volunteers didn't pick our own cases to investigate. They were handed out to us by the London office directors. We then did our research and reported our findings to AI London. They determined what action, if any, to take on each case, sometimes without further consulting us.

The first case they handed me was of a political prisoner in South Africa named Nelson Mandela. In 1960, police had massacred sixty-nine peacefully protesting Black South Africans in Sharpeville. For Mandela, a lawyer who had, with Oliver Tambo, opened the only Black law firm in Johannesburg and fought against apartheid in the courts since the 1950s, the time for peaceful protest had ended. After the African National Congress was banned in 1960, Mandela founded and became the head of uMkhonto we Sizwe, the armed wing of the ANC. In 1962, he was arrested and imprisoned, and in 1964 he was sentenced to life in jail. He'd been in the Robben Island prison for five years when I was assigned his case.

I corresponded with his wife, Winnie Mandela, among others. She went three or four times a year to Robben Island to visit her husband, and would tell me what was going on. I would pass all the information I gathered to London. It was years before I actually met Winnie in person, in New York.

Notwithstanding my reports, Nelson Mandela remained on Robben Island for many years. It wasn't until nearly a decade after he was freed, in 1990, that I found out why my work had so little impact on his case. It turned out to be Amnesty's policy not to adopt prisoners of conscience who had borne arms. But why had London failed to inform me?

In the mid-1980s, I began contemplating a book I might write featuring mostly men who while political prisoners had determined that on their release they would endeavor to lead their countries toward democracy. My research included some who not only survived the prison experience but through it became better educated, even learning new languages. The smartest went on to be presidents of their countries. The unluckiest went into depressions, maybe had failed lives, maybe killed themselves. I wanted to make a philosophical and psychological inquiry into the moments when particular prisoners decided they could use imprisonment as a crucible for their visions of leadership.

Among those I planned to include, each of whom I'd been fortunate enough to meet, were Václav Havel, the playwright who had been interned as a dissident and emerged to become president of Czechoslovakia; Gerry Adams, the feisty young negotiator and writer who, after prison, became the leader of Northern Ireland's Sinn Féin; Jacobo Timerman, the influential Argentine journalist-publisher and effective dissident; Breyten Breytenbach, the South African anti-apartheid rebel-activist—writer and painter—who spent seven years in solitary confinement; Sergei Kovalev, the Jewish former Cossack deemed anti-Soviet; Nobel Prize recipient Kim Dae-jung, president of South Korea, whom I'd met during his activist's exile in the United States before my colleague Patt Derian, Jimmy Carter's (and the first) secretary of human rights, accompanied him home; Adam Michnik, esteemed writer and courageous dissident leader in Poland (still that country's leading journalist), whom I'd spent time with twice in his country, then in New York; Árpád Göncz (Bill's translator), who learned English as a political prisoner and (to his surprise) was elected president of Hungary; and Nelson Mandela, whom I met in his office, post-release, on a visit with David Rockefeller as part of a small delegation from the Council on Foreign Relations. Later, I met President Mandela again, with President Bill Clinton and an entourage of South African and American youth. We met again in Johannesburg, though I can't claim that we became friends.

All the people I contacted were happy to speak with me, except Nelson Mandela. When Charlayne Hunter-Gault moved to South Africa in 1997 to be National Public Radio's chief correspondent in Africa and then CNN's bureau chief in Johannesburg, I went to visit her more than once. I knew Charlayne had become a friend of the Mandelas. Having been received in Nelson Mandela's office when I was part of the Council on Foreign Relations delegation, I asked Charlayne if she would contact him for me. I wanted ten minutes of his time for a quote about the moment in prison when he determined what his life, his political leadership, could be if he were released, and the book he planned to write after his release.

One day Charlayne and I boarded a small boat in Cape Town to go to Robben Island, which by then had been emptied of prisoners, but not yet set up for visitors. On the small craft with us was Ahmed Kathrada, another ANC leader who'd been sentenced to life in prison, and had even shared a cell with Mandela. Charlayne asked him if he could help me get a few minutes with South Africa's new leader. I had written both him and his secretary with my request, and got no response. Mr. Kathrada said he'd be happy to. Then Charlayne added, "He was Rose's first Amnesty International case."

Kathrada frowned. "In that case I can't help her," he said. That was when I learned that Amnesty had never taken on Mandela's case.

"He's never forgiven them for that," Kathrada said. "He won't see you."

Even though during his almost three decades of imprisonment, Nelson Mandela became the world's most famous political prisoner, Amnesty International had not adopted him. They had thanked me for my ongoing reports, but never told me. I was outraged.

From Joburg, I phoned and wrote the top Amnesty officials in

London and expressed my incredulity, suggesting that they find a way to try to reengage Mandela and honor him publicly, if he would consent. I learned that AI had accepted him as a prisoner of conscience in 1962, when he was charged with incitement and leaving the country without a passport. But when he was charged with "sabotage and armed struggle against the apartheid government," Amnesty decided against considering Mandela a prisoner of conscience, asserting their stance against the bearing of arms and potential violence. I don't know if AI has publicly changed its policy. They did offer Mandela their Ambassador of Conscience Award, and he accepted. Amnesty traveled to Johannesburg to honor Mandela in person on November 1, 2006. I was on Martha's Vineyard. It was the very day that Bill died.

Later, when I was lucky enough to be in a room with Mandela as part of the delegation that accompanied President Clinton to South Africa—with Eli Segal, the founder of AmeriCorps, to promote AfriCorps—I did not repeat my request or probably even identify myself. Nor did I go on with that particular book. I gave some of the material I'd intended to use to Kerry Kennedy, who included parts of it in her stellar volume *Speak Truth to Power,* which was later adapted into a play by Chilean novelist and essayist Ariel Dorfman. He became a top professor at Duke. The play was launched at the Kennedy Center with an extraordinary cast: Alec Baldwin, Julia Louis-Dreyfus, Giancarlo Esposito, Héctor Elizondo, Kevin Kline, John Malkovich, Rita Moreno, Sigourney Weaver, and Alfre Woodard. Ariel and Kerry traveled near and far with it, so I hear. He and I have been in touch recently during the fraught new election for the president of Chile. His young candidate won! He's retiring as a professor at Duke, where I hope to see him before long.

In January 1977, eight and a half years after Soviet tanks rolled into Czechoslovakia to crush the reforms of the Prague Spring of '68, the writers Václav Havel and Pavel Kohout, with more than two hundred other activists, artists, and intellectuals, signed and distributed a declaration of rights known as Charter 77. It became the foundation of the Czech dissident movement. The immediate spark of the move-

With Ginetta Sagan at Joan Baez tea party for Václav Havel, September 1994.

ment had been the arrest and imprisonment of the rock band Plastic People of the Universe, which had become a hugely popular symbol of underground resistance to Soviet control of the Czech people and their culture. Charged with disturbing the peace, the band members received prison sentences of up to eighteen months.

The Charter 77 declaration deplored the government's systematic abuses of basic human rights and democratic freedoms. It noted that in Soviet Czechoslovakia, freedom of expression and assembly, the right to privacy, religious freedom, and freedom from fear all "exist, regrettably, on paper alone."

The document went on to describe the movement that had produced it:

> Charter 77 is a loose, informal and open association of people of various shades of opinion, faiths and professions united by the will to strive individually and collectively for the respecting of civic and human rights in our own country and throughout the world . . . Charter 77 springs from a background of friendship and solidarity among people who share our concern for those ideals that have inspired, and continue to inspire, their lives and their work. Charter 77 is not an organization; it has no rules, permanent bodies or formal membership. It embraces everyone who agrees with its ideas and participates

in its work. It does not form the basis for any oppositional political activity. Like many similar citizen initiatives in various countries, West and East, it seeks to promote the general public interest.

Václav Havel and others were detained as they tried to deliver the document to the government. The original was seized and denounced as "an anti-state, antisocialist, demagogic, abusive piece of writing." Dissidents spread samizdat reproductions by hand. The signatories were variously jailed, exiled, removed from their jobs, their books banned. Havel would be imprisoned for much of the period from 1977 to 1983. He didn't become president until December 1989. Pavel Kohout narrowly escaped execution by the secret police when the two agents sent to assassinate him refused to carry out their orders. Forced to leave Prague, he and his wife fled to Vienna in 1978.

Amnesty sent me on my first of several trips with Ginetta Sagan, the Italian-born activist and key Amnesty member (later the honorary chair of the board of directors). As I mentioned earlier, Ginetta had given Amnesty its logo, inspired by the matchbox thrown to her by a guard after she was caught helping Jews escape from Mussolini's Blackshirts during World War II, and imprisoned, raped, and tortured. The message inside the matchbox: *"Coraggio!"*

I took Polly along with me to Prague to provide cover, as Susanna had in Chile, assuming that this time we would surely not be in danger. Ginetta and I arranged to meet dissidents on park benches, in the Jewish cemetery behind a specific tombstone—places where we hoped neither they nor we were under surveillance. Sometimes Ginetta and I went together, other times we split up. We weren't scared. We were on a mission, figuring out how to make things work.

Once Polly and I were in a taxi going to meet a dissident when the driver, clearly a government agent, tried to get us into an accident. This was a standard ploy for disrupting missions that seemed possibly suspicious, which would mean we'd be taken to a police station and miss our appointment. As the driver was obviously about to run us into a ditch on a side road, Polly and I jumped out of the cab and ran.

Another day, I went to see Pavel Kohout in his high-windowed apartment atop the Swiss embassy. It was sad to watch him packing the one box of books he was allowed to take into exile. The police arrived that evening to close his apartment and accompany him and his wife far out of the city.

At the end of our stay in Prague, as we got ready to leave the hotel, Ginetta stopped me and said, "Give me all your papers and notes. We can't keep them. I'm going to the basement. I'll tear them up and flush them down the toilet. Then we'll leave." We were planning to travel home separately, she with her husband by train to Germany, Polly and I by plane to New York.

Flushing written notes was normal procedure on these trips. We always tried to commit our notes to memory or keep a vital minimum in personal code, destroying the rest. Had certain ones been discovered, the results might have been dire for our contacts in that country.

I waited at the head of the stairs in the lobby for Ginetta to come back up from the basement. I waited and waited. If she took much longer, Polly and I would miss our flight. Finally I trudged down the narrow steps and found her standing still, small and round, with two armfuls of wet paper scraps—a comical sight.

"Both the toilets down here are blocked," she said in her high accented voice that Joan Baez used to imitate, to my repeated pleasure. "So I fished it all out. Here, you take half and I'll take half."

She gleefully stuffed large wads of wet papers in my coat pockets. Polly and I left central Prague laden with soggy secrets.

My first trip to South Africa, a brief one, was months later. The year before, Victor Emanuel, a Harvard graduate and instructor of politics, had abandoned that track to become a renowned ornithologist. In his native Texas, he founded the Victor Emanuel Nature Tours aimed at organizing bird-watching and general wildlife trips around the globe. Victor's new friend Peter Matthiessen was enlisted to invite his friends and help lead the first tour.

Their first big trip was to explore the birds of Kenya and Botswana. I was clueless about ornithology—and Victor—but at Peter's urging, I signed up with mutual friends and took along Polly and Tommy (a present for Tommy's eighteenth birthday).

We had a marvelous time in Kenya. Tom and Polly and John Marquand's son James were the three teenagers on the excursion, and became best friends. Offbeat incidents occurred, including John Marquand being instructed to set up his tent far from our little circle because he snored so loudly. When we awoke the first morning in our encampment we looked for John, still asleep. We saw his tent surrounded by a variety of attentive animals listening with obvious curiosity to him snore, but not invading his premises. It was a good omen for the rest of our journey.

As the weeks progressed, I was enchanted by the views of birds and animals identified instantly for us by our leaders. I think I became a "birder" (though I don't keep serious lists) after watching the crowned cranes do their mating dance. This was my first safari experience. Naturally I fell for the elephants. I realized my mother must have as well, because she had elephant decorations everywhere in our home in Baltimore. It's hard to find the words for my delight in the streams of zebras, the sightings of giraffes going by, and the occasional stately lion and lioness and their brood. Because I loved to fly, one day I found a way to be in a very small plane with a careful pilot and watch the herds from the sky. Though I'd planned to be a pilot and soloed, I never got enough hours in the air to earn my license. I felt safe copiloting.

When Amnesty learned I was in or near Nairobi, they requested that I see the head of the Ford Foundation in Kenya, John Gerhart. I told Victor and Peter I was going to abandon them for the moment and meet with John, and to my surprise, Victor said, "He's a good friend of mine, a birder from Texas, so we'll come with you." And they did for the beginning of my meeting.

John explained Amnesty's request. He advised me that when our group was on its way to Botswana, and changing planes in Johannesburg to get there, I instead go into more remote places in South Africa to look for Breyten Breytenbach, who they knew was a political prisoner, held mostly in solitary confinement. At the time, his condition and location were unknown. My task was to find out any information I could about where he was being held. It now crosses my mind that maybe the Ford Foundation, which helped me escape from Chile years before, might have some serious Amnesty connection.

Breyten, a poet and painter, later acclaimed for his memoirs, essays, and novels, had been imprisoned in 1975, no one knew where. He left Cape Town after college to travel in Europe when he was twenty, and while living in Paris he married Yolande Ngo Thi Hoang Lien. Because Yolande was Vietnamese and mixed-race marriages were illegal in South Africa, he was forbidden to return home (even to accept poetry awards he had received there). With other anti-apartheid activists in France, Breyten organized the resistance group Okhela. When, incognito, he traveled back to Johannesburg to bring funds for the underground, he was arrested. Many believe that members of his pro-apartheid family turned him in.

John told me that if I became aware of anyone being searched or arrested ahead of me as we were being processed in the Johannesburg airport as we changed planes for Botswana, I should, immediately, calmly go into the ladies' room and tear up and flush down the toilet all my notes (names, publications, and any other related material). He told me I should then fly directly to Botswana and look for a refugee camp where I might be lucky enough to get useful information. John warned me that I was not to reenter South Africa from there.

In the Johannesburg airport, I stood in the customs line with Polly and Tommy. The dark-skinned man two places ahead of us in line was taken away in manacles. And a white man right in front of us had his papers searched before being forcibly hustled off for questioning. That was enough for me. I was afraid to leave the kids, but couldn't bring Tommy into the ladies' room. I left them together at the side of the line and casually headed to the restroom, where I tore up all of my papers into small pieces and successfully flushed them down the toilet. Thankfully, we weren't questioned by customs, and off we flew to Botswana with Victor's group.

In Maun, Botswana, the first moment I could, I left Victor and Peter, Polly, and Tom and the rest of our group, so I could follow John Gerhart's instructions. I was told about a refugee camp where several young South Africans who had recently escaped from prison were being held. I got myself a ride there and found two young men who'd met Breyten in the prison they escaped from. They told me where he was currently held and that his condition was pretty good physically. I passed that information on to Amnesty, which followed up from London, and went back to join the children and my pals for a few glorious last days in the Botswana countryside. I will never forget the beautiful spreading sunrises that looked as if they were coming out of a huge hat, or the variety of birds. Tommy's actual birthday occurred there, and I happened to watch him that morning as a group of local boys gave him a turn playing a bow-and-arrow game. While I held my breath, terrified, too late to stop him, he shot an apple off the head of a teenager. Was William Tell looking down on the boys?

Breyten remained in prison awhile longer, frequently in solitary confinement, for what became a total of seven years. He later wrote a fine book about those years, *The True Confessions of an Albino Terrorist.* More books followed. One, *Return to Paradise,* I found particularly meaningful. And he had international exhibits of his original paintings. I helped Breyten secure a several-year appointment at NYU when he was released, and visited him in his home near Cape Town on one of my South Africa trips.

In 1995 I interviewed him during a series of radio programs called *The Writer's World* that I hosted for Voice of America. He told me there was a tiny window in his cell and minuscule creatures would alight on its sill to keep him company. He talked about how his years of forced isolation in prison honed and focused both his poetry and his politics:

> One should not bad-mouth the experience of prison, which brings me to the incongruous thought that perhaps prison is a way of cleaning the mouth . . . You know what it's like, being a poet yourself, that in the hustle and bustle of our daily lives, we seem to find so little time to withdraw to those essential areas of quietness where these things start to happen . . . One could make a case for prison being an essential poetic experience. Linguistically speaking. It pushes you right down to the roots of words, for instance, the root of language. And how very intimately and how very deeply experiences link up to words, those secret places where words and experiences are still the same, because everything is stripped there. There was no social nicety that could enrobe what's taking place.

. . .

After I came home from my summer trip to Botswana, which the kids and I still reminisce about, I returned to Russia to do work for Amnesty. I arranged for writer Francine du Plessix Gray, my Connecticut neighbor, and her son Thaddeus and my son, Tom, to travel to Russia with me. Francine and I had first met when we double-dated in Paris. It was the early 1950s, I with Bill and she with Tom Guinzburg: *Paris Review* days. She went on to be a Pulitzer Prize nominee, her subjects everyone from her parents to the Marquis de Sade. She married the painter Cleve Gray and moved to Warren, Connecticut, a half hour from Roxbury. Tom Guinzburg took over Viking Press from his father, and became my first publisher. He soon married actress Rita Gam.

This was Francine's first trip to Moscow. Both her mother and stepfather were Russian and had lived there before they separately fled from the Soviet Union to Paris. Her mother, Tatiana, had been engaged to the poet Vladimir Mayakovsky in Moscow. He tried to follow her to Paris, but was prevented by Stalin from leaving. Tatiana met and quickly married the Vicomte du Plessix, a French diplomat stationed in Warsaw, where Francine was born in 1930. Because of the timing of Francine's birth, there were rumors that Mayakovsky (who committed suicide in Moscow a few months before Francine was born) was her father. Tatiana denied it.

Francine grew up in Paris. In 1940, the Vicomte du Plessix, who had joined the French Resistance as a pilot, was shot down and killed by the Nazis. Tatiana fled occupied France for New York with Francine and Alex Liberman, another Russian émigré, a sculptor, and charming. They married and remained together the rest of their lives. He proved a splendid stepfather to Francine. For thirty years he was the editor at Condé Nast while Tatiana became a famous designer of hats for Saks Fifth Avenue. She was the center of a lively social and literary circle. They too settled in Connecticut. Dinner at the Libermans' was always substantive and fun. Once, when Bill and I arrived for dinner at their house, she stared at me briefly and said, "You look different, you look so happy. Are you having an affair?" I laughed and said, "Of course not." But I had actually just spent a surprising single night with a fellow poet.

Francine and I decided it would be a great trip for us, with Thaddeus and Tom, who was a classmate at Rumsey Hall, to go to Moscow and a good cover for me in case the Soviets were suspicious of my comings and goings. When their consulate in New York refused me a visa, I suggested Francine fly with the boys to Moscow, while I left the same day for San Francisco. I figured the consulate there had never seen and probably never heard of me, and since the New York offices were closed that day (a local holiday), there was no one with whom they could check my record. It worked: They gave me my visa and I flew that day to Moscow. We all learned many tricks and dodges working for Amnesty.

On my flight to Moscow I happened to sit beside a man I knew slightly from the political world. Aware of my Amnesty work, he said, "They're never going to let you in, even if they gave you a visa." But they did let me through at the Moscow airport—although they mysteriously lost my baggage, which contained not only my clothes but also medicines, a girdle, and some magazines I was ferrying to the mother of dissident Pavel Kahout, who had recently fled to the United States. For ten days in Moscow I wore clothes that Francine lent to me. She was a head taller than I and had a figure like Twiggy, which I did not, but she was generous and didn't laugh at my appearance too often.

My particular mission in Moscow was to meet Lev Kopelev (an ex–Cossack officer, an unusual post for a Jew). Originally from Ukraine, he had become a writer and well-known dissident. In 1945, after criticizing the atrocities committed by the Red Army as it swept through Germany, he was sent to the Gulag, where he was imprisoned for almost ten years and wrote a gripping book about it. He met fellow prisoner Alexander Solzhenitsyn during this time and in 1962 was instrumental in getting *One Day in the Life of Ivan Denisovich* published. As a dissident in the 1960s and '70s he was unable to find work, and his writing was published only in samizdat, underground.

I was not allowed to phone Lev to say I was coming, but I had an address for an apartment house at the end of a Moscow street where he was living on the top floor. I took Francine and the boys with me to the entrance of the building and said, "Wait here. I'll go upstairs and see if he's there and will receive me and let you come up." I walked up the stairs and knocked on the door. A great bear of a man threw the door open and loomed over me. When I told him

Amnesty's fiftieth anniversary celebration on Martha's Vineyard, summer 2011:
Wendy Luers, Rose, Harry and Pam Belafonte, Bill Shipsey, Nancy Rubin, Shalil Shetty.

my name, he grinned broadly and threw his long arms around me in a hug, hoisting me off my feet and carrying me around the room.

When he finally put me down, I said, "I have friends downstairs. Can they come up?"

His mood darkened. "Who are they?"

"My son, and my friend Francine du Plessix Gray and her son."

He whooped. "Mayakovsky's daughter? Bring her up!"

I fetched them and we had a wonderful conversation. He kept telling Francine, "You look just like him!" I couldn't tell if she was embarrassed or amused. I got the information I needed, and he warmly sent us on our way. Two years later, while he was traveling to West Germany, his Soviet citizenship was revoked. He never returned to Russia, even after Gorbachev restored his citizenship in 1990. He died in Cologne in 1997.

The rest of our time in Moscow we spent as tourists. Francine, a mushroom expert, took us mushroom hunting in the woods outside the city. We shepherded the boys around the Kremlin and museum sights.

The day I was scheduled to leave, I got a call from the airport.

"Mrs. Styron, we found your luggage. It went to Lebanon. It's here now."

How convenient for it to show up on my last day. I hopped in a cab, went to the airport, picked up my bag, and came back to Moscow. I still had three hours before my flight. I met a friend of Pavel Kahout's mother on the road, handed over my packages for her right out of the cab, then had the driver turn around and drive me back to the airport, where I joined Tom, Thaddeus, and Francine for the flight out.

The abolition of the death penalty has been my longtime crusade, one that I shared with Bill from our earliest months together in Rome. In the 1980s, with Larry Cox, I helped guide the Program to Abolish the Death Penalty in this country. In the mid-1980s, Larry went to work in AI's London office, following that with stints at the Rainforest Foundation and the Ford Foundation, where he provided funding and other support for human rights activists around the world. He returned to AIUSA and became its capable executive director in 2006. In my mind, he was the best director Amnesty ever had. Earlier, Jack Healey had been its long-term fine guide. I hear he is well, and writing. Larry and I continue to meet socially and reminisce.

Larry recently recalled how controversial a position it was at the time to be against capital punishment, both in the United States and within Amnesty. Some members who had joined Amnesty to focus on political prisoners in other countries felt that opposing the death penalty in the United States was outside the organization's mandate. Some did not share our opposition to capital punishment. William Buckley, an early member of AIUSA's board, resigned over the issue. Larry and I made several trips to the South together, where capital punishment was most often meted out and where the movement against it was small but very active. We spoke at anti–death penalty conferences, debated pro–death penalty advocates, and spoke when we could with often hostile lawmakers and prison officials. We met with prisoners' rights groups such as the Southern Coalition for Jails and Prisons, then led by the colorful, outspoken North Carolina minister Joe Ingle. Joe has remained a moral presence from New York to the South. Larry and I sat up with young activists far into the night, discussing issues and singing peace songs.

Through the South, into Texas, and on to California, I went to prisons, meeting with death row inmates and interviewing them about their lives. In these past decades, many have been proven innocent and released, thanks to the efforts of the Exonerateds. This dedicated group of activists began small public conversations in New York, and quickly and effectively expanded across the country, getting prisoners off death row using DNA and other tests. They pursued justice in cases when the inmates had not received proper legal defense and support. They often showed, in addition to DNA tests, that some convicts were not mentally sound enough or possibly old enough to have been held responsible for their crimes.

So many of the men on death row told me about abuses and brutalities they'd suffered as children. By the time they were six or seven years old, dozens were well on their way to becoming violent too. Meeting them reaffirmed my convictions about the injustice of capital punishment. Even for serial killers. Why not keep them alive, study their unique brain patterns when they enter prison and then after years of incarceration, to see how major crimes might be avoided or the criminals rehabilitated to varying extents? I feel that would possibly be much more of a protection for current and future society. I have friends who teach in maximum-security prisons and alert me to profound changes that they observe. One friend, Brooke Allen, has recently quit her major position as a professor at Bennington College in order to teach full-time at a maximum-security facility, where she feels that some of the long-term inmates are the brightest and most dedicated students she could have.

At last, thanks to Bryan Stevenson (among the individuals who offer me hope for the future), our government is rethinking the sentencing of teenagers to life behind bars. Their brains are not yet fully formed. Massachusetts and California lead the way at the moment. Bryan, in Alabama, founded the Equal Justice Initiative to protect young offenders long-term. Recently he has also established the truly important National Memorial for Peace and Justice and the Legacy

Museum in Montgomery—highlighting the brutal and illegal executions in our American past. I am planning to visit it, first the "lynching museum," when he is available to guide me. Bill Styron would have heartily approved and wanted to join us.

When Mitterrand abolished capital punishment in France, I went to Paris and persuaded his justice minister, Robert Badinter, to come to the United States to tell us how we could accomplish that feat. I arrived just when he found out about the murder of his father, who had been a leader of the Resistance during World War II, and how, where, and why he had grown up in Paris with his mother after the Nazi invasion.

Robert was convinced that if we could produce a case or two in which someone had been unfairly executed, the time would be ripe to abolish it. He came to the United States, we went to several cities to talk with professionals, and nothing happened. Discouraged, he returned to France. I was deeply disheartened.

Circling back to the '70s and my early involvement with Amnesty, in 1975, I attended one of the Bertrand Russell Tribunals, this one held in Mexico City's Chapultepec Castle, where a number of us agreed to present papers to publicize Pinochet's crimes against humanity. There I met and became friends with Orlando Letelier and Gabriel García

Amnesty death penalty march, 1976—with Vinnie McGee, Franca Scuita,
Jack Healey, Paul Hoffman, Charles Henry, et al.

Amnesty death penalty rally, 1976—with Dennis Brutus, Franca Scuita, et al.

Márquez. Letelier, a diplomat and Allende minister, had been imprisoned from September 1973 to September 1974, when U.S. and international pressure on the Pinochet regime finally got him released. Attorney General Levi used his parole authority to let him into the United States. When we met, he was preparing to accept a post in Washington, D.C., at the Institute for Policy Studies.

García Márquez and I had written back-to-back articles about Chile for the magazine *Ramparts*, which was an American political and literary magazine published from 1962 to 1975 and closely associated with the New Left political movement. My article, entitled "Chile: The Spain of Our Generation," appeared in one of its final issues in 1975. As I joined a lunch table in Chapultepec Castle, "Gabo," as he's known to his friends and fans, famously announced that he would never write another word until Pinochet was out of power. Thank God he didn't stick to that, because Pinochet ran Chile for another fifteen years. Carlos Fuentes, whom I'd met with Bill when he had been a participant in the North-South writers' gathering a year or so earlier in Mérida, came to sit beside me. Gabo smiled broadly under his black mustache, sat on my other side, and put an arm around my shoulders. Gabo's English was not much better than my Spanish, and

Unknown participant, Rose, Gabriel García Márquez, and Carlos Fuentes,
Russell Tribunal, Mexico City, 1975.

Carlos cheerfully translated as needed. We talked briefly of our experiences in Chile, of international responses to the coup, and then, as
I recall, of recent fiction. (As one of his millions of fans, I remember
well the week I read *One Hundred Years of Solitude* in galleys brought
me by Tom Guinzburg on our joint vacation with family: I never
left my porch chair in Jamaica except to eat and sleep, not even for
tennis.) In Mexico City, his characters seemed to intrude as he talked
passionately, often amusingly: the magic realist. It was the start of a
friendship between us that was augmented by meetings and social
events in Cartagena, New York, and on Martha's Vineyard.

I was not thinking of home at that point. Alexandra, my nine-
year-old, was in school in Washington, Connecticut, and by that time
Tommy was sixteen and a junior at Taft. Polly and Susanna were at
college at Brown and Yale. Was it much of an adjustment for Bill to
get used to my travels, even though he clearly supported my activism?
Did he have brief liaisons while I was gone? Our marriage was secure,
but I guess my relationship with our youngest was not, to my eternal
regret. Even now I look back and realize she did not look favorably
on her status as a child born a decade later than her siblings, often
alone, as I had been . . . I did not have a "mean father." I remembered
enjoying my childhood years "alone," and made sure Al had fine care-
givers and babysitters and team riding companions and a neighborhood of school pals, but clearly she was not like me.

Son Tom with his dad at Al's graduation from Taft, 1983.

In September 1976, Secretary Simon called me and said, "This is ridiculous. I'm going to Chile in a few days and I think I need to meet with Orlando personally. But I can't have him seen coming into my office. Will you bring him to the back door at two o'clock this Thursday? We'll sneak him in that way."

I called Orlando and told him I'd be landing at National Airport in D.C. at noon that Tuesday, September 21. I'd come in to Sheridan Circle to meet him at the institute offices, and we'd drive together over to the Treasury.

When I came down the ramp at National at noon that day, I was met by a friend and fellow Amnesty USA board member, poet Tom Jones. I was stunned as he told me the meeting was off—Orlando had just been killed, along with his young American assistant Ronni Moffitt, in a car bombing in Sheridan Circle. Ronni's husband, Michael, a lawyer, was in the backseat. He was injured in the blast, but not killed.

In succeeding seasons, Michael and I would help investigate the bombing. It was tracked back to DINA agents, sent by Pinochet. One of them, Michael Townley, was an American expatriate formerly with CIA. He was convicted in 1978 but released the following year under the witness protection program. Others involved weren't convicted until almost twenty years later, after Pinochet was out of power.

At National Airport I told Tom I wanted to go see Isabel right away.

"No, don't do that," he said. He reminded me that I was an Amnesty member, and Amnesty had a strict policy of maintaining a posture of political neutrality, so that no government, whether Fascist or Communist, democracy or monarchy, could get off the hook by accusing us of bias.

Tom told me that Amnesty wanted me to get on a plane and go to Strasbourg, where they were having their annual international meeting.

As I remember it, I met my mother somewhere for lunch as planned, called Bill to tell him I was leaving. An hour or so later, an amnesty lawyer put me on a flight to Europe. When I arrived in Strasbourg that evening, the first thing I did was go to the cathedral and just sit and try to collect myself. I was undone by what had happened. I wasn't Catholic or in any way religious, but it was the right place to be—dark, shimmering, empty—and I found comfort there. I thought about how Orlando had planned to set up a Chilean government in exile in Amsterdam. Ariel Dorfman, the Chilean novelist, cartoonist, and playwright who wrote *Death and the Maiden,* would be his deputy. Orlando had asked me to help them run it. He knew I wasn't going to leave my family and move to Holland, but I seriously considered commuting back and forth. Now, suddenly, those were no longer considerations.

After midnight, I arrived at Vinnie McGee's home and he gave me his bed (he slept on the couch). Vinnie was philanthropist Irene Diamond's assistant and connected to others who supported our varied human rights ventures, especially Bob Bernstein's Human Rights Watch, which I served on the board of. Bob had been a senior member of the AIUSA advisory board I chaired when he took the first group of American writers to the Moscow Book Fair, then augmented the Helsinki Accords by forming the Helsinki Watch. It expanded worldwide, becoming the invaluable U.S.-based Human Rights Watch.

Joan Baez called Strasbourg and told me there was going to be a funeral procession for Orlando in D.C. in a couple of days, and she and I were asked to be there, in the lead. We had each bonded with Orlando Letelier when he was asylumed.

Joan and I were good friends and fellow Amnesty members. I first met her in the '60s in Cambridge when she was performing at Club Passim. We connected often, especially through Ginetta Sagan, who was Joan's neighbor in Palo Alto. I remember sitting between Joan and film director Costa-Gavras at the 1972 Paris conference launching the Campaign for the Abolition of Torture. Costa-Gavras was quite smitten with Joan and kept leaning past me to flirt with her. Amused, I kept inching my chair back and back until the two of them leaned together like a pair of courting cranes.

Now Joan urged me to come to D.C. for Orlando's funeral. This was followed quickly by a call from the World Council of Churches in Geneva. They told me there were all sorts of reasons why I should not be getting on any plane to the United States in the immediate future. They were telling Bill Wipfler, then in Geneva, the same. My life would be in danger. I was debating whether to go or not when Susanna, in Europe then, called and said forcefully, "Mom, don't you dare get on a plane. It's much too dangerous. Drive with me to Paris. Who's more important, me or Orlando? He's dead. I'm your child and I'm alive."

I called Joan back and told her I wasn't coming. She was incredulous. She said it was just a bunch of scare stories, that nothing would happen to me, that I owed it to Isabel and Orlando to be there. I thought I owed more to my wonderful daughter. I didn't go to Washington, and I harbored guilt about it for years. Susanna came to Strasbourg and we drove to Paris and down to Spain, mother and daughter bonding again, as in Chile. I thought perhaps Orlando would have approved.

In Chicago, Joanne Fox-Przeworski and the Chicago Commission of Inquiry had also been making public the crimes of the Pinochet regime. The *New York Review of Books* published the commission's report and my report together in May 1974, calling them "Terror in Chile I" and "Terror in Chile II." Joanne and others were trying to start a Chicago chapter of Amnesty. It's a measure of how little known Amnesty still was in this country in the mid-'70s that when she called a reporter at the *Chicago Tribune* about it, he slammed the phone down on her, thinking she wanted to talk about amnesty for Vietnam War draft dodgers. I went to Chicago to talk to Joanne's group, and we met for the first time. In a few years, she'd join me on the board of Amnesty International USA.

Thirty years later, when Joanne and I had both long since retired from the Amnesty board (and I had stayed with her in Paris during her career with the UN's Economic Social Council), she asked me to come speak at Bard College, where she had founded the Center for Environmental Policy. Bard was planning an extensive human rights program, as Trinity College had done. Joanne organized a panel of what she called AI pioneers, eight of us who were original or early members of the New York chapter. She wanted our memories of Amnesty USA's early activities to be recorded. Most of us hadn't seen one another in a while, and we were all quite surprised by how little we'd known of one another's activities on behalf of AI, beyond our group meetings and local events. We had followed the organization's effective policies of silence and extreme discretion for decades.

After the panel, we stayed up all night sharing stories. It was only then that Joanne said to me, "Did you realize that when you and your daughter were in that pool in Chile, I was there watching?"

What a revelation! We'd been visiting each other in Paris and New York for years and she'd said nothing. Amnesty had a powerful hold on each of us. Silence about our individual activities had been paramount. Google says those born in my year were the last of the "Silent Generation." But now, aided by the internet as well as intimate meetings, we could converse and deepen our knowledge of our history.

11

More Wildlife Adventures

N ATURE IS MY INSPIRATION. Since my trip to Botswana and Kenya with Victor Emanuel and Peter Matthiessen, I have pursued many birding and general wildlife excursions with them, exploring the out-of-doors, land and sea, far and near. Tom and Polly accompanied me several times, as did a few good friends. I even persuaded Bill to go on a couple of later trips—to India and to Tanzania. Rain-soaked tents and open-fire-heated tents, with outdoor plumbing, frozen and canned food, excessively bumpy flights, and jeep excursions I took in stride, but they provoked negative reactions from sensitive Bill and incited his hasty bowing out early to return home. George Plimpton replaced him the last couple weeks in India, and Mike Wallace's wife, Mary, became my new tentmate in Tanzania. George, Peter, and I actually delayed everyone's trip from India to Bhutan because as published writers we were each forced to receive and sign documents that promised we would not write about the country (even though all our writings would have been positive, admiring). My favorite souvenir is a photograph of Peter in a long formal robe presented to him in the countryside there. I assume they knew that he was a Buddhist priest.

On a memorable Mexico trip in 1978, the year after Botswana,

Tom, Polly, and I climbed El Triunfo in the Sierra Madre peaks, in the Chiapas region of Mexico. I got hooked on the azure-rumped tanager, name and all. It reminded me of my fascination with the prothonotary warbler, whose odd name stuck in my mind in Whittaker Chambers's book condemning Alger Hiss. Chambers claimed they went birding together. Hiss denied any such companionship. When I read the testimony, I wondered why seeing this rare bird was evidence to condemn Hiss. At the time I thought Chambers had invented it, but I've more than once seen the oddly named warblers by now. And in Hiss's last years, I came to think, grudgingly, that the man I'd long championed and once dined with was guilty of a kind of espionage after all. The colorful azure-rumped tanager and its name were definitely more appealing. It was Polly who first saw one, to Victor's delight and identification.

We'd started the El Triunfo trip in Chiapas on a Sunday morning. I had lost a filling, a very deep one in a near-front tooth, and wasn't keen on climbing up into the jungle in impossible pain. I was pointed toward the local clinic, where I stood in a long line of local people. The dentist came out in a white smock covered with blood. That scared me, but I took a deep breath and went in. Without a word or even cleaning the tooth out, he filled it with some kind of cement. It lasted for years.

Sunday bells pealed, and we set off. On El Triunfo, Victor hoped to spot a horned guan—a large, very rare, turkey-like black bird with a red horn. The top of El Triunfo was one of the very few places it was known to live. Before beginning the ascent, we camped out on the grass at the finca of our guide, Don Rodrigo. I woke up in the early hours of the morning to see a pig straddling my sleeping bag, peering into my face.

In the morning, as we loaded our bags on Don Rodrigo's pack-horses, he told us we couldn't take the usual route up the mountain because local peasants were squatting up there in a protest and the police had blocked that trail. We'd have to use a much more rigorous trail that went right up the other side of the mountain, very steep and narrow. Instead of four or five hours to the summit, it took three days. One of the horses plunged over a cliff and down the hillside with our food and gear. Miraculously, it survived.

We climbed and climbed. I had persuaded artists Jack Zajac and his painter wife, Corda, friends from Rome, to come along on this trip. I'd hoped in vain that our mutual friend Peter Matthiessen would join us. The Zajacs were miserable. (Did they ever forgive me? The Styrons and Zajacs had memorable trips together in Italy and America in the years after.) We climbed all day, it rained a great deal, we slept in soggy tents, and ate packaged food heated over an open fire, which the Zajacs did not pretend tasted good. Polly and Tommy were once so hungry they stole a can of tuna from the supplies. (Victor has never let them forget it.) Nightly body checks were necessary for ticks and other insects. Tentmates became good friends. Victor today refers to the Zajacs as his worst climbers, and when I visit them in Umbria or at their American home in Santa Cruz, we still laugh about it.

One morning my tentmate, Cindy Bumstead, and I got up early and started out ahead of the others. We took a wrong fork on the trail, which began to lead us down instead of up, and were soon lost. We descended into a thick forest while the rest of the team went on climbing. Finally Tommy said, "Where's my mother?" A posse came down and rescued us. Victor continued upward, of course, still excited that he might see a horned guan. Suddenly we all met a hunter coming down the narrow trail with a dead horned guan over his shoulder. Warbler, as Victor refers to himself, looked sad for hours. He was sure there was not a live horned guan still to be found at the mountaintop. We did spot a spectacled owl and a flock of as many as two hundred orange-footed parakeets, and a pair of bright-feathered caracaras—Mexico's national bird. Today the area is a game preserve, but Victor realized on subsequent trips that much of the forest was destroyed at the top.

As we came back down, it rained and rained. Everyone but I wore climbing boots, which I don't like, so I hiked in sneakers. My sneakers shrank, and by the time we got to the bottom I was on my way to losing both big toenails. The Zajacs never came on another trip into the wild.

One year Victor gave his favorite birding regulars bird names. His: the hooded warbler, because he often appeared before dawn in our cold open trucks, a blanket over his head until sunrise. Peter: the curlew, because the curlew is a swift-running shorebird and Peter's first big successful book was *The Shorebirds of North America*. (I am still aware of trying to keep up with Peter on shores and frozen lakes on various continents.) Me: the scarlet tanager. I asked him why, having expected him to call me the Baltimore oriole. He said, no, you're the scarlet tanager because like Scarlett O'Hara you always put off making decisions until tomorrow. He was right. I realize I've missed more than one swell opportunity, pondering.

In 1980, again with Peter, Tommy, and Polly, we ventured to Peru. In Lima I went first to the big art museum. There I found myself discussing a painting with the man standing next to me, who turned out to be Mario Vargas Llosa. We'd never met before, though we have on several occasions since. (I cheered when he ran for president of Peru, and again when he won the Nobel Prize in Literature. He is brilliant, vigorous, attractive, dedicated, deserving.)

In Peru, our group flew first over the strange Nazca Lines in the desert to Explorer's Inn, where the remarkable ornithologist Ted Parker awaited us. His girlfriend was conducting a bat workshop, which fascinated me. (Decades later, on the Vineyard, I helped organize a night bat hunt for the Nature Conservancy.)

One morning, alone at dawn as was my wont, I went for a walk into the jungle on a well-trodden trail. I was standing rapt, admiring a troop of shiny red ants climbing sheets of shining filaments up toward the sun, into the high flowering bromeliads, when I heard strange footfalls in the leaves. I looked down to find a harpy eagle at my side. It was huge, half my size, and had a majestic white head crowned with feathers, a dark gray chest and wings. We stared at each other awhile and walked on apace together. Our leaders were pretty skeptical of my tale at breakfast, branding it a poet's creation. Thankfully, at dusk they all spotted him or his cousin in a tree.

Our next stop was to be Machu Picchu. We chugged in a crowded, noisy, dirty train through the valley, looking out as Victor, excited, identified countless birds. Polly was anointed the star of the trip when she spotted a bright orange cock-of-the-rock.

As Victor led the group through the Machu Picchu site, he asked the guard if we could stay a little past the usual closing time so that Peter Matthiessen could give the group a talk about its history. Everyone but Victor and I left with Peter after his tutorial, which was terrific:

graphic and funny. When the two of us, still exploring and chatting as usual, tried to leave, we discovered that the guard had gone off to play soccer and locked us in. I can't remember how we eventually managed to emerge in the darkness. Victor was the soul of invention.

I decided to join a few hardy men, tourists, the next day as we climbed Huayna Picchu, the steep peak that rises behind Machu Picchu. An extra height-view (no little plane for me this time) was my silly reason. On the way back down I had my first ever intimation of vertigo. The path's extreme height and the narrowness of the ledge, just a footpath with nothing to hold on to, was suddenly frightening. I realized how shameful my former teasing of my husband and other travel companions with acrophobia had been. Victor actually had us sign release forms so that he couldn't be sued if any of us lost our footing. Returning, safe at last, I foolishly joined the men scaling a small peak close to the ruins. For my hubris I had to descend backward. I've gotten vertigo more than once since—when I was not climbing.

A decade or more later, a number of us (no kids invited) embarked on an incredible excursion to the Antarctic. Peter wrote refreshingly about the trip in *End of the Earth*. The book included photos by tripmate Birgit Bateman, who, with her premier nature-artist husband, Robert Bateman (both Canadian), became frequent treasured trip companions. We sailed on a Russian research vessel named the *Akademik Ioffe* for the physicist Abram Federovich Ioffe. We were told it was the only Russian ship ever named for somebody Jewish. The captain, Nikolai Apekhtin, was a man who knew poetry and spoke English. I spent more than one splendid hour talking with him on the bow and in the ever-interesting control room. He'd been given the keys to American cities including Baltimore and San Francisco when he'd docked there. His crew seemed to consist of scientists and engineers who wanted to get out of Moscow and had signed on to this ship so they might be away for months at a time together.

Before boarding, our group stopped in Santiago, Chile, on the way down. How different this visit was from my mission there in 1974! Now I took Peter and Victor to meet Orlando Letelier's widow, Isabel, and Matilde, Pablo Neruda's widow—the latter at Neruda's house on the water, Isla Negra. (A play I saw on the Vineyard in 2022 highlighting Neruda was set on Isla Negra.) The impressive shell collection there and the mementos from the poet's life—even his suits and hats in the closet—mesmerized me. I wished again I'd found that mysterious buried manuscript. For a whole day we went birding quietly along a river. From there we flew down to Punta Arenas, at Chile's southern tip, where Orlando, Ángel Parra, and other pro-Allende citizens I knew had been imprisoned in 1973: Pinochet's time. My emotions raced.

A bird-frequented park was our habitat for a day, before we set sail through the Strait of Magellan and around Cape Horn. Along the way I had a stupid accident. I got up the first night to go to the john, and did not properly secure the heavy door. The ship heaved. The door sliced my middle finger to the bone. No one answered my frantic midnight cry for help. I managed to extricate my hand myself. At 7:00 a.m., still in pain, I went to the infirmary and found the ship's doctor, an elderly gentleman who had long retired from the medical profession. Properly horrified, he stitched me up with thick black thread and bound the finger. It was a white signpost reminding me to be careful the rest of the journey. On the last day, he painstakingly removed the undissolved black thread. My tiny scar reminds me how lucky I am to still have the finger, and brings back memories of the extraordinary trip's glory.

Soon we sailed on to the island of South Georgia where in the whaling port of Grytviken we visited the simple grave of Sir Ernest Shackleton. In 1914, Shackleton set out from Grytviken aboard the *Endurance,* bound for the South Pole. After the *Endurance* was trapped and crushed by pack ice in Antarctica's Weddell Sea, Shackleton led his crew to the tiny Elephant Island. Then, in a small open lifeboat, he and five of his men sailed to South Georgia across eight hundred miles of one of the worst oceans on Earth in hopes of getting a ship to return other passengers. I mean to read his book someday.

We climbed up, over, and down to a promontory into the camp where Shackleton's little group had waited all that winter, using only two overturned small boats for cover. In spring a ship finally appeared and they were rescued. Shackleton returned to South Georgia in 1922 to start a new Antarctic expedition, but died of a heart attack in Grytviken. He was only forty-seven.

From South Georgia, we followed the *Endurance*'s route to Antarctica. Periodically we put down from the ship in Zodiac inflatables and scooted over to visit small islands that are home to vast and varied penguin colonies. On one of them I sat watching scores of Adelie penguins around me. Sitting on the sand at the edge of the water, I watched them dive in and out, while a pair of large males stood near me, like tuxedoed guards, just a few feet away. Each cradled an egg between his feet while their wives had gone off to find fish. Little baby penguins surrounded me, curious, even climbing into my lap and gazing up at me. I was enchanted. Suddenly the two males began to squabble with each other, still standing over their eggs while batting each other with their wings and squawking. One leaned over and batted too hard, and his egg slipped out from between his feet. Instantly a small scavenger bird raced over, poked its long beak into the egg and sucked out the fetal baby. The two fathers fell silent, stricken looks on their faces that I have never forgotten, more than human as they anticipated the mothers' return.

On another island, the penguins gathered all their young in a ravine, hundreds of chicks with just two adults guarding, while the rest went off for food. In the water at the bottom of the ravine, three or four huge seals lounged like pontoons. I stood up on the high rim of the ravine (not sure where my companions had wandered). I was marveling at this penguin nursery when a skua, a large, brown, gull-like bird of prey, swooped down from the sky toward the chicks. The adult penguins raised a terrible alarm, and all the little ones ran down to the water and out onto the backs of the seals for protection. I guessed that the skua must avoid seals. Happily, I did not see it devour a single penguin.

12

The Council on Foreign Relations

I BECAME A MEMBER of the prestigious Council on Foreign Relations in 1983. Few women were on the council at the time. Kay Graham, publisher of the *Washington Post* and close friend, was among the first nine invited to join a couple of years earlier. I wish I'd known then. I actually turned the council down that first time I was invited, thinking there were no women and I wouldn't want to be active in a men's-only club. The second time they asked, when I knew other women had agreed to join, I accepted. It was a swell decision. Bill Luers had nominated me, Arthur Schlesinger Jr. seconded. I was more than pleased. By then I was deeply engaged with Amnesty and human rights, traveling on missions, writing essays and articles for a number of periodicals.

Joining the CFR seemed an excellent opportunity to promote human rights issues because in those days the council was small, and it was easy to meet heads of state and policymakers. It took me a while to fit in there among all the established government leaders and businessmen. Petra Kelly, a founder of the Green Party in Germany and a phenomenal promoter of peace, spoke at the first meeting I attended. Petra and I were the only women in the room with about fifty men, and they were rough on her, questioning her sharply, arguing with her. I remained silent. She looked at me as though for support, but being brand-new and quite intimidated, I didn't say a word.

Afterward, when I went up to speak with her, she said, "I kept looking at you because I needed another woman to relate to." This was an unsettling new environment for me, a country girl by now. I often thought later how important the increasing number of women's voices were on the council. For example, in 2002, Jewelle Bickford founded the Women and Foreign Policy Advisory Council at CFR.

At a council gathering in 1990, I was speaking with Peter Tarnoff, then president of the council, and Richard Holbrooke, who'd been an assistant secretary of state in the Carter administration, when Peter suggested that the three of us should go to Vietnam and Cambodia. There were ample human rights issues for me to gather information on there and in neighboring Thailand, and traveling with those two smart guys would be exciting. We made plans. In the late 1970s, Vietnam had invaded Cambodia and ousted Pol Pot and the Khmer Rouge, who had massacred an estimated two hundred thousand citizens during their brutal four-year reign. The Vietnamese had removed their last troops from the country in 1989, and in 1991 Prince Sihanouk, who had been in exile since the 1970s, returned to become president and later king. Vietnam, meanwhile, spent the 1990s in a tense border standoff with China, which had backed the Khmer Rouge against the Vietnamese in Cambodia, and considered the Vietnamese government a dangerous Soviet puppet state on its flank.

In addition to Peter Tarnoff, Dick Holbrooke, and me, our group included former ambassador to Thailand Mort Abramowitz, and Peter's wife, Mathea Falco, plus their son Ben, then five years old. Smart, affectionate Ben and I became great friends on this trip and remain so. I'm amused that he remembers that I taught him how to swim in the hotel pool in Phnom Penh. Today he's written his second successful book, this one on the young Mark Twain and his literary circle.

From New York, we flew first to the Philippines, where ambassador Frank Wisner II hosted us. His French wife, Christine, who had previously been married to the father of French president Nicholas Sarkozy, joined our group for the rest of the trip—to Thailand, Cambodia, and South and North Vietnam. She and Frank divorced soon after. Frank's "new" wife is a very special woman and friend.

We arrived at Camp C, the Cambodian refugee camp on the Thai side of the border, just as hundreds who had fled the Khmer Rouge and spent over a decade inventing a viable community were being forced to go back, through deadly minefields, to resettle. I was impressed that they made villages out of muddy streets and small tin houses. Big clay-carved posters of men with legs blown off and carried on stretchers instructed the returnees wordlessly on how to deal with possible disaster caused by exploding mines. It was frightening for the refugees and certainly for me.

In Phnom Penh we met a man I've never forgotten: Sérgio Vieira de Mello, the handsome, smiling Brazilian hero of human rights, a remarkable UN diplomat. He was bravely working in all the hot spots, from Bangladesh to Cyprus to Mozambique to Lebanon to Kosovo, helping refugees and war victims. In Cambodia in the 1970s he was the first UN representative to hold talks with the Khmer Rouge. We stayed in touch over the years. He was an inspiration to me.

In 2003, Sergio was killed in a hotel in Baghdad. I had spoken with him at a Harvard gathering scant weeks before. He appeared there in an intimate space with Bernard Kouchner, the founder of Doctors Without Borders, and they had laughed about the difficulty of accomplishing anything quickly at the UN. De Mello declared that Baghdad would be his last trip before retiring, although by then he was a candidate to be the UN's next secretary-general. Samantha Power's *Chasing the Flame* chronicles his heroism.

From Phnom Penh, we went with Sergio out to the well-named Killing Fields, where the Khmer Rouge had massacred and buried thousands. It was devastating to walk that ground. I watched Sergio working his magic, comforting and advising the returning refugees. We toured the Tuol Sleng Genocide Museum, a former school that the Khmer Rouge had turned into a prison. The torture chambers and instruments attached to sagging bed slats were still on display. Photographs of some of the victims, who included poets, artists, and musicians, were on the walls. I realized I had published a long article for *Ms.* on one of the women. Her picture startled me; I mourned anew.

While we were still at the Genocide Museum, a messenger arrived and said that Prince Sihanouk, who had just returned that day from exile in China, wanted to see us in two hours at the royal palace. We raced back to our hotel, where I put on a dress and heels. We trooped into Sihanouk's beautiful palace and into the blue-domed throne room, where we were settled on low, richly brocaded divans and gilded chairs. I remember thinking we were like Dorothy and her friends waiting to meet the Wizard.

Soon the pomp began. The prince made his entrance in regal robes. He went straight to Ben, patted him on the head and made a fuss over him, then nodded to each of us in turn and went to sit on his throne on a high dais. We were served drinks and very elegant hors d'oeuvres. Then the prince cleared his throat and asked each of us to say something or pose a question. Dick Holbrooke went first and talked, I think, about financial matters. I believe Mort spoke about the Carnegie Endowment for International Peace, of which he was the president, and Peter about the Council on Foreign Relations. I don't remember their words. I was too nervous planning what I'd say. Then Dick introduced me as an American human rights expert.

Prince Sihanouk went up in smoke. Before I'd said a word, he was loudly defending himself against any charges of wrongdoing, declaring, "I didn't do it, I'm not responsible," and launching into a litany of blame against others, including a nephew. I knew he was referring to allegations of certain abuses, but I had not said anything. It was the mere mention of "human rights" that elicited his outcry. It made me realize how far the human rights movement had come in the twenty years since I first joined the little Amnesty group in Ivan Morris's mom's New York apartment—and how much the Powerful wanted to appear Good.

A few years after this trip, a young survivor of the Killing Fields, Arn Chorn-Pond, came to visit me on Martha's Vineyard. I was on the tennis court with Judge Mark Wolf, who welcomed him. Mark and his son Matthew were always immensely kind to Arn, helping him establish a Cambodian outpost near Boston, supporting his eventual return to Cambodia to create a Youth Corps and a music school. I was on the board of advisors of the Reebok Human Rights Foundation when we presented Arn with an award in 1988. He'd been a boy when the Khmer Rouge took over Cambodia, killing most of his family but keeping him alive in a work camp to play the flute for them. He still plays it professionally. Arn was one of the few children who survived the camp.

When the Vietnamese attacked Cambodia, the Khmer Rouge cynically put the boys in the front line to stop the bullets. Arn escaped into the jungle and eventually made his way to a refugee camp in Thailand. Quite ill, lying on a dirt floor, he was actually stepped on by a visiting American, a minister from New Hampshire named Peter Pond, who was in Thailand trying to document the plight of the Cambodian refugees. He and the recovering boy bonded. He brought Arn to the United States and adopted him, along with several other young Cambodians. (Arn's story is told in the PBS documentary *The Flute Player*.) I'd first met Arn in D.C. when he spoke at an Amnesty general meeting. He was still a young teenager. Much of the audience dissolved in tears.

With another American, Judith Thompson, Arn went on to start the organization the Children of War, which brought Palestinians and Israelis, English and Irish and other groups in conflict together through their young people. The effects of such reconciliations are more crucial than ever. In 1998, while watching Arn work with gangs of youth in Lowell, Massachusetts, Mark Wolf, now founder of the International Anti-Corruption Court, got an idea to help his son Matt and Arn start a camp to try to keep urban kids out of violent gangs. Matt continued the Red Auerbach Future Stars camp (free for boys and girls ages eight to fourteen) for years. Today Arn divides his time between the United States and Cambodia, where he runs an organization he founded, Cambodian Volunteers for Community Development—also, I have heard, a fine music school. Matt Wolf married a Cambodian woman, Chanda Ouk, and comes to Martha's Vineyard each summer with his kids and parents, a happy reunion for us all.

From Cambodia we went to Vietnam. The last American soldiers had evacuated Ho Chi Minh City (formerly Saigon) more than fifteen years earlier, but it still felt like a postwar town, with people on the streets peddling American souvenir dog tags and other memorabilia. When we stepped off the train in Hanoi, we were greeted by an enormous image of Ho Chi Minh gazing down over the city from one of its tallest buildings. Hanoi was a beautiful old colonial city with crumbling pale yellow and white Palladian villas and palaces on the banks of the wide Red River. I used to worry that the old residential and public buildings would all be torn down, but I understand that much has been preserved and restored.

In both cities in Vietnam, our group met with various government officials, and my role was always to bring up human rights issues. I had a list prepared by Amnesty of unjustly jailed prisoners—political, of course—and where they were being held. The government officials routinely said to me, "We have no political prisoners in Vietnam." I would produce my list of names and leave it with them, and weeks or months later a few would often be quietly released.

PEN had tried to send a delegation of writers to North Vietnam and asked me to find out why they had been turned down. (They did not seem to have been discouraged by my failure to find a Neruda manuscript in Santiago.) I put in a request to meet with the Union of Vietnamese Writers, the official government organization, and found myself at a long table with perhaps a dozen writers who were not forthcoming, giving me stock answers but no real information. Dick Holbrooke surprised me by asking to come along. He played my secretary, seated at my right hand, recording on a little portable typewriter he'd brought with him.

I was able to get them to talk about safe topics like their literary history and the French and American influences on it, but not about more current or personal subjects. Those, I gathered, might get them in hot water.

Not willing to give up quite yet, I thought to ask, "Have you read any American writers lately?"

One of them, seated at the far end of the table, volunteered, "I just read a long, interesting piece in an American magazine, about our war, called 'Love Day.'"

Without looking up or pausing in his typing, Dick said, "That was in *Esquire,* and it was by her husband, William Styron." He pointed at me. I was taken aback, but gratified.

That opened the floodgates. They all knew who William Styron was, and suddenly they were eager to talk and tell me their stories, which I brought back to PEN. I was asked to send my poems there to be translated. Stupidly, perhaps with my outdated vestige of self-effacement, I never did.

13

Reebok and Human Rights Watch and Amnesty

A LAN PAKULA had consulted Bill about making *Sophie's Choice*. Alan wanted him to do the screenplay, but Bill said he had no idea how to write a film script and told Alan that he should write it. Which he did, consulting with Bill once or twice. We were thrilled when Alan decided to cast Meryl Streep as Sophie. She had called asking Bill to contact Alan so he would audition her for the role. Bill told her it had already been cast. But Meryl persisted, and Bill did. She put on false teeth caps and had a perfect accent. She blew Alan away and was hired, despite the fact that a beautiful dark-haired, rather voluptuous European actress had been promised the role.

I had seen Kevin Kline onstage in *The Pirates of Penzance* and was really impressed. I called Alan and said, "Wouldn't he make a wonderful Nathan?" I imagine Alan had already seen *Pirates,* but I like to think my suggestion helped prompt the audition that gave Kevin the part. It was the first film in Kevin's long, brilliant career.

Bill and I were disappointed not to be invited to watch the filming of *Sophie* in Dubrovnik, but we did have brief fun observing a one-day shoot in Brooklyn. Later, Bill advised cutting a sequence in which Nathan rode a big white horse onto the Brooklyn Bridge, and Alan

Bill and Meryl Streep and Mark Morris
backstage at Lincoln Center for Poetry & the Creative Mind, 2002.

cut it. Bill thought highly of the finished film. Alas, Alan was killed in
a bizarre Long Island road accident years after—a long, heavy pipe
bounced off an open truck just ahead of him. It went through the
windshield and his forehead. Death was instantaneous. I happened to
be in his apartment with his wife, Hannah, and others for a meeting
when the terrible news arrived by phone.

Meryl later told us there were sequences cut that she thought
excellent, especially rough scenes between Sophie and Nathan, especially one on the staircase up from Stingo's room. Kevin agreed. We
assumed the cut footage was at Yale and tried every avenue to find
the abandoned hour or two that Alan shot, but nothing turned up
anywhere. We haven't quite given up hope.

Meryl, Kevin, and I still meet from time to time, though too infre-
quently now. Meryl and I see each other in New York or Connecticut for events we're both involved in, such as the annual Academy
of American Poets' program Poetry & the Creative Mind at Lincoln
Center, which we started together with Jorie Graham in 2002. Kevin
was a star at a recent performance there, footloose and fun. I still
smile remembering my disbelief when the gentleman who posed as
a waiter, bowing, taking the coat off my shoulders in a city restaurant,
turned out to be Kevin playing a prank. Any excuse to see Kevin is
fine with me.

. . .

Starting in the mid-1970s, Amnesty International in London, with the help of Monty Python's John Cleese, organized gala benefit performances to raise funds and public awareness for human rights. The first one in 1976 was called *A Poke in the Eye (With a Sharp Stick)*, then in 1977 it was *The Mermaid Frolics*. In June 1979 came *The Secret Policeman's Ball*. I had a terrible case of poison ivy that made me miss the last—the only one I tried to attend.

Amnesty USA's director, Jack Healey, looked for similar ways to raise money and awareness here. When the film adaptation of *Sophie's Choice* was completed in 1982, Jack asked me if I could get Universal to do the premiere in New York as a fund-raiser for Amnesty. "If you can do that," he said to me, "we'll get the theater and throw a big sit-down dinner party afterward for everybody we've invited to the screening."

I said, "Jack, I can do all this fieldwork and travel for you, but I live in the country. I don't have a clue as to how to organize an event like that in New York. It's a wonderful idea, and I'll try to secure the movie for you, but you're on your own as far as producing the event."

"Don't worry, I have the perfect person," he replied. "My friend Nancy Rubin in Washington."

With Bill, Meryl Streep, and Kevin Kline on the set of Sophie's Choice.

Marching with Nancy Rubin in D.C., early '90s.

I got us the film, and Nancy organized a fabulous evening. She and I have been co-conspirators and the best of friends ever since. She has served as the U.S. ambassador to the UN Human Rights Council and has done terrific work through other organizations, including Amnesty, the International Human Rights Law Group, the Women's Commission for Refugee Women and Children, and the Project on Justice, plus her private Didi Hirsh Mental Health Services. In recent years she's founded organizations in California focusing on youth with mental health challenges, featuring suicide prevention. I have found Nancy to be unfailingly caring and generous. I *still* regret not going with her to the Fourth World Conference on Women. I was scheduled to be part of a small Council on Foreign Relations group with David Rockefeller and Pete Peterson to meet Nelson Mandela a few days later, and was told I'd have trouble getting from China to South Africa, so I opted out. Of course meeting Mandela was hugely important to me. His was my first Amnesty case. I always think I can do everything—a trait that makes my friends shake their heads. This time I was forced to make a choice: Mandela.

In 1986, Mary Daley, a first-class public relations specialist and events organizer and friend of Peter Gabriel, prompted by AIUSA director Jack Healey, devised another way to promote Amnesty and human rights: a star-studded rock tour of six U.S. cities, called A Conspiracy of Hope. The rock promoter Bill Graham (no relation to Kay Graham) of Fillmore East and West fame ran it. Peter Gabriel, Sting, U2, Bryan Adams, and others waived their usual fees to perform. It was a huge success, raising much more than we'd imagined, and we were all delighted. I was nearly deafened sitting in the front row at the Los Angeles concert. The deafening was repeated when I was onstage, on tour, but it was worth it, even as I explore hearing aids today.

We began thinking in a hopeful way about doing it again, but this time on a grander, international scale. We didn't have much of a plan. One day Mary and I were talking about it, sitting by a pool before an Amnesty meeting in Los Angeles, when we were approached by a young Reebok vice president, Angel Martinez. Angel had emigrated from Cuba, sent by his parents as a boy, and after graduating from the University of California, Davis, he had begun a stellar career in the fitness industry. He got excited about the possibility of Reebok funding a tour and took it to his CEO, Paul Fireman.

The result was Reebok putting up $20 million to fund Amnesty's 1988 world rock tour, Human Rights Now!, which coincided with the fortieth anniversary of the UN's Universal Declaration of Human Rights. Because of Amnesty's policy of not being publicly allied with any organization, corporation, or government (always maintaining its position of political neutrality), Reebok was not allowed to put its logo on anything associated with the tour, or even to announce its funding. It was quite remarkable that Reebok agreed to put so many millions into this tour anonymously.

Once again Bill Graham was the organizer of a massive undertaking, and it was definitely a more spectacular success than the '86 U.S. tour. It began at Wembley Stadium in London in early September and went around the world to twenty cities, including Paris, Budapest, Barcelona, Tokyo, New Delhi, Harare (Zimbabwe), and São Paulo, before the final concerts in Argentina. The core group of performers who donated their time included Peter Gabriel and Sting again, plus Bruce Springsteen, Tracy Chapman, and Youssou N'Dour, with guest artists in each of the different countries along the way, such as Roy Orbison in the United States, Ravi Shankar in India, Milton Nascimento in Brazil, and many others.

A couple of months in advance, Meryl Streep and I flew to Stockholm, where Amnesty had been awarded a Nobel Prize back in 1977. We joined Bruce Springsteen, who was there performing, to announce the upcoming tour. Meryl had the magnificent idea of bringing along a popular troupe of break-dancers, teenagers from New York City. They leaped, twirled, and spun on their bottoms, impressing and charming the Swedes and me. Their agile and graceful performance, their exuberance and calisthenic choreography were amazing.

When, a bit later, Amnesty asked me to go to the Barcelona concert to be a liaison with media there, Tess Bramhall, my dear pal from the Vineyard, said she'd go with me if we could stop in Madrid first and see the Prado. I was more than happy. Tess and I had been friends for almost thirty years by then and had enjoyed countless games of tennis, family beach picnics, visits to our tennis partners' winter homes, and excursions local and foreign to famous museums, each of us interested in art. Tess had been a docent at Boston's Museum of Fine Art. We flew to Madrid and took a taxi straight from the airport to the Prado, trusting our bags with the unknown taxi driver's friend who owned a bar nearby. We had about two and a half hours at the Prado, then the driver returned, collected our bags, and drove us back to the airport for our flight to Barcelona. I was tremendously happy to have finally seen before my eyes the original Velázquez's *Las Meninas* and Goya's *The Third of May*. I'd once been at the Madrid airport with Bill on a four-and-a-half-hour layover, and I'd said to my husband, "Let's grab a cab and go to the Prado." Bill characteristically said, "Not on your life. We'd never get back in time." I spent the time in the airport, quietly fuming at him, even though I knew he might be absolutely right. His negativity frequently conflicted with my determined forays, too often making a put-upon wife of me. But I loved him and we both hated confrontation.

The Barcelona concert was held in Camp Nou, the large soccer stadium on the outskirts of the city. It was quite an evening, the entire stadium jammed, maybe a hundred thousand young people on their feet, jumping up and down in time to the music. In the middle of it, I was whisked away to be interviewed on TV and radio as an Amnesty representative. Being on camera has never been easy for me, but I was willing to do anything for Amnesty. Tess was endlessly patient.

While still in Barcelona, I got an urgent telegram from Jerome

Wiesner, the president of MIT, who had been JFK's science advisor, declaring that I must meet him in Moscow in two days, because Andrei Sakharov had suddenly requested to see us both. Sakharov, one of Russia's most brilliant physicists, was also one of its most outspoken political dissidents, criticizing his government for its nuclear arms buildup and the invasions of Czechoslovakia in 1968 and Afghanistan in 1979. The Soviet authorities were hesitant to jail such a public figure. Instead they sequestered him in a mental institution, injecting him with debilitating drugs, and then banished him and his wife to internal exile in the remote city of Gorky from 1980 to 1986, when Gorbachev's new regime allowed him to return to Moscow and public life. Sakharov was seizing the opportunity to talk with the West. This, I realized, was an amazing opportunity, since Amnesty had not been able to get into the Soviet Union legally. I called Jerry, saying yes I'd come from Barcelona, and asked where to pick up my visa.

"Oh, I just sent it to Martha's Vineyard," he replied. "You'll have to come back to get it. I'll wait for you in Moscow and we'll go together."

I groaned. It was the weekend, Friday. Tess and I decided we would spend the afternoon going to museums in Barcelona, and leave the next morning for Boston and the Vineyard. On the street, I saw heading toward us a very handsome young Spaniard—black hair, flashing blue eyes—in a loose white poet's shirt, tight black pants, and shiny boots. He was staring right at me and giving me a big smile, and I stared back, transfixed by his good looks. As he passed us, he suddenly grabbed the purse off my shoulder, pulling down hard, leaving me only the strap. He ran off under an archway and through an alley just ahead. On impulse, I ran after him, with Tess behind me crying, "No, no! Let him go!" Then she was running too, chasing me as I chased this young thief down a narrowing alley.

Being quite a good runner in those days, I actually thought I could catch him. Then, as we chased him down the partly covered alleyway and around a corner, a woman stepped out from a doorway and blocked my path. In Spanish, of course, she pleaded with me to stop. It only took a few seconds for me to lose him. I was pretty despairing, convinced that she was part of his operation. But having no other choice, I turned around and walked back toward Tess. I was more than chagrined by my original flattered take on the thief: that he was flirting with me, as the unfortunate Italian postman had actually tried to.

Now I had to recalculate how I could leave Spain with no identification, passport, or money. And how I would ever get into Russia without ID. We went straight to a police station, where they said I'd have to wait until Monday morning and go to the U.S. embassy. I knew from experience that European thieves always operated best on weekends. The embassy opened at 8:00 a.m. Monday. I was there at 7:00, the fifth in line. All four of the Americans ahead of me had had their purses or bags snatched over the weekend too. Preying on tourists seemed to be a thriving business in Barcelona. The man directly in front of me had his arm in a high-angled cast. I asked how that came about. He said his important briefcase had been snatched from his hand on the street; he and the thief struggled, and the thief bashed him on the arm with the briefcase hard enough to break it. Maybe, I thought belatedly, that woman who stopped me was trying to protect me.

I got my credentials and we flew back to Boston and then to Martha's Vineyard. There I discovered that because I wasn't home when the messenger brought the visa, it had been sent to Amnesty's Boston office. Unhappy but determined, I went back to Boston, retrieved it, and flew to Moscow. Bill, accustomed to my crazy travel schedule, had welcomed me with kisses in the Vineyard, and not seeming as nonplussed as I, dear man, waved me on.

Jerry had waited for me. When we met, Robert McNamara was at his side. He wanted to come see Sakharov with Jerry and me. The three of us spent incredible hours with the great man at his house the next day. Sakharov told us how he had been forcibly hospitalized for long months and given mind-altering drugs. I almost fell in love with him—with this bravery and the clarity of his mind and his remarkable recovery from all the trials he'd been through, his imposing moral stature. Jerry had recently proposed to his American colleagues that he and Sakharov start a Russian–American foundation that would provide funding for dissidents, suppressed or impoverished Russian intellectuals and humanitarians. The money could easily be raised in the United States, he said, if Sakharov, who was a hero there (Reagan had declared May 21 Sakharov Day a few years earlier), would come and speak to the National Academy of Sciences and to wealthy, concerned people in Washington and New York.

Sakharov demurred, saying that he didn't want to leave the Soviet Union while his friend Sergei Kovalev was in internal exile, not a free man. Kovalev was a biologist and another leading dissident, one of the founders of the Soviet Union's first human rights organization in the late 1960s. He had spent much of the '70s in prisons and labor camps, followed by banishment in the '80s to the small city of Kalinin.

That night, Jerry, Bob McNamara, and I went to a little diner that offered us just the potatoes that had been trucked into Moscow that day, plus vodka. The three of us sat talking over the day, with Jerry musing about a plan to call Gorbachev about championing not only Sakharov but Kovalev (which he did the next day, successfully). Suddenly McNamara started to cry and went on crying, wordlessly. Finally he began telling us how moved he was by Sakharov, "that great moral man," and how bad he felt about his own less-than-noble role in the Vietnam War. This was long before his public mea culpas. Jerry and I decided to keep mum about this for the time being. It was a strange evening.

Bob headed back to Washington the next day. Jerry had a stopover in Paris and persuaded me to accompany him there. I changed my flight. I would fly economy, he first class. I was in line at the check-in when he rushed up to me.

"I'm having a really bad problem," he said. "I left my passport at the hotel, and they won't let me on the plane without it. I'm taking a cab back to Moscow. I'll have time to get it from the desk and come back, but please hold the plane. Do anything you can to hold the plane."

I checked in and waited in the lounge. Jerry had not returned when they called our flight. I walked down the ramp to the plane. Still no Jerry. I waited there, while everyone else was ushered in past me. Now everyone was on board and the flight attendants were all but pushing me into the plane.

"I'm waiting here for Professor Jerome Wiesner, who is President Gorbachev's friend. He must make this flight. I'm not moving until he gets here."

I actually had my foot in the door. They'd have to chop off my foot to close it. We stood there for thirty minutes, the plane full of passengers and the flight attendants increasingly agitated with me. Finally they sent a man off to look for Jerry. The man came back down the ramp and said, "Dr. Wiesner's here. He's checking in now. You can get onto the plane."

So I did—and they slammed the door shut behind me. I'd fallen for the oldest trick in the book.

Poor Jerry was stuck back in Moscow while the hotel staff looked for his passport. He'd lost his room, and all the hotels were now booked solid because a big convention had swooped into town. A housekeeper who'd pressed his shirts stashed Jerry secretly on a mattress she had made up in a top-floor linen closet. I, meanwhile, having landed, slept at the Paris airport, waiting to change planes in the morning, lacking the French visa that would have enabled me to book a hotel or visit a friend. Jerry and I did not catch up with each other till fall. Would Sakharov come to the United States soon?

Meanwhile, in late September and early October, the Human Rights Now! tour went on without me—from Europe to Africa and Asia. I rejoined it in mid-October for the last few concerts in Argentina and Brazil. While we were in concert in São Paulo, Michael Dukakis, who was running for president, was going to be giving a talk on TV. Bill and I knew and liked Michael and his wife, Kitty, and had supported his campaign. Our daughter Al had worked hard for it in his office. I was sure he was going to win, and I convinced everybody I could—Sting, Gabriel, others—to sit in an auditorium with a large TV screen to watch his speech. What they saw was Michael Dukakis looking silly in a military helmet emerging from a tank, looking and sounding like anything but a president. I was embarrassed for him and my colleagues teased me no end. I guess he thought he was showing his support for the military or the military's support for him.

While we were still gathered in the auditorium, Raoni Metuktire, a chief of the Amazonian Kayapo people, came into the space in full tribal chief regalia—a feathered headdress, a circular plate in his lower lip. He wanted to meet Sting, who jumped up to greet him. He asked Sting to come to the rainforest with him to meet his people and see what terrible things were being done to them and their land. Sting told him he had to do the last two concerts of the tour, then he'd go with him. And he did.

After São Paulo, the tour went to the small city of Mendoza in Argentina, on the border with Chile. We couldn't get into Chile because Pinochet was still in power when the tour was being organized, and neither Lloyd's of London nor any other insurer would cover the musicians. So we decided we'd get as close as we could and beam the concert into Chile on TV.

Pinochet, under increasing international pressure, had agreed earlier in 1988 to allow a national plebiscite, in which the people of Chile would vote on whether he should serve another eight-year term. The vote was on October 5, just a week before our Mendoza concert, and the Chileans voted No. It would be more than a year before Pinochet actually stepped down, but his reign of terror was over, and he was on his way out.

The night before the concert, hundreds, perhaps thousands, of young Chileans who had never been allowed to leave their country walked across their border into Mendoza. Among them were a few older attendees whom I'd met with in Santiago and Valparaíso back in January 1974, fourteen years earlier. (We had a fine reunion after the concert.) Also in the audience were members of the Mothers of the Plaza de Mayo, who'd come up from Buenos Aires. They were the women whose sons and daughters and grandchildren had been "disappeared" under Argentina's own reign of terror after a military coup in 1976. Sting sang his song "They Dance Alone," written specifically for the Mothers. Peter Gabriel joined in. Everyone in the stadium, estimated at thirty thousand people, seemed to know the words and sang the first chorus with him, standing up on their seats. All the young people on the right side of the stadium were Argentinean, and we had placed little flashlights on all their seats, which they waved in the air as they swayed and sang. No flashlights had been distributed on the other side of the stadium, where all the Chileans had surprised us and just settled. Immediately, hastily, we had managed to pass them paper petitions to the United Nations, and when the song reached the second chorus, the left side of the stadium looked like it was going up in flames. The kids there had lit the petitions as torches they could wave, along with the others' flashlights. A giant roar of delight rose up into the night. It was an extraordinary, exhilarating moment.

The tour ended the following night with another hugely successful concert in Buenos Aires. Then we all dispersed to our respective homes—except Sting, who went up into the rainforest with Chief Raoni as promised. That visit prompted Sting to start his Rainforest Foundation, which helps provide legal and medical assistance for indigenous peoples in the Brazilian and Peruvian Amazon regions. They are often helpless in the face of their governments' decisions affecting their lands and are plagued by disease frequently contracted from white developers. I cheered them on from afar. Sting's foundation blossomed and raised big funds for twenty or thirty years. I wish that I had gone with Sting to see the rainforest and its inhabitants for myself, but at least I continue to advocate for them.

By November, Jerry Wiesner had persuaded Gorbachev to encourage Sakharov and Kovalev to visit the United States, and he arranged for Sakharov to speak at the National Academy of Sciences in Washington and at the Metropolitan Museum of Art in New York to announce and raise funds for Jerry's proposed Russian–American foundation. Sakharov went first to the academy in D.C., where he stood up in front of scores of scientists and powerful people like Colin Powell and David Rockefeller. He said why he thought the foundation was a *lousy* idea and why it would never work from the Russian end. Jerry and his backers were stunned and left. Then Sakharov went to New York and, at the Metropolitan, said essentially the same thing to an audience of intellectuals and patrons and wealthy interested people from across the United States. Everyone left— puzzled, disappointed. No one gave a nickel.

Jerry went home to Boston and had a heart attack, from which he never fully recovered. Sakharov went back to Russia. There was no explanation for his speeches that I could determine. I was shocked and felt incredible sorrow for Jerry and for the wonderful opportunity lost to help the Russian dissidents. At Sakharov's side on the brief U.S. trip was Kovalev, who looked like he had just gotten out of prison. Everything about him was gray—his hair, his skin, his clothes. But he soon pulled himself together and became a human rights champion.

My last year as chief judge of the RFK Human Rights Award, I pressed to give Kovalev our lifetime achievement award, especially as we'd never had a Russian awardee. Our judges agreed that a Russian flag would be added to the array of others of past awardees' nations. We did not succeed. Ethel and the RFK board pressed us to give it to a group of deserving Latin American teachers. It was a good ceremony, though I admit regrets. I saw Kovalev a couple of times later in the West, looking rejuvenated (and well dressed); I interviewed him in Salzburg in 1992, and applauded him when, after the Russians invaded Chechnya, he fought there and was dubbed "the Hero of Chechnya."

When the accounting was done after the Human Rights Now! tour, Angel Martinez discovered that Reebok had spent only $10 million of the $20 million they'd earmarked for it. Paul Fireman wanted to do more under Reebok's name. At my suggestion and the board's approval, Paul decided to take those extra funds and use them to publicly sponsor something for human rights. Angel and I talked with Paul and other people about it. I already had experience doing the RFK Human Rights Award, and suggested that Reebok could do something similar, but for stellar young activists, perhaps "under thirty." They eventually put human rights messages inside their sneakers.

Reebok—Rose, Peter Gabriel, Rafer Johnson, Sting, Paul Fireman,
and Mike Posner—the original board, early '80s.

The Reebok Human Rights Foundation was started in 1988. It would give an annual Reebok Human Rights Award to exceptional young activists around the world who'd actually jump-started human rights organizations.

In 2005, Reebok and the German-owned Adidas agreed to merge. Our 2006 awards ceremony, held at NYU, was an especially moving one, with people standing to applaud and cheer and shed more than a few tears as former and current winners shared the stage. In the audience Paul Fireman sat me just behind the new German owner of Reebok and asked me if, when the ceremony was over, Mike Posner and I would accompany this man to the reception and talk to him about the history of the awards. Throughout the ceremony I stared at the back of his head, and he was as still as a stick figure, very thin, his dark hair close-cropped, bespectacled, wearing a slim-cut suit and narrow tie, an erect German who never got up to cheer, never clapped, never turned his head, had no reaction whatsoever to the whole ceremony.

I knew we were in trouble. Mike and I tried to engage him afterward, and he showed not a flicker of interest until I mentioned that Bruce Springsteen was on the Amnesty tour. Then he lit up a little bit, telling us that Bruce was coming to *his* Olympic ceremonies in Berlin. After that he never said another word, never came to the reception, and we never saw him again. Eventually Adidas formally informed us it would not be continuing our Reebok Foundation.

We didn't want to disband. The foundation had supported so many good people. We had a program that was by then running smoothly for years. Through Kathleen Ryan we asked Jimmy Carter, who was still on our board though we rarely saw him, if the program could possibly be run out of the Carter Center in Atlanta. Paul Fireman said if that could be arranged he would personally fund it for a few years and see what happened. A year went by and we didn't hear anything from Carter. Meanwhile, his book *Palestine: Peace Not Apartheid* came out. I thought it fair, although the title gave me pause. Many American Jews were offended by it, including Paul Fireman, who withdrew his offer of funding. Our Reebok adventure was over—at least until February 2021, when the Reebok Human Rights Award was revived through the collaboration of Alabama State University and the ACLU.

I am excited to learn about the work of the newest award recipients, who are combating systemic racism: LaTonya Myers, Hernán Carvente-Martinez, and Eva Maria Lewis in 2021 and Dieter Cantu in 2022. Some of us who bonded so closely at the foundation still hope to join this adventure together again. We will wait and see what is possible.

14

My Orwellian Year

THE MID-1980s were years filled with travel for me. In 1985, Pulitzer Prize–winning poet Galway Kinnell and I were part of a delegation that traveled to war-torn El Salvador. I had first met Galway on the tennis courts of the Vineyard Haven Yacht Club, when I was asked to arrive for a 7:00 a.m. game with him before he presented the first Nathan Mayhew Seminar in the summer program on our island. I was the only person the organizers knew who got up early enough to play at that hour. Galway and I became instant friends. Over the years, I went to his poetry readings and lectures and we signed up for silly tennis championships in New England. I joined him to walk across the Brooklyn Bridge for a Poets House annual fund-raiser. He joined me for a goodwill trip to El Salvador, where I mostly remember him sitting on a curb writing poetry when we weren't working with children together.

The trip included Robert Kennedy's daughter Kathleen Kennedy Townsend, a couple of Democratic congressmen, the actors Mandy Patinkin and Peter Horton, and Dr. Charles Clements, who ran the Salvadoran Medical Relief Fund and was a founder of Physicians for Human Rights. By 2011 he was director of the Carr Center for Human Rights at Harvard's Kennedy School of Government. He was its chief operating officer when I was a fellow there. He took over when Rory Stewart, in 2000, left to run for office in England.

The military in El Salvador staged a successful coup from 1979 until 1992, the government fighting an ongoing war with various guerrilla groups. Thousands of civilians were brutalized, raped, murdered, or made refugees. In 1980, three American nuns and one lay worker had been abducted, raped, and murdered for aiding the rebels.

Not surprisingly, the Reagan administration was fully on the side of the military junta. Our group was organized and led by Margery Tabankin, director of the Arca Foundation, with the goal of showing some influential Americans the effect that U.S. financial and military support of the government was having on the lives of poor Salvadorans.

Charlie Clements, an extraordinary humanitarian and peace activist, had graduated with distinction from the U.S. Air Force Academy and volunteered to fly in Vietnam. After nine months there, he concluded it was an immoral war and refused to fly anymore. Following his discharge, he became a Quaker and went to medical school. In the early 1980s, seeing what he feared was another Vietnam starting in El Salvador, he volunteered to go there and offer medical assistance. He worked in a rural area about twenty-five miles from the capital on the slopes of a volcano called Guazapa, and by the end of 1982, the villages and guerrilla encampments surrounding it were bombed, rocketed, or strafed daily by U.S.-supplied aircraft. By 1985, the ten thousand civilians who lived in the villages surrounding the volcano had been turned into refugees by repeated assaults by the Salvadoran military.

We went to their refugee camp, taking wheelchairs and medical supplies. Charlie had heard that a boy whom he had cared for in Guazapa was in that camp. When the military attacked Guazapa, all the civilians fled en masse into the surrounding mountains or across a large lake, moving at night so as not to attract the attention of military spotter planes. This boy was always more vulnerable than most, because he lived in a small three-sided wooden box that fit around his narrow buttocks. He had been left paralyzed below the waist by what Charlie assumed was polio. He dragged himself along the ground, lifting himself up slightly as he slid, cheerful and uncomplaining.

Charlie found the child a collapsible wheelchair. After they exchanged hugs and tears, he picked the boy up out of his box and placed him in the wheelchair. It was amazing, because no one had to show him anything about it. Within seconds the boy was flying around the refugee camp with a huge grin on his face, moving (perhaps for the first time in his life) at a pace faster than dragging his box across the dirt or pavement. They laughed and cried together, both experiencing the boy's joy.

Then Charlie and I met other sick and injured children, many of whom had been separated from their families. With the crayons and paper we brought, they made drawings for us of their horrific experiences. One child drew her scary dream. In San Salvador, we met with the Mothers of the Disappeared, CoMadres—a group of mothers who had courageously banded together to seek information on sons and husbands who went missing during the long, vicious civil war—to give them their RFK Human Rights Award. They showed us grisly photos of the disfigured corpses of their sons, daughters, husbands, and fathers that the government's death squads had left lying in public places. Kathleen Kennedy Townsend presented them with one of the sculpted bronze busts of her father that was always given to award winners. We were in tears.

Not long after returning from El Salvador, in October 1985, I was in Budapest, being briefed for a Human Rights Watch mission across the border in the Romanian province of Transylvania. Under Nicolae Ceauşescu's Communist regime, certain ethnic writers were in dire situations. Young British journalist Tim Garton Ash and Sweden's Gabi Gleichmann were part of an intimate conference I attended, headed by Jeri Laber, senior American human rights activist and writer. As Tim and I were preparing to cross the border, we were warned that the last westerners to enter and meet with dissidents had been involved in a car crash arranged by Romanian security forces as a way to hold them for two weeks and thwart their plans. We knew this tactic had been used in Soviet countries before, and I had personally experienced the foiled attempt in Prague when my Polly and I were on the Amnesty mission with Ginetta Sagan.

Before leaving with Tim, I called home to Bill to say he might not hear from me for a couple of weeks, but not to worry. He replied, pleading, "Come home. I need you. I'm breaking down. You remember I was in Albany to give a talk. I just fell apart—I don't know what's going on."

His tone and his words worried me, of course. Bill sounded much darker than what I'd become used to at home or on other missions. I could usually negotiate with him. Just before I left, he'd panicked uncharacteristically over his impending speech in Albany for Bill Kennedy, with whom he had an easy relationship. Now I weighed promises and duties, but not for long. I told Tim I couldn't go to Transylvania with him, that I needed to rush home, and I'd give him my copious notes. I promised I'd help him write whatever kind of piece he thought appropriate on his return. Tim said, "I can't go alone. You know all the contacts and procedures. Dissidents are waiting on street corners to meet *you*. Besides, my wife and I are expecting a baby and she'd never forgive me if I were delayed." I thought he was absolutely right, but the urgency in Bill's voice forced me to abandon the mission.

It never happened. I've wondered how long the Romanians waited on our designated street corners. My initial feelings of guilt and concern were drowned out by waves of worry for Bill and thoughts about what I might need to do when I got home.

I arrived in Roxbury to find Bill in the grip of a full-on breakdown. From late 1984 there had, I realized too late, been warning signs. For instance, while he had always cherished separate quiet time, in recent months he'd come to demand real solitude. He complained (usually with success) if I suggested we invite guests to join us or if I wanted to arrange some celebration. He wrote in the afternoons and then drank whiskey at dinner and after a while he reviewed his day's work, often into the wee hours as he listened over and over to favorite symphonies by Mozart and Beethoven or country music. He read to me less after dinner, and soon not at all, abandoning our yearslong ritual. He became increasingly irritated by noise—any traffic, excessive conversation, even the clatter of dropped cooking utensils. As, acerbically, he had years earlier tried to shut out the bright voices and physical noises of our four high-spirited children. Unpredictable, he would lash out—especially at the younger ones, Tom, and later Alexandra. I knew he loved us all, but, progressively, I was rarely able to protect the children from his untoward anger, as I had often seemed able to in earlier years.

Having been raised by steady, affectionate parents who encouraged my independent judgment, I was baffled by Bill's outbursts and his need to control the children and me. Had he lifted a finger against any of us, I would have left, but he kept any such inclinations for his fictional characters.

I knew that despite a statement or two uttered in his dad's presence to the contrary, his childhood had not been a happy one. He had feared and anticipated his mother's death as she suffered with cancer throughout his boyhood. By the time she died when he was thirteen, he had lived years of dread intensified by his dad insisting he come home from school each day to immediately light a fire and guide his mother toward the hearth. He had no siblings. His sweet, distraught father, we discovered much later, had signed himself in to the Buxton Hospital in Newport News after Bill's mother, Pauline, died. He was doubtless suffering from depression. Bill's father soon married Elizabeth Buxton, the hospital's head nurse, who had attended Bill's mother. Elizabeth was ever jealous of the two Bills' obvious mutual affection, and she was always disapproving of "Billy." Luckily, Bill was sent off to Christchurch boarding school on the lovely banks of the Rappahannock River, and he found his way to friendship through his humor and to developing skills in sailing and writing.

But love did not prepare me for 1985. As Bill's sixtieth birthday (June 11) loomed, he—a well-known, well-teased hypochondriac, with both the *Merck Manual* and *Physicians' Desk Reference* on a table on his side of the bed—became insanely hypochondriacal. He saw THE END on every horizon. Death was on his mind, not only for himself but also for cherished others. As before, if I returned from a visit with friends later than I'd suggested, he'd be standing in our doorway, stating how worried he'd been about my fate. Now he simply followed me everywhere. When his favorite golden retriever was sick, he was certain she would die, and he left her with me in Roxbury while he escaped to the Vineyard. (She lived three more years, to his joy. An avid chaser of squirrels, she miraculously caught one during their daily walk, lay down next to it, and expired.)

When Polly fell off her runaway horse onto the Vineyard asphalt, and then when Alexandra was in a car accident one Connecticut New Year's Eve, both requiring stitches in their heads, he assumed death was imminent for each. Agonizing over our daughters, Bill often reproached me. I felt genuinely guilty, fearing somehow it was my fault that I had not always supervised them more carefully, as today's mothers doubtless would have. I recalled my own unsupervised adventures in Baltimore and Atlantic City, and concluded I really was a laissez-faire mother, for better or worse.

Of course, Bill blamed me when I went out for an errand and ten-year-old Susanna swam into the harbor to get a closer look at Frank Sinatra's imposing ship *Southern Breeze*.

Years later, the kids told me that the sweet young helper I had allowed to drive them to Rumsey Hall School in the next town, Washington, Connecticut, some mornings when I was off to a meeting had let them stand up in our convertible as she sped along the hilly country roads. I certainly was not vigilant enough. Whether the fact that the driver lived with us because she was Bill's old girlfriend's daughter and needed a job blinded me, I'm not sure. I finally caught on to her obvious troubles when she once spent an entire day running the noisy vacuum cleaner up and down our old attic rug. She was an artist of some talent, very dear, devoted to her own differently troubled siblings. I loved her and failed to calculate the obvious. I did not monitor Bill's mood swings or disturbing decisions as closely in those days, cherishing his affectionate hours with me. Later I surely would.

Bill never drank during the day, but he had always indulged just before dinner and, I guess, drank excessively often later, well after midnight while I slept. Before I left for Hungary in October, he had stopped his habitual drinking as suddenly and completely as he had given up smoking twenty-odd years before. His old pal liquor had deserted him, making him nauseated, he said. His insomnia—for which a careless Vineyard doctor, impressed by "William Styron," had prescribed

Ativan, as much and often as Bill wanted, two years earlier—became far worse. A New York doctor switched him to Halcion, lots of it. Bill paced in doctors' offices for this or that real or imagined physical ailment. He spent long hours lying on the bed staring at the ceiling, not writing. Or, if he did summon the energy to write, he described characters consumed by their own fears of failing health and fortune or approaching death. I noted, bemused at first, that every one of his fictional heroines was a victim of suicide or murder, but I had not understood that it was a disguise for his own apprehensions. For the first time, his editor, Bob Loomis, confided in me that Bill's writing had deteriorated, and that it had been hard to talk with him about it.

In the months when I was attempting to understand and to keep my own balance, our Vineyard friend Stan Hart, a successfully recovered alcoholic, convinced me that Bill's state was caused by his sudden, complete withdrawal from alcohol. Bill's withdrawal from smoking in 1963 had produced a frenetic need for chocolate and the repeated theft of our children's gumdrops, but nothing worse. This year, plying him with sweets did no good. Nothing did. He took pleasure in nothing and no one. His conversations—always far ranging and spontaneous—became self-centered, labored, obsessive. Bill stopped urging me to leave him alone at home to think and work. He stopped going off without me on enticing trips to Paris to see the Joneses, or to Moscow with the Robert Lowells again, or down the Mississippi for a special literary boat trip, jaunts on which I too had been invited but from which I had been left summarily behind (to my resentment). I had kept going on missions for Amnesty or Human Rights Watch or PEN, which he encouraged me to do. But no more.

Bill stopped railing at me for my peccadilloes and Pollyanna turns of phrase in 1985. He suddenly wanted me there all the time, exclusively at home. He didn't want me out of his sight, and he *wanted* to talk. If we went to the supermarket he—the usual enthusiastic food shopper—padded, ridiculous, behind me. If I took laundry to the basement, following me down the steps was too humiliating or scary, so he'd stay upstairs and fret, calling down repeatedly, "What are you doing down there?" The contrast was odd, extreme, yet sometimes endearing and almost comforting to me, starkly different from his litany of declarations that he needed to be alone.

With Bill, Martha's Vineyard porch, 1967.

Before this we had always been discreet, by tacit agreement, about certain personal activities when we were each "alone." I had a few one- or two-night stands with sometimes well-known guys, which I enjoyed but did not wish to continue and possibly complicate or ruin our marriage. I suspected Bill did the same (once with a friend's sister-in-law, an unhappy neighbor, the unfortunate woman I caught with him in bed in his studio when I arrived home a day early from an Amnesty mission). We two sophisticated artists had until now lived comfortably in our rural world, perhaps clinging to our parents' Victorian codes of silence about any possibly disturbing family matters. We both wanted our marriage to continue.

Bill asked me to accompany him on long walks with the dogs, during which he talked about his hatred of the world and winter, his fears about work and aging. I have to admit that on those walks, as the leaves turned in New England, when he seemed newly intimate and affectionate toward me, my heart was full, wifely, despite the disturbing nagging apprehension in my brain. September was a deceptively good month for me as far as my marriage was concerned. I was sad for Bill, but I was guiltily happy for us. How could I have been so stupid, so selfish? I understood nothing about breakdowns' psychiatric needs. I guess I believed that when alcohol withdrawal played itself out, he'd see the colors of the leaves, the beauty of the world again, and our renewed intimacy would last, flourish.

During this time, I seesawed hopelessly between bafflement and anger at our situation, between immediate compassion for Bill and despair for him, for our future. I began a long poem. These lines appear halfway through:

> *The man who lies beside me as he's lain*
> *night after moonless night*
> *this season staring at the ceiling does not*
> *feel my hand. No longer do I fear*
> *he'll deafen me or crush*
> *these thinning bones. He and his*
> *blood-red storm-black energy I've ridden*
> *up and down the bucking hills*
> *reveling in the sun's companionship*
> *have left me.*

When I finally figured out that Bill was clinically depressed—not just moody or in withdrawal or angry at life, but *clinically depressed*— I knew we needed professional help. Neither of us had explored being steadily counseled by psychiatrists. I called Art Buchwald and Peter Matthiessen and Jean Stein, writer pals who had experienced mood swings since youth, and asked them to make such a suggestion directly to Bill. When Bill's pain was at its worst, he was able to take advice from friends who had been through something similar more easily than from me. I became the scholar of Bill's moods and behavior, too interested and curious to turn off entirely even when I could not reach him. I knew that this man I had married was never boring, always brilliant, mesmerizingly mercurial. I'd often thought that a marriage as long as ours was like several marriages, each partner growing and changing throughout. Now a delicate balancing act ensued. One thing depressives are good at is keeping you off-balance, and I realized I must look around the corner to be ready for what was coming next onto our windswept, waterlogged path if health and sanity were ever to return.

At that time our trusted family doctor died, and a local GP suggested a psychiatrist in New Haven. We went to his ugly, seedy office, which harbored a big three-quarters-dead overwatered potted tree on the damp gray indoor-outdoor frayed carpet in the tiny waiting room. I sat on a bench two feet from the plywood-doored wall to his office. Through the wall, I could hear the psychiatrist droning at Bill about age, about lowering his creative expectations—maybe Bill shouldn't write anymore and should think of other things to do— meanwhile instructing him not to think about hospitalization because it would only stigmatize him. Bill emerged with three prescriptions: an anti-anxiety pill, Xanax; an MAO inhibitor, Nardil; and an "upper" called Desyrel, which in combination with the Halcion pushed Bill down further, fast. Looking defeated, believing the prognosis, Bill insisted on being driven back at least weekly to see the doctor. "Just don't let him out of your sight," the psychiatrist told me. Whenever I phoned him to say, "This isn't working," he prescribed more medication. I kept a diary, observing every pill, every conversation, and every change in Bill's voice or gait, every doctor's order. (I've looked for the diary in vain. I remember it started with my new motto at the time: Stop. Look. Listen. Hang On.)

There *were* a few comic moments. Backstage at a downtown New York PEN event Bill was to speak at, he frantically persuaded his dear friend and editor, Bob Loomis, to taxi uptown and ransack our apartment for a pill Bill had forgotten while another author scrambled to sew a button on Bill's jacket, at his insistence, so he would feel presentable onstage. Less comic, except in retrospect, was an hour in Paris when Bill repeatedly refused to join an award luncheon in his honor with the grandiose Madame Del Duca and crusty academicians after he received the Prix mondial Cino Del Duca and a fat check, and had his name inscribed in marble on the Del Duca Mansion wall. Bill's publisher was visibly embarrassed and Madame flounced out. And flounced back. We finally persuaded Bill to attend the luncheon briefly, so as to accept the grand award. But later that night, at the splendid restaurant for dinner with the publisher and her family, Bill lost the $25,000 check, and the five of us reacted, crawling under the table and around the walkway until we found it. Bill promptly signed it away, I think it was to an Italian or French medical center's cause. These scenes were really much more humorous than those that Bill recalls in *Darkness Visible.* So was our last New York visit pre-hospital: Poets and Writers had concocted a theatrical fund-raising evening where several of its premier authors performed in the Big Apple Circus, while others (like Bill) applauded from the first row. When Norman Mailer, clad in a Speedo, flexed his tattoo-painted muscles and rolled by on a bongo board, and Erica Jong, dressed as a fairy and perched atop an elephant, rode too near him, the look of horror on Bill's face beat any clown's.

Surely it is logical that a depressive's memory, even one as prodigious as Bill's, could be skewed by trauma. A novelist prompted by the dialogue in his head and by the imagination that creates and controls a story might intuitively choose a meaningful ending. Bill's description two-thirds of the way through *Darkness Visible* of his determination one night to commit suicide, then of watching a film in the living room as I slept upstairs, hearing in it the gorgeous Alto Rhapsody his mother had performed, and thinking suddenly of his children and the past joys in our house, and deciding to *live,* to wake me up, then allow me to take him to the hospital, might be indelible in a reader's mind. It is in mine. In *my* mind, I never slept if Bill was not in bed beside me. And, possibly, the piercing of his heart by Brahms actually might have taken place hours earlier. Still, I am convinced that this was the moment that saved him, and I'm certain his thoughts of our family did finally nullify his resolve to kill himself.

Moreover, prescient, deeply thoughtful, attentive daughter Polly came to our bedroom in those early hours toward daylight, urging him to go to Yale New Haven Hospital rather than return to the unfortunate doctor. He agreed. I quoted her excellent writing about it in *Unholy Ghost,* a collection of essays edited by Nell Casey, on living with depressives. Polly's jotted notes struck me as wholly accurate:

So, I guess I should write this down, or I won't believe it. I came to the house Friday evening because I'd heard Daddy had had a terrible night on Thursday and that he and Mum were fairly shaken. I was prepared for a morbid gloom, but not for what the night actually turned out to be. When I went upstairs to his room he was lying there with his long gray hair all tangled and wild. I took his hand, which was trembling.

"I'm a goner, darling," he said, first thing. His eyes had a startled look, and he seemed to be not quite there. His cool, trembling hand kept fumbling over mine. "The agony's too great now darling. I'm sorry. I'm a goner."

For the next hour, he raved about his miserable past and his sins and the waste of his life and how, when they published the scandal of his life, we should try not to hate him. "You'll hate me. You'll hate me," he said in a whisper. Everything was repeated over and over:

"I love you so much. And the other children. And your mother. You'll hate me for what I am going to do to myself. My head is exploding. I can't stand the agony anymore. It's over now. Tell the others how much I love them. I've betrayed my life. All my books have been about suicide. What a miserable waste of a life. I'm dying! I'm dying! I'm dying!" And on and on, and over and over, while grabbing me to come closer, taking my head to his breast, holding me closer. My father.

When Mum finally came upstairs again, as he held me next to him with his eyes closed I mouthed the words, "HOS-PI-TAL" to her.

Thank heavens for Polly! I called a doctor friend at Yale New Haven Hospital immediately. He contacted the right authority and the three of us drove there. Fifty minutes of silence as I recall.

Bill's hospital stay began agonizingly for me. Visiting each day, I would listen to hours of his nightmares, sorrows, disorientation, then watch him shuffle down the hall like a figure from *One Flew Over the Cuckoo's Nest*. When I spoke to the doctor, he warned me that electroconvulsive therapy (ECT) might be advisable. Filled with *Cuckoo* images, it didn't occur to me that techniques had been improved, and I protested emphatically. Even at his most medicated, Bill begged me to keep protesting so his creative brain would not be permanently altered. I pursued this mission so annoyingly that the doctors urged me to go on vacation. I declined.

A comical episode took place at Yale Hospital. Bill had entered weeks earlier, and the kids were determined that this time, despite

Bill Styron and Lauren Bacall at the Poets & Writers fortieth anniversary celebration, 1980.

our collective panic, they would make Christmas Day fun (perhaps they understood that Dad was helpless to derail their plans). Susanna made a film for her father, splicing together the amateur reels from childhood that he and she had shot, and she badgered the guard on duty to let us take the huge forbidden TV set in at noon. So tearfully persuasive was she that he looked the other way, and we lugged it up the stairs.

Bill's roommate politely went to the lounge as twelve of us set up flimsy red-and-green paper plates on a bed, unwrapped Christmas dinner—twenty-pound turkey, pies, everything—and proceeded to spill most of the gravy and cranberries on the sheets. What could we do but giggle? Tension relieved, Bill smiled his first smile—at such ridiculousness—and actually enjoyed the proceedings. The poignant cinema memories made a couple of us cry.

No Christmas with Bill was ever a bummer after that. I can't overstate the importance of family love and support in helping the depressive find his or her way back from the Darkness. The activity, the distraction, the companionship does wonders for each body and soul, probably for the addled brain too. If only temporarily.

What we did, after all, was to buy time, foiling the fantasies or plans for suicide. So we told Bill over and over that we wouldn't go away, but the depression would. That the beauty of the day would surely return. And the full moon, and the songs.

Slowly but surely, with time, therapy, and medication, Bill improved. Polly wrote eloquently:

> He survived the seven weeks there though at times we wondered if they'd given him a lobotomy without consulting us. As his anxiety subsided, he became increasingly goofy and zombielike, but then slowly he became more coherent, more animated, and finally more willful. When his temper returned, we let out a collective sigh of relief; he was better.

When a noisy plane or spring birds destroyed the country stillness, and Bill would bark, "BE QUIET," I could laugh again. Slowly we resumed our seasonal routine between Roxbury and Vineyard Haven. I went with Amnesty on the Amnesty World Rock Tour, traveling

Party time at dix Quai d'Orleans, Jim Jones's Paris apartment with Gloria "Moss" Jones and Irwin Shaw, early '60s.

to Madrid and Barcelona. Then Jerry Wiesner asked me to come to Moscow because Sakharov wanted to meet him and me. Bill went to Paris to stay with Jim Jones, settling into their long, comfortable companionship.

We Styrons all survived Bill's first depression. When he recovered, he began to smile, enjoy public and private conversation, travel with friends, and write again. In 1989, Bill published a first version of *Darkness Visible* for *Vanity Fair*, and the following year Random House published the book. He thought he was home free and concluded, firmly upbeat, that other victims of depression would recover too. He stopped all medication, which worried me a bit.

Bill did have a fairly brief relapse, probably triggered by his acute apprehension concerning a scheduled major operation on his neck. The surgery was being delayed a fortnight due to Mass General's busy schedule. How many scheduled operations delayed in these Covid years have sent potential patients into despair? Having been treated by a new local doctor who prescribed Halcion for his recurring insomnia, Bill took the drug again just before traveling to Claremont College to fulfill a speaking/teaching engagement, and in sunny California, his gloom again descended. He became alternately obsessed, distracted, or mute before the students he had been invited to address. The Halcion caused, in Bill's words, "a chemical commotion" in his brain. He was suicidal again and scared, and scared *me*. Eddie Bunker, our beloved friend who had survived reform school, a wild life, and prison to emerge as a successful screenwriter and actor, was at Bill's side. Eddie was convinced that methadone, which had stabilized him, would save Bill. Knowing Bill would resist—he by now hated any drug—Eddie sent me off with an ex-gang pal and a big, fierce-looking dog for a walk, while he tried to coax and cheer Bill. He failed.

I immediately called a psychiatrist both Bill and I admired, Dr. Peter Whybrow. We'd both read his book on mood disorders, the only one that made sense to us. We'd met him in Philly at Sheldon Hackney's home when Sheldon was president of the University of Pennsylvania. (Whybrow's spot-on diagnosis of *me* during a lunch conversation was that I had seasonal affective disorder. He was a pioneer in identifying SAD, and he recommended that I use a light box during our New England winters, which my son, Tom, and I both used for a few winters.)

Dr. Whybrow had been spot-on for Bill. I'd more than once heard that Dr. Whybrow was now living nearby in California near Claremont, so I thought I'd try to have him see Bill. He was great, came promptly, and said, "Get on a plane and take Bill straight to Mass General. I'll arrange for him to stay in the psychiatric wing until his neck operation." Bill was admitted days early, and the whole stay was a success.

There were no fantasies of death for more than a dozen years. Almost every day, Bill was in contact with fellow depression sufferers by mail or by phone. People who were moved by his book wrote to him, but those in desperate need of help telephoned. He was invariably sympathetic, expansive, and ready with crucial advice. One memorable letter he received was from a young Chilean professor and political activist (female) in Nevada who had been severely injured in an accident. The anesthesia and subsequent drugs administered caused horrifying memories to resurface of her student days under Pinochet. Life was an isolating nightmare, she said, until *Darkness Visible* helped her understand that recovery was possible.

I also recall Bill speaking on the phone for a long time to a man who was apparently standing outside his house brandishing a gun, pointing it alternately at his head and at the police, who were trying to dissuade him from shooting. A savvy policeman phoned Bill, who then literally talked the distressed citizen out of a suicide or murder. A cop grabbed the phone and thanked Bill. Another time, a woman with acute insomnia, threatening suicide, was put on the phone by her son, a minister at his wit's end. Within thirty minutes, Bill had persuaded her to go to a sleep center he knew about in Alabama. And once, following a caregiver's pleading, he convinced a young man not to jump off a roof.

It used to be that when I'd hear Bill closing the bedroom door and speaking in soft dulcet tones, affectionate tones, to the person on the other end of the phone, I was certain he was speaking with a pretty groupie he'd flirted with at a southern literary festival or a woman around the corner in Connecticut he might be driving somewhere on a Sunday or loaning his car to, or—you name it. My jealousy instantly registered 106 degrees. In those days, my pride would not let me listen in. But after 1985, when he had pretty much recovered from his battle with depression and began the whispery calls again, he'd prudently say, "I'll phone you back," if I surprised him or he heard my footfall on the stairs. After all we'd been through, without our marriage (or me) cracking up, I was resentful but silent. Once I picked up the other extension and listened for a minute; a few days later, I did so again. What I heard was not old tryst arrangements but the comforting of one or another young woman in the throes of depression—he labeled them his "patients"—who received the full complement of his sympathy and enlightenment.

Bill's spoken and written words of encouragement to countless individuals, and the speeches he gave to groups of people suffering from depression, surely contributed to his own sense of well-being, and perhaps even stimulated his continuing creativity. Thus, the vision of a writer whose premier demand had been respect for his privacy, his need for solitude, and control of his environment slowly altered. As he improved and changed, my anxieties, and those of the children, subsided. I read Kay Jamison's first-rate book on artists with depression. I conversed with her often. I relaxed.

Looking back, I would say that sticking with the person you love through the stresses of a mood disorder can eventually be incredibly rewarding. Depression, Johns Hopkins psychiatrist Ray DePaulo notes, eats at the heart of every relationship. One must be sensitive, nurture the fragile connections, humor the sufferer like a baby. Do not say, "Pull up your socks, you're fine." Each case is as different as each person's suffering—and as different as each spousal relationship—but I know from my friends that the significant numbers of manifestations and underlying patterns of thought and behavior can be quite similar. Perhaps the best thing one can do is to act on intuition. And keep intuition's third eye open forever, after recovery, to note the first trembling turning leaves of a change of season.

In an interview for *Le Figaro,* after Bill recovered from the first depression, he surprised me by talking of himself as an alcoholic. He worried about how he probably decided to drown himself in alcohol at some point. He likened depression to not being able to breathe and believed it was curable 95 percent of the time, noting that poets and writers often have suicidal tendencies, e.g., Virginia Woolf, Romain Gary, Hemingway. He defended Primo Levi, whose suicide was dissed by the press, which set Bill off. He argued that Levi must have always been haunted by his early death camp experience.

I observed, and Bill agreed, that many depressed people develop profound emotional dependence, and the latent infantilism that lies below dependence surfaces. I think we're all infantile in our most vulnerable times—certainly I am, and not always latently. While one assumes that in the course of a decent marriage, emotional dependence and support are mutual and free-floating, depression breaks down the easy give-and-take, and the prime sufferer can become obsessed. Bill's obsession almost undid me.

I credit my ability to survive, such as it was, to my stable Baltimore childhood. I felt safe with and blessed by my family, even in my days of rebellion. I was challenged to try and fail, and try again—blindly, since I had no model of stormy ancestors or contemporary brain stars to guide me. I had not even read certain memoirs or scientific essays that might have illuminated or predicted the world I found myself in. But I think a big dose of my usual curiosity kept me going.

The Burgunders had practiced the Victorian "code of silence" about less savory personal affairs—relatives involved in publicized social capers, or a marriage considered politically unfortunate, or a close neighbor who evidenced mental aberrations and went off to be hospitalized. When I found myself the pedant of Bill's successive medication disasters, I guess I avoided drawing certain conclusions. Bill had tried repeatedly to convince me of the worst. I was initially in denial, uninformed denial.

(Only years later, when Mike Nichols—at the height of public success—begged Bill and me to take care of his children because he was "bankrupt, incompetent, and dying," did I understand the frequency of downward mental patterns that could evolve, possibly fatally.)

From our individual family observations, doctors might have conceived a treatment shortcut or longcut or two, or at least kept us better informed on what to anticipate, which might have lessened the despair that often engulfed us in this painful time. If only I'd been wiser and somehow found a concerned, devoted genius of a doctor. If only I still had the Johns Hopkins Hospital connections of my youth. If only we'd had a family mentor who'd journey to rural Connecticut. If, if, if! Often guilt had swamped my usual sensation of just being at sea.

Saving oneself and one's family is human (and animal) in nature. In our case, all four kids, who had been terrified by Bill's earlier rages, disapproval, disconnection, and diabolical humor, suddenly, when he was hospitalized and labeled ill with depression, responded with concern and compassion. They pulled together, for his sake, and for mine. Their attention and advice to me were invaluable and instructive. They still are sweetly, constantly ready to protect and comfort and entertain me as I age. Kids, after all, can be the best witnesses to their parents' behavior and problems. Incredible son Tom became a clinical psychologist, a professor at Yale Medical School, and the director of Yale's New Haven outreach programs to the less fortunate. Youngest daughter Alexandra explored her childhood in her book *Reading My Father*.

I wish the doctors Bill saw in 1985 had shown interest in my recorded observations of his symptoms, or in the kids' feelings and insights and conjectures. They didn't. We knew nothing of their experience with patients like Bill or their analyses of him. We had only suspicions of what might be happening inside that complex, pain-ridden head, behind that sad face.

Thank heavens now there is a field, a burgeoning one called (among other things) narrative medicine, that helps doctors and nurses communicate with patients, their families, and their support systems, to assist with the diagnosis, treatment, and care of patients. I wish we had experienced that kind of support. It would have benefited Bill, me, and the children.

Protective armors can be thick. The mind deep inside the depressive's armor can be especially quick to defend itself—by tactics that mislead, push away, stab, trivialize, unravel—from the family force it irrationally perceives as threatening.

Through our family's experience of Bill's depression, the children and I learned to be especially watchful on holidays and impending celebrations. Novelist J. P. Marquand's son John told us how in the midst of Christmas dinner his father arose and in a rage picked up the lighted and bedecked tree and hurled it out the door. Bill did threaten to kill himself one Christmas noon, so dark was his mood. But the anticipation of evening hoopla with Lenny and pals thankfully infused him with holiday cheer in time for the evening's singing. The kids and I paid attention, knowing what to look for. We did our best to adapt to our new awareness. At least no suicide.

When Bill returned fully to our family and the world and the kids' lives, my life resumed. I finished the poem I quoted earlier:

> *We have arrived:*
> *it is a calmer day.*
> *The light surf rambles with us*
> *along the fine grained sand.*
> *The sun reclines on his longest*
> *cloud-raft, glow fanning*
> *the horizon (Curry's Line Storm*
> *turned away from rain),*
> *catching the sky-tuned gulls,*
> *smooth perched slipper shells*
> *broadside, as in late afternoon*
> *it will catch white sailboats*
> *stilled in our eastern harbor.*
> *Love that lay hidden under*
> *yesterday's monstrous breakers*
> *in the pounded dunes*
> *walks with us, quietly.*
> *Retrievers black and golden*
> *chase tiptoed sanderlings*
> *at a dead run, across the ledge*
> *left by the last high tide.*

15

Intrigue in Eastern Europe

A COUPLE OF SEASONS before Bill's breakdown, I had traveled to Poland, Germany, and Czechoslovakia with Kurt Vonnegut. Kurt was a PEN member and I was chair of the PEN American Center Freedom to Write Committee. We were charged with meeting writers in Eastern Europe and inviting them to PEN's upcoming international meeting in New York. PEN knew that countries "behind the Iron Curtain" would send government-approved writers and official PEN representatives. Our job was to find dissident underground writers and figure out how to get them to New York. Amnesty also asked me to gather information while I was there.

Bill joined us for the Poland leg of the trip. He'd been to Kraków and Auschwitz while working on *Sophie's Choice* and wanted to share experiences there with us. Bill led Kurt and me on a day trip to Auschwitz. At one point, I wandered more slowly than the men, moving among the ruins and monuments and displays of the cremated victims' clothes, and I lost sight of them. I suddenly was aware of being Jewish and became afraid. Shaken as I walked through Auschwitz, I eventually found the guys, but that hour infected my dreams and waking moments for a long time.

After our important, emotionally charged visit together, Kurt and I would go to East and West Germany without Bill. He'd go to his beloved Paris, then we'd all meet again in Prague, where Ambassador Bill Luers had arranged a screening of *Sophie's Choice*.

Kurt turned out to be a marvelous traveling companion—wry, chuckling, reserved unless you poked, which I hadn't known. His writing was very popular in Eastern Europe. Although he was of German descent, there was an Eastern European sensibility and humor in his work that I hadn't thought about before. He really flowered among the underground writers we met there. His good humor put them at ease. Of course, they were nervous about meeting with us, worrying that we were under surveillance and might lead government agents to their hiding places. (We did not.)

Poland had been a Soviet satellite since the end of World War II. By 1980, the severe food shortages and general restrictions on life prompted Lech Wałęsa and others to found the trade union Solidarność (Solidarity), which grew into an umbrella dissident organization with ten million members. In 1981, General Wojciech Jaruzelski, leader of the Communist Party, cracked down, declaring Solidarność an illegal organization and instituting martial law. Wałęsa and many others were imprisoned. He was released in 1982, and was awarded the Nobel Peace Prize the following year.

Martial law was lifted in 1983, but when we visited in 1985, Jaruzelski's regime was still stifling dissent through arrests, imprisonment, and even killings. Wałęsa was watched like a hawk, his movements restricted. As everywhere in the Soviet Bloc, free speech in Poland was severely suppressed, driving writers, publishers, and presses underground. "Underground publishing" was alive and well.

The morning after we three arrived, Warsaw was gray, with rain and wet snow coating the bare trees and streets. We saw a church sporting a banner that declared BOG-I-OJCZYNSKA—GOD HONOR FATHERLAND. Windows were artificially lit as we drove to St. Stanislaus Church. Father Popiełuszko's weekly sermons there had been attended by as many as three thousand people, plus crowds for poetry readings. He had been a friend of Lech Wałęsa. A quarter of a million people had come to his funeral the year before. Popiełuszko was a quiet young saint to them. Police had accused him falsely of harboring weapons after a parishioner told authorities that she saw men bring guns and hide them under his mattress. Supporters slept in his living room to protect him for several nights after that. We were told his killing was not planned, only a police kidnapping that went awry.

That afternoon, our second in Warsaw, Kurt and I set off on a dubious adventure. On arrival the afternoon before, I had been standing in line behind Kurt and Bill to register in the lobby of the hotel when from the left a man in a flowing black cape darted across the lobby and pressed into my hand a small square of folded and taped graph paper. He whispered to me in English, "Don't open it until you're upstairs," and left as quickly as he had come. Used to Amnesty adventures by now, I took his instruction seriously. Upstairs, I went into the bathroom and opened the folded paper. It contained a small hand-drawn map and a note that said in effect, "Read this, memorize, and destroy it. Come to the entrance of Warsaw University tomorrow at 1300 hours, bring Mr. Vonnegut and your husband if you can." Then it gave specific instruction for us to leave the hotel with a tourist book and follow the map to a person carrying a copy of *Wampeters, Foma and Granfalloons,* Kurt's early book. I memorized the note, tore it up, and flushed it down the toilet, as was my habit on such missions.

Bill refused to accompany me. He didn't like intrigue. He hated to travel in the first place and didn't want anything unexpected to happen. He was not adventurous, but usually wished me well, and friends said he was proud of my work. Kurt said he'd go with me. At the appointed hour we set off, followed the map, and found our man, who took us on a brief tour of the Warsaw University campus and gave us further instructions. When we parted from him, we strolled, walked down four concrete steps, and entered a certain green door, climbed a certain stair, locked eyes briefly with a man who stood statue-like in a Sherlock Holmes cap and pipe by a high window—at which point it was very hard not to look surprised, even amused—and then followed him out another door, keeping our distance until we rounded a corner to see another man opening a car door and ushering us in. Wordlessly, the driver took us to contact #4, who took us in another car to #5, and he to #6, crisscrossing highways and streets to our mysterious destination—a tall gray-and-mustard Soviet Modern box of a building.

As we pulled up, Kurt casually asked, "Is this what you always do?" My apprehension had been sprouting as these maneuvers went on for an hour and a half, but Kurt's big, bluff presence kept me reasonably calm. I'd concentrated on memorizing road signs and mile markers like dropped breadcrumbs. When I admitted that this was unique, Kurt looked startled, then quite worried.

Our last guide carried a hardcover edition of *Sophie's Choice,* the fat volume in English under his arm. Inside the building he signaled us to an apartment on a high floor. When we knocked, the door half opened and a huge puppy jumped on me, truly scaring me for the first time. A woman opened the door fully, grabbed the dog, and ushered us through a curtain. We found ourselves (behind the Arras, I thought) in a small room with five men, one of whom invited us in English to sit down, assuring us he was only a translator, not a member of the group, nor was this his apartment. He quickly identified the other four as the most elusive, hunted men in Poland. They had been in hiding since the Jaruzelski crackdown in 1981. I recognized two of the names immediately. The face of one was quite changed, perhaps by plastic surgery. He was Zbigniew Bujak, twenty-eight or twenty-nine, and clearly the leader of the group. He was effectively Wałęsa's counterpart in Warsaw. All were being sought by the police; none had papers or lived with their families. They were articulate, intelligent, at our service, ready to answer any questions we had, and wanting to ask lots of their own about what was happening in the Western world, especially in the United States. It seemed they had no newspapers or radio broadcasts from the West. They particularly asked if people in the United States knew about them and the underground Solidarność movement, and what the opinions of our American friends were.

We talked for hours. They told us of a new law pending in parliament that would allow the government to imprison and fine anyone without a trial and with no recourse to counsel. And the problems miners were having under martial law. During the sixteen months that Solidarność had been legal, there was only one fatal accident in Polish mines. Under martial law, more than two hundred accidents had occurred.

Like other Poles, they spoke highly of President Reagan. His tough attitude toward the Soviets made dissidents and Solidarity-supporting Poles feel safer, and they liked his policies of containment. "Communism destroys even language," one said. Solidarność understood the need to work within the Communist system, at least for the time being, but in all elections after World War II, workers had never voted more than 10 percent Communist. They were ready for democracy. "Communism is just a slogan now for the Soviet empire," they said. And, "Communism makes people cheat and be dishonest. In its sixteen months Solidarność made truth fashionable."

In all matters, Kurt was the supreme diplomat, the enlightened questioner and answerer. After nightfall, when we'd been with them for four and a half hours, we persuaded them to let us leave. We knew Bill would be frantic (was he ever!) and our evening hosts worried. We left reluctantly, driven this time to a taxi stand. They breathed sighs of relief that we had not been followed. It had taken us well over an hour to get to our assignation, which we assumed was far out of town. It took us ten minutes to get back.

We arrived late to a party in our honor given by envoy Jim Hutchison and his wife at their new apartment. Bill was extremely relieved. He had persuaded the hosts to call the police, which they assured us they had been about to. That would have been a disaster.

The next morning we left early for Gdańsk, formerly the heart of the Solidarność movement. It was a six-hour drive through foggy flatlands, neat houses, and farms along the Vistula. A Solidarność member nicknamed Anna the Bad drove us, then turned us over to a sour young Anthony Quinn look-alike just back from Oxford, who mentioned his aristocratic lineage and was clearly pained at being required to waste his time on us.

Wałęsa appeared, smiling, gentle, in a soft V-neck sweater over a white shirt, scrubbed after the full day's work he kept up in order to be part of his Solidarność group. After seeing us, he would go to an office to receive calls, then home to be father and husband. A large pin with the face of the Black Madonna of Częstochowa was on his chest. (He had chosen the Madonna, devoutly revered by

Polish Catholics, as an implicitly subversive, anti-Communist symbol for Solidarność.) Fine featured, mustache and hair neatly trimmed, Wałęsa looked relaxed, not determined or angry as in his pictures. He offered us a delicious meal—actually in his mother's house.

Among the guests at our dinner with Wałęsa were Marek Nowakowski, author of *The Canary and Other Tales of Martial Law,* which I liked very much, and Svetlana Stone's friend Osenka, both articulate and good-humored. Conversation ranged from Poland's similarity to the U.S. South (Bill) to rich Americans (Kurt with his Polish zlotys), Kurt's books (most popular), and the newly translated excerpts from *Sophie's Choice.* The Poles would never publish all of *Sophie,* everyone said, because they considered its references to Polish antisemitism slanderous. (Twelve years later it was fully translated.) The arms race was discussed. They all loved Reagan.

Our audience ended with Wałęsa's expressing the faith that the Polish people's long march would end well. I don't think he could have predicted that five years later he would be elected president of a free and independent Poland!

In Kraków we stayed with Mike Metrinko, our consul there, who had been one of the American hostages in Iran. We met foreign editor Maria Starz-Kanska, and had dinner with William Harwood. A month later, accused of participating in antigovernment demonstrations on May Day, Harwood would be expelled from the country. We talked of Jerzy Kosiński as Zinoviev in the film *Reds.* Some Poles didn't know of him; others said he was a nice Jewish boy who had made good in the United States. I smiled to myself, recalling Jerzy's grandstanding and his ever-changing tales of intrigue and escape. Other evenings we met the officers of PEN, other members of the literary community, a film director, a teacher of English, student fans of Bill and Kurt, and others. We learned that in all Eastern European countries, writers subsisted by translating. Theirs was a hard lot. Several PEN officials told Bill they resented the implication in *Sophie's Choice* that all Poland was antisemitic. Proud and perhaps oversensitive, they said that they had personally hidden and defended Jews. Bill tried to explain that he had not intended to imply that all Poles were antisemitic, and that

*Gdańsk, Council on Foreign Relations, 1987—with Lech Wałęsa (center, in checked jacket)
and Peter Tarnoff (fourth from right) et al.*

the characters in the book were fictional. They insisted that what was fiction to an American was history to a Pole.

A later encounter with a professor echoed this for me. A few years later I would return to Warsaw without Bill to attend a conference as a member of the Council on Foreign Relations. Through the first morning's discussion I became aware of an older Polish man across the table staring at me intently. He leaned across and said, "I need to talk to you." When the group broke for lunch and stepped outside, he approached me, gesticulating and speaking in a disturbed tone. "Your husband got it all wrong! I did not turn in those Jews to the Nazis! None of us professors from Kraków would do a thing like that!" He was convinced he was the model for Sophie's father. He was not. Bill had based the character partly on two other men, one he had met. But it was a graphic display of how effective the book had been if it aroused distress and guilt about the unfortunate practices of the time.

Meanwhile, how wonderful it was to be in the beautiful old Kraków Bill had evoked so well in his book, to walk the streets and see the castle, the cathedral, the tombs of great Polish poets and kings, the dragon statue on the Vistula guarding the high fortress, the palace with its crowned eagle gargoyles, the baroque spires.

After Bill left for Paris, Kurt and I and Kurt's friend Stanislaus, a physics professor, walked Warsaw's Old Town, the medieval heart of the city. It had been bombed to rubble by the Germans in World War II. Now meticulously reconstructed, it was a perfect stage set. The restored royal palace, just reopened, was glorious. The Poles were said to be the best historical restorers in Europe, their skills much in demand in other countries.

In D.C., in 1984, Teddy Kennedy asked me to help him start the RFK Human Rights Awards program. I was already one of the judges of the Journalism Awards, which the RFK Memorial Foundation had been giving since 1969, recognizing reporters who focus on issues of race and poverty, the disenfranchised, and the victimized. When I said I'd be chief judge but not run it, Ted chose Caroline Croft to be its executive director.

During my eighteen-year tenure as chief judge there, the fellow judges I chose included Patricia Derian, Preston Williams, Mike Posner, and John Shattuck. The awards were presented annually to brave human rights activists around the world, providing funding and abundant publicity for their causes. We gave the first award in 1985 to CoMadres, the mothers who sought information on their sons and husbands who had disappeared. In Argentina, the Mothers of the Plaza de Mayo, several of whom I would meet, did the same for years. They wore white headscarves, many of them diapers stitched with the name of the missing relative, as they marched around government buildings with signs held high, identifying the "disappeared" closest to each one.

In 1986, Polish dissidents Zbigniew Bujak and respected journalist and newspaper publisher Adam Michnik were awarded the RFK prize. Adam was able to remain above ground some of the time and became an effective link with his friends in hiding.

Poland's years in the grip of the Soviet Union were already coming to an end by the time Michnik and Bujak won their awards. Gorbachev began loosening the reins on the entire Eastern Bloc of satellite nations and spoke of perestroika, a restructuring of the empire. Jaruzelski, impressive behind his bronze-colored sunglasses, was forced to come to terms with Solidarność, which became legal again in 1989. In elections the following year, Lech Wałęsa succeeded Jaruzelski as Poland's leader.

Revisiting Warsaw for the Council on Foreign Relations conference, I saw a sight I'll never forget. As my train pulled into the station, Adam Michnik ran along the platform under my window with a big bunch of flowers for me. The next morning, we had coffee at Juri Becker's great apartment. A splendid thinker and writer, Adam was one of the few allowed to travel between East and West on his passport. He hadn't abandoned Socialist ideals, yet he envied American poets who had so many flowing rivers to write about. He had been a Communist for years and chose the West for literary, not political reasons. He said he was beginning to write like an underground fighter and thought he'd best get out. He didn't care if he could travel anymore. West Berlin's borders were enough.

In Prague, Ambassador William Luers and his wife, Wendy, put Bill (who had just arrived from Paris) and me up at the grand U.S. embassy, a sixty-five-room seventeenth-century palace. They had befriended Prague's dissident writers, artists, and activists as they had done when Bill was ambassador to Venezuela from 1978 to 1982, and again invited many American writers and artists to visit.

I met Václav Havel and other dissidents secretly during the daytime. At dinner, Bill Luers would kick me under the table if he thought I was about to say something we wouldn't want the government to hear, and we had to watch what we said in the embassy car because the driver would report it.

I remember waking the first morning to birds in the garden beyond the huge French windows. It was April Fools' Day, light rain, the city gold and amber. Under arches and around corners of old cobbled streets we walked or were driven. We went to the marvelous home of Jiří Mucha, journalist, short story writer, and former political prisoner. The house was filled with the art nouveau paintings of Mucha's father, Alfons, and the stuffed birds he hunted. We also saw the ancient typewriter Arthur Miller liked to type a little on when he visited Prague not long after the Soviet crackdown in 1968, when he met Mucha, Havel, and Kohout. Mucha did not know Arthur had written the play *The Archbishop's Ceiling* about a building on his square and its proprietor. We lunched with Jiří—handsome, lively, outspoken about the impossibility of accepting invitations to the United States because he feared he would not be allowed to return. I have heard that expressed by many who were considered dissidents in other countries. Every writer said the same: Poet, playwright, novelist, translator all wished to come, but none could. At least none who'd either signed Charter 77 or published in the West dared to.

That evening, we went to see *Sophie's Choice,* a private showing the Luers had arranged for a select group of officials and friends. It was the first American film the embassy had been permitted to show. They had not been allowed to screen *Amadeus,* although much of it was filmed in Prague, because Miloš Forman was persona non grata.

The following day, Bill signed books at a bookstore dedicated to playwright Karel Čapek. Bill, Kurt, and John Updike were among the first American writers who gave signings in Soviet Prague. It was courageous of the bookstore managers to arrange it—the bookstores were, of course, state-run. It was equally courageous of Prague's citizens to attend these events, always under the watchful eye and cameras of the secret police.

Hundreds would line up with string bags filled with dog-eared translations by distinguished foreign authors they had bought. Bill was apparently a hero to them, and he sat patiently signing all the books. It took courage for people to even line up. He was truly gratified.

While Bill gave a talk for university students the following morning, I had coffee with the journalist Jiří Dienstbier, an intelligent, soft-spoken, serious man who'd been jailed from 1979 to 1982 for signing Charter 77 and was now the underground movement's official spokesperson. (Years later I was surprised to meet him in Mia Farrow's Connecticut garden. How worlds connect!) I then lunched with the writer Ivan Klíma, dark-haired, dark-eyed, and dashing, and his pretty wife, Helene. Ivan, Jewish, was ten when the occupying Nazis sent him and his parents to the Terezin concentration camp. I learned from reading his book *My Crazy Century* that they survived because his father was such a skilled special engineer that the Nazis needed him and kept delaying the family's transfer to Auschwitz. When they finally returned to Prague, all his schoolmates had perished. In 1968, when the Soviets invaded Czechoslovakia, he and Helene and their young daughters were in London, on their way to the United States, where Ivan had been given a teaching fellowship. When that position ended in 1970, they could have sought asylum, but opted bravely to return to Prague.

When the Luers were visiting Václav Havel in 1989, at the height of the Velvet Revolution, Bill Luers apparently asked him what he thought of all the students demonstrating for freedom, and Václav replied, "I don't think much of them, because every time they demonstrate I get put into jail." I was told by Wendy that Havel's brother Ivan predicted to her Bill that it would all come to naught. Instead, it helped to end Communism in Czechoslovakia and catapult Václav Havel to the presidency. Faced with writing a new constitution, he and the other leaders—most of whom were intellectuals and writers, not politicians or lawyers—asked the assistance of outsiders. The aid of American lawyer Lloyd Cutler, who was White House counsel in the Carter administration and, later, the Clinton administration, was enlisted. Lloyd brought jurists from all the major European parliamentary countries to Prague, where they met with the parliamentary commission and helped them write what soon became the constitutions of the Czech Republic and of Slovakia.

Havel spoke of a wonderful feeling of freedom and success, despite the political anxiety of the split. He and Michael Žantovský, the Czech ambassador, responded to my questions about their time in prison with tales they told each other in Czech, punctuated with laughter. I caught little of it and soon gave up trying, happy to see them enjoying a brief respite from the political crisis. Certain funny episodes—one with Václav hiding under a commandant's desk—were translated for me, courtesy of Michael.

I recall now how excited, touched, and elated Bill Styron and I were years later, receiving a holiday phone call from Václav Havel and Mia Farrow during Bill's last illness. They toasted us from our favorite café in Prague, where a picture of Bill apparently still hangs. I was immeasurably sad later that evening, knowing how down Bill must be. We talked no more of Prague. How I miss evenings in places far and near with Bill, and with special men like Havel.

16

The Best of Friends:
Kay Graham, "Les Girls,"
Mike Wallace, and Art Buchwald

E ACH SUMMER, the world comes to Martha's Vineyard. The quiet place we know in other seasons rings bells of welcome to family, lovers, campaigners of every type, activists, plus the best of friends. Entering the landscape of summer again, in the place we care about most, can be bemusing as well as great fun. Our horizons fill with tennis, water sports, kids' games, dinners, and lawn parties, complex political agendas revealed in support gatherings or in earnest, intimate talk.

The Vineyard this past half century has awarded me scores of close friends and interesting co-conspirators young and old, besides my beautiful burgeoning family. I think of the late evening calls I would get from one of the young Washington officials whose summer dwellings were on the island of Chappaquiddick. The last ferry from Edgartown to Chappy is before midnight. If games such as Trivial Pursuit were still going on at 10:30 p.m., the phone would ring and I'd be asked to fill in and play in Vineyard Haven. They knew I was a night owl and enjoyed delving into cultural memory. I had seen them sporadically in the daytime at the Yacht Club or in the water, and the night games were always a pretty jolly affair.

I think also of Kay Graham's arrival on-island and our ever-

*"The ladies who lunch," mid-'90s. Back row: Lucy Hackney, Rose, Ann Jordan,
Kay Graham, Tess Bramhall, Penny Janeway, Hillary Clinton, Charlayne Hunter-Gault.
Front row: Diane Sawyer, Wendy Luers, Carly Simon, Mary Wallace, Constance Ellis.*

increasing friendship. Kay, first I admired, then loved. Didn't everyone? I always felt she had a special "thing" for Warren Buffett and
one for Bob McNamara. She shone when either was around. I knew
Bob casually after his wife died, when he and his then current inamo-
rata invited Bill and me up to his house once and we entertained
him at a lawn gathering. I have long been close to his son Craig, who
differed with his father's political actions so keenly that he fled to
Latin America in his early twenties, became a farmer, and today owns
and oversees a magnificent walnut and olive plantation that I visited
in Northern California. He still comes to the Vineyard each summer. Our breakfasts, conversations, and even canoe rides are legion
in August. His family house, recently sold, has lively memories for
me because of Kay Graham. She called one Monday in midsummer
many years ago and said, "I just learned that President Clinton and
Hillary are coming to the island and that Bob McNamara has given
them his house for the month. Have you been there?"

"Not lately," I replied.

"Well, I think Bob lived there out of a backpack. There is no
respectable bedding or tableware or linens. Everything is ugly. And

With Mike Nichols and Diane Sawyer, early '90s.

there are no curtains on the huge glass windows. The Secret Service will be right outside peering in! Could you help me fix it up?"

"Of course," I replied, happy to share any experience with Kay.

"Okay, we need multiple huge drapes for the windows by Friday. Who can make them?"

Luckily, I thought of a talented Vineyarder who had made cushions and more for me, Julie Robinson, and she got to work and made quite attractive pale, unpatterned "drapes" in four days.

"Now, where should we go for table mats and napkins and glasses and silverware?"

"Bramhall & Dunn," I replied. "Emily Bramhall has wonderful taste and can even guide us to sheets and blankets." So off we went on a girly shopping spree, choosing perhaps a dozen of each item we particularly liked since we'd agreed to divide them up and take them to our homes in the fall. We had fun setting it all up. It even had a degree of charm. Bill and Hillary seemed quite content with our choices.

When Kay had decided to look for a summer house on the Vineyard, years before we decorated Bob's house for the Clintons, she called me and asked if I would meet her to go house hunting. (Kay's husband, Phil, had been a friend of my father's in Washington. I had met him when I was a teen and he gave me a summer job drawing fashion ads at the *Washington Post*. Phil's connection with my father is probably why Kay sought me out.)

House hunting was my favorite sport, first accompanying Mia Far-

row, then Mike Nichols in their successful searches, with both ending
up in our neighboring village of Bridgewater, Connecticut. I surely
advised Kay not to buy the ramshackle, brown-shingled, long one-
story building that, according to George Plimpton's father, had been
a men's club in the nineteenth century. It had no views because the
house faced huge unpruned trees, and inside, the structure was so
full of dust that we sneezed when we opened the door. In front of
us were stacks and stacks of old books on the cracked floor. I said
(as I'd said to Mike in Connecticut), "You sure don't want to buy this
one, Kay!" She bought it the next day (as Mike did his) and created the
most beautiful all-white home one could imagine, adding a kitchen
wing and bedrooms and dining room. The house was so inviting and
comfortable I wanted to stay in it forever. The spacious porch soon
had a splendid view of the water. The unpromising trees had been cut
down and the lawn, with a flower-bordered walk, descended to a little
wooden structure where we changed our clothes to swim and enjoyed
an occasional light lunch.

Before becoming a real girlfriend, Kay asked more than once why
four or five of my tennis partners and I wanted to play with her on
her court when she was so much older! She was truly shy and self-
doubting (as I learned she'd always been) in her early Vineyard days,
several years after the death of her charming, dominant husband,
Phil. We adored her, and she let her hair down with us during lunches,
sharing her opinions and certain details of her current life, as well as
regrets. Once she told me how sorry she was that she left her youngest child, Stevie, at home when she had gone away on a boat trip
soon after Phil's suicide. She knew we respected each other's privacy.

I've wondered recently if Kay and I had a special connection
because both of our husbands suffered from severe depression. Phil
was clearly manic-depressive. One psychiatrist had speculated that
Bill was too. It wasn't something we talked about, but it was a ground
note in both of our lives. Perhaps that was one of our unspoken
bonds.

Weekends and dinners soon became grander and more intriguing. At Kay's, I found myself playing tennis with a head of the CIA,
having dinner with President Reagan and Nancy, being tricked into
arriving to find Henry Kissinger waiting for me outside, and with a

With "Les Girls": Mary Wallace, Tess Bramhall, Constance Ellis, Wendy Luers, Lucy Hackney at Seven Gates post-picnic, mid-'90s.

cameraman. I had pointedly refused Kay's repeated invitations to join her for Henry's annual weekend visits. I used to think she forgot why I told her *no* each summer—that it was because of my knowledge of Henry's perfidy in Chile, his support of tyranny, and much more. I once thought Kay understood power better than politics. But later I concluded she was simply being her perfect hostess self, trying to make her guests' requests a reality.

Henry tried and tried to make a friend of me on the Vineyard, at the Council on Foreign Relations, and, once, to my amusement and softening, when we found ourselves the only two people in the Brussels airport's baggage claim at a rerouted day trip (during an air strike) from Paris to London. He had looked at me across the uncrowded room we waited in, and quipped, "I know you hate me, but here we are!" We both laughed. The bags came. I departed.

Having recently heard that he suggested that Zelensky should cede Ukraine to Russia, I now know why I never trusted or liked Henry.

On the Vineyard, when Kay came one afternoon to my porch to welcome her ex-daughter-in-law, poet Jorie Graham, who was visiting me, Henry phoned and asked gruffly, "Why haven't you invited *me*?

With Kay Graham, 1980s, on Martha's Vineyard.

I'm Kay's guest. Your friends in East Hampton always invite me!" I replied, "Henry, you know why," and hung up. I trust he was as good-humored about it as I.

Kay was drawn to and treasured the company of movers and shakers, and could not possibly have shared all their political views. She understood the personal and usually kept her political thoughts to herself. Her trusted editor Ben Bradlee filtered his and hers successfully, then impressively, for the *Washington Post*. They certainly came out on the right side when they published the Pentagon Papers.

Kay phoned me late one night and begged me not to give an interview I had promised to a stellar writer based in the UK, who was compiling a book about Kissinger. I assume Henry had called Kay and asked her to discourage me from talking to the writer, who had phoned me that morning. I had agreed to express my views, in print. It was clear to me that the writer was on my side politically. Kay obviously knew how I felt about Henry, and I realized then that I cared a lot more about my friendship with her than I did about stating my Kissinger opinions. I agreed to say nothing. My thought was: Henry is her dear friend; she does not want him vilified in print by someone else who is a friend. But how did she and Henry know I'd been contacted?

Kay successfully tricked me twice into appearing at her home with him. I was not cross, just found it humorous, and chalked one up for Kay both times. Once she asked if I could replace her at tennis, playing with three of her Washington guests. I'd retorted something like "Kay, you know I won't come during Henry's visit."

"But the point," she came back with, "is that I want to show Henry

At Kay's—Kay Graham and Ann Buchwald and Mike Nichols and Styrons, early '90s.

the piece of land I bought on Oyster Watcha Pond, so he'll be gone and you can be our fourth on the court."

Gullible me! I parked, walked up the grassy slope to her court, where I could see she was still playing. Who was sitting outside the court, waiting for me? Henry! In Boy Scout uniform, black shoes and socks, planted in a chair. I knew I'd been had, and thought, "Touché, Kay!" I sat on the grass before his chair, near enough to converse. As I recall, we talked about current sports championships, and then about Chile's tall ships coming soon to our island. I made some quip about looking forward to seeing them here and not in the Valparaíso harbor as I had in 1974. Good-humored enough, I thought. I knew Pinochet's political prisoners had been held there, the fleet protected by the U.S. Navy Kissinger had sent down. But Kay heard me, dropped her racquet, and said, "Henry, we're out of here: It's late!" They left in a hurry. I filled in on court with top Washington brass. Our compact was complete. (I've never gotten angry with friends I cared about as much as Kay. There seems to be a select group of my best friends from childhood, tennis, wildlife, from Connecticut, the Vineyard, even abroad, including special writers, who are family to me, with whom I have totally unconditional affection, even if their perspectives differ from mine, as of course some are bound to.)

Just once, with misgivings, I relented to Kay's dinner invitation to us with Henry because our friends Wendy and Bill Luers were visiting and Bill wanted to meet Henry to talk over a proposed ambassador-ship. Bill Styron and I did not sit near them, not at Kay's table. Even if outwardly I seemed content or amused to encounter Henry Kissinger socially, inside I seethed. At Bill Luers's ninetieth birthday party in Washington, Connecticut, a couple of years ago, I was seated at Bill's table and there was a space across from me that suddenly, halfway through dinner, was filled by Henry Kissinger. When he sat down, I grabbed the big vase of flowers decorating the middle of the table and pulled it right in front of me so we did not have to look at each other. I wonder if he knew I was there . . .

My last lunch with Kay still makes me sad. She had invited me on a sunny noon, saying two of her sons, Bill and Steve, were dining with her, and they often didn't get along well but would surely be on their best behavior if I joined them.

Bill and Steve were a pleasure to share the hour with. When they left, Kay commented, "This was fun." Then she added, "I always assumed Stevie was your favorite member of my family, since he was with you so frequently. Well, I've come to value Stevie more and more. He seems to be the one who cares about me most and under-stands me best." Kay was right. Stevie was the most creative of Kay's four fine children. Bill and I enjoyed his company and cheered him on for the founding of the New York Theatre Workshop and his profes-sorships at Columbia and Bard. Bill always chose or at least approved our guest lists. I wondered if he and Kay's Billy had had a falling-out. Billy could be charismatic, charming, very smart, forceful. I actually consider three of his accomplished wives my friends. Perhaps Kay felt he was most like her husband. Wasn't he also manic-depressive?

The next week, Kay, on a business trip, fell on her head and died. How I mourned. Kay's property had long been willed to neighboring Billy. One day soon after, I returned to Kay's lawn with our friends Tess Bramhall and Connie Ellis to reminisce about our wonderful times there with Kay. Billy appeared and said sharply, "Leave and *do not* ever come back." We were dumbfounded. And obeyed. He tore down her house, guesthouse, tennis court, pool, everything but one chimney soon after she died. Following the destruction, he sued the town of West Tisbury to lower his taxes on Kay's property, which no longer included her glorious house, all the property's structures gone. Billy lost his suit year after year, then he became ill, stayed in

With Art Buchwald, Bob Brustein, and Lucy Hackney, Martha's Vineyard, early '80s.

California, and—like his dad—committed suicide, shooting himself (coincidentally?) the day before the history-laden film *The Post* was to be released.

Stevie still sails over from his Nantucket perch almost every summer. He, Peter Sacks, Peter's wife, Jorie Graham (once married to Billy), and I meet for a day on our seaside dock and porch, often recalling our times together in Stevie's New York town house, or Kay's joining Styron croquet games on the lawn, Kay girlish, and as noncompetitive as ever. We are so pleased Stevie is having a romance with Laura Bickford, Al Styron's very special, sweet, talented friend who visits us each summer from California. Kay would have been cheering them on!

When we first arrived on the Vineyard and rented a house, Lillian Hellman, the John Herseys, and the Charles Guggenheims were our impressive neighbors. Soon journalists Art Buchwald and Mike Wallace appeared and became our most entertaining pals along our shore. And for two summers, at least, the Leonard Bernstein family and Mike Nichols rented nearby. Their children continue to come to the Vineyard most summers.

Once I appeared in Washington still in my tennis garb fresh from a

With Nancy Rubin, Mary Wallace, and Ann Buchwald—rehearsing for a show in Florida, 1980s.

Vineyard tournament, having grabbed my suitcase, planning to dress formally in the Washington airport. But on arrival, I was informed my checked bag had gotten left on the plane and would be back in a few hours. I decided not to wait and so appeared, once again, improperly dressed at a fancy D.C. political event. This time I was to be a speaker on human rights. My vanity was definitely in check.

Mixed tennis doubles produced fun traditions, on- and off-season, some social, some not! An annual tradition was Bob Brustein and Art Buchwald playing against Lucy Hackney and me. A favor was required of the losers. One year when the boys defeated us, they said we must clean their houses. Lucy and I donned maids' uniforms head to toe and entered Art's house after midnight with our noisy vacuum cleaner, mops, and full water bucket. Art and Ann, asleep upstairs, heard the noise and cautiously crept barefoot down the steps. I remember seeing their little bare legs and feet first. When they saw us they burst out laughing. Arty insisted he accompany us to Bob Brustein's house to perform the same chores, and witness serious Bob's reaction. It was perfect! The next year we beat them. They had to be elegant waiters for us at a large luncheon on the Yacht Club deck.

Another year, with Bob and Mike Wallace opposite Lucy and me on the court, Arty umpired and soon wrote a song about Mike, which was played at Mike's large seaside birthday party to the tune of "He Walks the Line." The lyrics of the song told the following story: Mike called his opponents' ball "OUT" of the court's lines when it was verifiably "IN." Arty asked passersby, including sailors beyond the shore and a helicopter pilot above, what they had seen, and each confirmed that the ball was definitely in. Mike had cheated. He had to be the winner. Arty tutored Bob, Lucy, and me in singing the song for the evening gathering. It was pretty funny. Mike and Mary were the ideal audience.

A big part of my year-round life developed and continues (though not on the tennis court recently) through my early tennis partners: Tess Bramhall, Constance Ellis, Charlayne Hunter-Gault in particular, with Wendy Luers and Penny Janeway dropping in. Lucy, Mary, and Kay are gone (playing on God's court now?). We called each other Les Girls and met at each other's hometowns (Baltimore, New York, Atlanta, Philadelphia, D.C., Boston, and Greenville, Delaware) each winter, also arranging off-season trips together to France, England, and South Africa especially. Adventures abounded.

Many years ago, several of us traveled to Johannesburg to see Charlayne in her spacious, well-protected home and garden. Five of "Les Girls" went to the Phinda Reserve. When we entered the park, on the wall outside was a picture of the five animals we would see: the leopard, the water buffalo, the elephant, the lion, and the rhinoceros. Charlayne put the names of each of the five animals on pieces of paper she folded and dropped into her hat. We were each to draw one out to see what our animal names would be. When we pulled them out, a couple of us were distressed. I pulled the water buffalo. I remembered the big, ugly water buffalo leaning over my face as I awakened and opened my sleeping bag on the deck of the *Silver Fox* (which my friends called the *Silver Fax* because I was receiving so many faxes on our travels). Connie and I had been on the deck sleeping because the two men who ran the boat were snoozing in our assigned bunks. The boat had pulled into the little beach on the shore of a river in Zimbabwe and the water buffalo was right in our faces. I didn't want to be that ugly creature.

Charlayne put the pieces of paper with the five names of the animals all in the hat again and we each pulled a second time, with exactly the same results! These would be our nicknames forever. We address each other by phone and email as Dear Buffalo, Dear Elephant, and so on. Charlayne's leopard is pronounced "lay-o-par" because she was learning French for her South African job with CNN. Connie, the smallest of us, was l'éléphant since she was a French teacher and frequenter of Provence. Mary Wallace was Mary Roberts Rhino (named for the magazine journalist Mary Roberts Rinehart, sort of).

In the famed Stellenbosch Vineyards, not a major wine drinker, I sampled too much of each lovely wine offered, and passed out on the grass. My friends thought that hilarious, especially Charlayne's stellar husband, Ron, who had joined us there.

After Phinda, Charlayne was working and the four of us went off together on a little boat and then in a van to explore. One night we had dinner near Stellenbosch under a full moon with the memorable Govan Mbeki. We drove him home, guided by the full moon glittering invitingly along the river. When we returned to Charlayne's in Johannesburg, we instantly played tennis (our cohesive habit) in her yard while our hostess worked. Tess and Ron went golfing too. We had a splendid final dinner with Charlayne and Ron's friends (many important South Africans, including another Mbeki). Then we raced off to the airplane, which we almost—Tess in a panic—missed. We agreed it was the best excursion ever.

17

Poetry's Return, Belfast, Doolin, Dublin

M Y FRIENDS OFTEN TEASED ME about my extensive travels and enjoyment of any social events that came my way, occasionally not noticing that some of it was for important human rights ventures. In 1993, Bill and Wendy Luers hosted a celebration for me and Bill at the Metropolitan Museum of Art to toast our fortieth wedding anniversary. Bill Luers, after his years of dedicated work as a diplomat, was president of the museum at the time. Art Buchwald, who couldn't be present because he was presiding at a graduation ceremony in California, sent Mike Wallace a note for him to read aloud at the dinner:

> When I called Rose to explain my conflict she said, "I'll go with you. I have to change planes in LA en route to Indonesia anyway." I reminded her, "Rose, you have to be in New York for your anniversary party." "Oh, yes, you're right," she said. "But if I skip dessert I can catch the red eye and make a human rights breakfast in Santa Monica."
> Bill Luers then asked Bill Styron what he might have missed most in our forty years together. He replied, "The telephone. Whenever the phone rang during forty years, not once was it for

me. It hasn't been easy all these years for a happily married man to say to whoever called that he had no idea where his wife was. But, I am not complaining. Rose has been good to me. Every time she returns from a trip she brings me a present, like this T-shirt that says Stop Killing the Armenians."

How Bill and I laughed. (Bill Luers often said my middle name should have been "Ubiquitous.")

Actually, Bill—and my baby, Alexandra, in school at Rumsey Hall, then Taft—never complained aloud about my journeys. I loved them so. Often when I left I feared they might think I was abandoning them. Or (worse) they would not miss me. I surely missed my whole family whenever I was away from them. Sometimes I was in territories so remote I could not telephone them, which was especially hard. I always made sure that Stacy Bevans, who as a teenager and young woman was available to keep Al company, do any transportation needed, and lead or accompany her in the horseback riding they were both devoted to. We also had a loving housekeeper, Ettie, who could live in when needed. Bill actually encouraged my forays, and more than once wrote important pieces based on serious tales I brought back. Not so, however, in the midst of his depressions.

Having enjoyed and profited by my own lack of parental supervision as a child, I thought Alexandra would be as happy with Stacy as I was when I was with my own old teenage babysitter Irene Ferguson. Nevertheless I worried about her. And sometimes I believe she has never forgiven me my perceived absence of caring . . . she always keeps her own terrific parental and social life quite separate from mine. Our older three quite often invite or arrange for me to share in their activities, to my unfailing pleasure. And I try to always respect their needs for privacy. Christmas 2022 at Susanna's in Nyack with kids and grandma was my happiest recent weekend.

The early and mid-'90s offered a change of pace and vision for me. After a decade of abbreviated missions and the pervasive darkness of Bill's depression, I found myself conflicted when I was offered a UN post in Geneva. On a walk with Galway Kinnell, I expressed my reservations. He said, "Would you really rather do that and keep putting your poetry aside?" I discussed with him my reservations about a United Nations life, which was very different from going on individual missions. I occasionally went to the UN in New York to observe meetings, which were rarely inspiring. I was honored to be asked, but I was not immediately drawn to even part-time life in Geneva. And then, of course, there was my poetry, which I'd put on hold since my trip to Chile in 1974, twenty years earlier. Some poets are fueled by their activist engagements—Carolyn Forché, for instance. She has written powerful poems out of her important experience. But I could not. In response to Galway's question, I thought to myself that I did not really want to put my poetry aside any longer. He successfully lured me back into it.

I went out west to Squaw Valley to write under the leadership of Galway and Sharon Olds and Robert Hass. Each morning there the Poetry Police would pick up our previous twenty-four hours' work, type it, and pass it out to the participants for class discussion. After the retreat, poetry was the only thing I wanted to be involved in. Galway had offered me a way forward.

Poetry was my private way again, and in 1995 I published an island-inspired volume entitled *By Vineyard Light*. An excellent young photographer, Craig Dripps, who doubled as our tennis coach, asked if he could use some of my as-yet-unpublished lines to complement a large show of his island photographs. Of course, I agreed. And soon we went together to each other's favorite island spots and I produced my poems accompanied by his fine pictures to exhibit. George Plimpton, renting in Vineyard Haven that summer, came to the exhibit and insisted we should produce a book with distinguished international publisher Rizzoli: Rizzoli made us an offer and produced a beautiful volume, the only publication I ever made money on, in hardback and paperback. It was a memorable venture for Craig and me. I recently gave some leftover paperbacks to the Vineyard Museum for their gift shop.

By the end of the twentieth century I took myself seriously as a poet again. Except for a few forays into journalism, poetry became my writing focus, my emotional form of expression.

As noted before, Meryl Streep, Jorie Graham, and I—with no preconceived plans—looked for a way to raise money for the Academy of American Poets. Its funds had been drastically reduced when a splendid Black female poet had not been chosen by the chancellors to replace a chancellor who had died. Her white husband wrote damning letters that were printed in two prominent journals, and patrons suddenly disapproved of the all-white mostly male group of active poets and halted funding. The two women on the board promptly resigned. A Chancellors Group with new election roles was announced, widely expanded. Jorie, Meryl, and I started Poetry & the Creative Mind that April—National Poetry Month—featuring prominent nonpoet American leaders who onstage at Lincoln Center stood and recited favorite poems they or we chose. We sold out at Lincoln Center and have every year since with a totally different cast of presenters annually. We're back in business financially. The academy is, I believe, the world's oldest effective poetry organization. Its splendid director, Jen Benka, has devised and encouraged many national programs promoting poetry education at every level and financial support for poets in need plus annual awards for poets old and young. International support is ever increasing. Although by Covid Time I had resigned from most boards I'd long been involved with, surely not the vibrant AAP. Jen will be hard to replace.

Trips to Ireland kept poetry—all the arts—in the front of my mind. How could they not? I remember my emotional reaction to the amateur paintings on the walls all over Belfast during the Troubles in Northern Ireland. There were murals and scenes of both violence and peace and the arousal of passions on both sides. They brought the community together and let people of varying ages express themselves in art rather than physical conflict. That's one of the uses of art of all kinds. Music arouses us. Paintings and graphic art arouse us. I know how moved we and people around the world are when writers who use language in excellent ways highlight and illustrate the social ills and environmental concerns of their day. They're dealing with visual history, and its lessons, with social and political issues as seen through characters and images that can change the way people feel and think, even though it may not lead to action right away. The 2021 film *Belfast*, which sees life through the dominant child character's eyes, should not be missed.

Bill and Philip Roth at a New York party, '8os.

My first introduction to Ireland had been with Bill, Philip Roth, and Maggie (Philip's first wife) on our way back to the United States from Rome a few years after Bill and I moved to Roxbury. We and the Roths had found ourselves in Italy at the same time, and we planned the stop together. I remember a fine rainy summer afternoon the four of us shared beside the river Liffey.

I had a very different experience when, a few years later, I traveled to Belfast with Melanne Verveer, Hillary Clinton's right hand, who in time served as the first U.S. ambassador for Global Women's Issues and the U.S. representative to the UN Commission on the Status of Women, appointed by Obama. We were in Belfast to support the start of the Northern Ireland Women's Coalition, cofounded by smart, accomplished, vivacious Monica McWilliams. The major study Monica had conducted, assessing the experiences of women victims of assault, impressed me. It led to the UK's first policy recognizing domestic violence.

I was taken with Monica's assertion of women's involvement in the competing Catholic and Protestant unionist and nationalist identities. Her Women's Coalition crossed the sectarian divide and championed human rights and equality in a country totally politically dominated by men. I found her achievements inspiring. Monica's successful Irish coalition went on to help women in need of political strength internationally and guide them to power in places such as Bosnia. I always enjoyed meeting her on her subsequent trips to the United States. Our last couple of visits were in Boston and on Martha's Vineyard, chez Styron, both with Tim Phillips, who had anchored impressively one of my Northern Ireland trips. Tim recently bought me Monica's excellent new book.

Between meetings for the Women's Coalition, I had a free weekend and decided to take the train to Dublin. I had no plans other than to see the city. I stopped for tea at a hotel and read in a newspaper that Sinn Féin's Ard Fheis (pronounced *ardash*), or annual policy meeting, was to be held in a secret location in the woods beyond Dublin.

A woman who looked familiar came up to me with a big smile and said, "Are you Rose Styron? I'm Dot Tubridy, a friend of Ethel Kennedy's. We met at Hickory Hill."

Now I recognized her. Dot had been a friend of the Kennedys since JFK's presidency. She was apparently influential in getting him to visit Ireland in 1963.

"What are you doing here?" she asked. "Is there anything you'd like to do in Dublin?"

Joking, I replied, "I'd love to go to the Ard Fheis."

"Oh, I can set that up for you," she said. "I'll call my friend Rita O'Hare, Gerry Adams's right hand. You can take a taxi there. I'll ask her to meet you."

A taxi driver dropped me off at the edge of extensive woods. As I walked through the trees, wondering why I had got myself into this, a very nice man met me and took me to Rita. She had saved me a seat in the front row, right in front of Gerry Adams, Sinn Féin's president, and Martin McGuinness, who'd gone from being an IRA soldier in his youth to Sinn Féin's other leading figure. I learned he was also a poet. His words, when he spoke after Gerry, were quite moving.

In Gerry Adams's address to the crowd, he began, "We are meeting here this weekend at an historic juncture in the struggle for Irish democracy . . . At the center of the whirlpool of developments is the prize of peace, much sought after by all sensible people in both these islands." I did not realize then that in just a few years, in 1998, the IRA would announce its historic unilateral cease-fire and the Good Friday Agreement would be signed by the Irish and British governments and four of the Northern Ireland political parties, including Sinn Féin. Among the signatories was Monica McWilliams.

That day in the woods was my first sight of Gerry and Martin. We went on to become friends (despite something that happened on a subsequent trip to Belfast that might have gotten me into serious hot water with them). When Gerry was finally awarded a visa to the United States, I went up to visit him in Maine, where he stayed with John O'Leary, former mayor of Portland and later ambassador to Chile under Bill Clinton. On the day of his arrival, we sat in rocking chairs on the O'Leary porch, talking for hours. We have seen each other often. I went to the Clinton White House with him to celebrate Saint Patrick's Day in 1995, and a few years later got Carly Simon to sing "Happy Birthday" to him at a party in a New York nightclub. He spoke to my students at Harvard, and over breakfast in Boston, he asked if he could read me a few of his poems in Gaelic. He did, and followed it, smiling broadly, in English! I knew that Martin McGuinness was an established poet, but hadn't known that Gerry wrote poetry as well. Renowned Irish poets from Yeats to Heaney are among my favorite wordsmiths. John O'Leary's wife, a classmate of Susanna's at Yale, was Gabriel García Márquez's goddaughter and favorite translator. She and John were at our table when Gabo visited. (Talk about favorite wordsmiths!)

When I returned on my own to Northern Ireland in 1994, it was to visit Paul Hill, who was living with Courtney Kennedy (who would later become his wife) above a pub in Doolin. I've known Courtney since she and Polly were friends at Milton Academy.

In 1974, at the age of nineteen, Paul had been convicted along with three other youth for the Guildford bombing. Paul was also convicted for the murder of Brian Shaw, a former British soldier. After being physically and psychologically tortured, threatened at gunpoint, and held at a police station incommunicado, he had signed eight false confessions written by the Royal Ulster Constabulary. Paul was sentenced to life and moved repeatedly from prison to prison, spending much time in solitary confinement. It was Kafkaesque. Though the convictions of the Guildford Four were reversed on appeal due to gross misconduct by their accusers, Paul remained convicted of Shaw's murder. At the time we met in Doolin, he had been free on bail, working assiduously to clear his name.

As I sat in the pub reading the *Irish Press,* Paul came down from his apartment and offered me coffee and freshly baked Irish bread. I had read his autobiography, *Stolen Years* (his face had filled out a bit since the author photo was taken), and I'd seen Jim Sheridan's recent film *In the Name of the Father,* based on the memoir by Gerry Conlon, one of the other Guildford Four. As we talked, Paul referred to Zola, Dickens, Simone de Beauvoir, Kafka, Sholokhov, William Carlos Williams. I was amazed. When I asked him about his plans for the future, he responded immediately, "Get on with my life!" He had in the last couple of years traveled to Australia and England at the request of falsely accused young men who asked him to speak on their behalf. If Paul was at last acquitted, I wondered if he could possibly follow in the footsteps of Havel, Breytenbach, Mandela, and Adam Michnik, whom I still cheered for.

At the time, I remember thinking about the Joint Declaration for Anglo-Irish Peace that had just been published by Prime Minister John Major and Albert Reynolds.

Soon I attended Paul's new trial, in Belfast, and while there, Amnesty delegated me to observe the trial of the Ballymurphy Seven, another group of young Catholics who'd been arrested as teenagers following a massacre at the height of the Troubles. They too hoped to be exonerated.

At the end of the first day of Paul's trial, Kerry Kennedy, who was there for her sister, came up to me and said, "Rose, I don't think you ought to leave this courthouse without a bodyguard, preferably a strong young Irishman. You should go straight over to the Sinn Féin office, which isn't far, and explain."

"Explain what?" I asked.

"The op-ed piece."

"What do you mean?"

"You haven't seen it?"

She showed it to me. Just before I'd left for Ireland, the *New York Times* had accepted an op-ed piece of mine about what was going on in Northern Ireland, in which I tried to give fair play to both sides, but was clearly sympathetic to Sinn Féin. On my way to Ireland, I got a phone call at Heathrow Airport (announced loudly) from an op-ed page editor. He said they needed to cut the piece. I said he must let me know exactly how before it was printed, and told him how to reach me hours hence. What the *Times* had done to trim the piece *without consultation* was to remove some words from a key sentence to make it read as though I totally disapproved of Sinn Féin. It was a subtle change, but it completely reversed my position.

I understood why Kerry was alarmed. So was I. With a young tall Irishman as escort, I walked straight over to Sinn Féin's offices. I hoped Gerry Adams would receive me, and not be too angry to accept my explanation of the deceit. Gerry at his desk smiled at me cordially and, thank heavens, chuckled, seeming sympathetic.

A short time later, with Courtney Kennedy, Kerry, and their mother, Ethel, by Paul's side, Paul was finally cleared of the murder charge. He and Courtney married, moved to the D.C. area, had a beautiful daughter, and gave her the lovely Gaelic name Saoirse. Unfortunately, after years in prison, Paul would have trouble adjusting to the world outside. I had the impression he was something of a lost soul. He and Courtney later divorced. The ultimate tragedy of their lives was the sudden death of their beautiful scholar daughter at age twenty-two at the family compound in Hyannis, in 2019.

In Belfast in 1995, the Project on Justice held the first of a series of conferences and seminars designed to help the situation in Ireland move from conflict and intractability to negotiation and resolution. We brought together people from all sides—Catholic, Protestant, and a few British—to hear from people who had gone or were going through the process of reconciliation in South Africa, Eastern Europe, Latin America, and elsewhere. One of the goals was to show people in Ireland and England that other groups around the world had faced and worked through conflicts similar to their own, to make clear that their conflict wasn't unique or unsolvable. We were told the conference played a key role in helping to jump-start the peace process. It provided the first opportunity for the British government and the leaders of Sinn Féin to meet publicly. Hotel Europa, where we gathered, had the dubious distinction of being the most bombed hotel in Europe. Our leader, Tim Phillips, later found out that British intelligence services were concerned that the hotel would be a bombing target during the gathering, but thankfully all proceeded as planned.

The following year, Tim had the idea that it might be useful to bring the participants out of Ireland to a neutral setting, where for at least a few days they might start to see each other not as Sinn Féin or the Ulster Unionist Party but as human beings and individuals. In Northern Ireland the conflict had gone on for so many generations that it had hardened into a complete separation of Catholics and Protestants along not just religious but political and economic and social lines. The two sides often knew only dehumanizing and depersonalizing stereotypes of each other as the enemy and evil. They refused to converse. I had sat in the Northern Ireland parliament at Stormont and watched former U.S. senator George Mitchell, whom President Clinton had sent to Ireland to mediate negotiations between the Catholics and Protestants. George was positioned between the Protestant representative of the Democratic Unionist Party (DUP) and the Catholic representative of Sinn Féin. They would not speak to each other and would only communicate through George. He listened to the Protestant, then turned to the Catholic and repeated what the Protestant had just said. Then he listened to the Catholic's response and repeated it to the Protestant. It was like kindergarten, and it would have been hilarious if the stakes weren't so dire.

To help break down those barriers, the Project on Justice brought more than two dozen political players from Northern Ireland, the Republic of Ireland, and Great Britain for seminars at Harvard's Kennedy School of Government. At first they still weren't talking to each other at all. The Protestants clustered at one side of a room, the Catholics at the other. If you were in one group, you didn't speak to somebody from the other, because your friends and colleagues were watching. They even refused to be in group photos together. First the Protestants would have their group shot, then the Catholics.

To break up their groups, Tim began to seat them alphabetically in the seminars. Then Wendy Luers and I had the idea that it might be useful to bring them to Martha's Vineyard for a day just to relax, have some fun, and hopefully begin to see each other not as the DUP and Sinn Féin representatives but as people in swim trunks having a nice day. Tim got them up early in the morning, took them down to a boat, and brought them over to our island. Most of them had never been to the Vineyard before. They stopped first in Oak Bluffs, where Henry Louis Gates, our "Skip," who had a place there, had arranged a big lunch for them. When I arrived, somebody said to me, "Nobody will sit with Sinn Féin. They're over there by themselves. Will you go sit with them?" So I did.

They had the rest of the afternoon free to swim and walk along the beaches, and then were all invited to our place for cocktails and a buffet supper on our lawn. I invited a number of my Vineyard neighbors and friends too. Thus these Irishmen from Derry and Belfast, many from working-class backgrounds, many of whom had been imprisoned reputedly for acts of terrorism and violence, found themselves having cocktails and supper with Katharine Graham, Art Buchwald, Mike Nichols and Diane Sawyer, Charlayne Hunter-Gault and Ron, Walter Cronkite, and Mike Wallace. I sat Katharine Graham between an Ulsterman and a Sinn Féin man. Both of them wanted the *Washington Post* on their side, so they were forced to be polite to each other as they tried to influence Kay. Tim says that for some of the Irish it was the first time they'd ever felt that what was going on in their corner of the world map was important to, understood, and respected by people elsewhere. They were not used to being shown such respect (especially by the likes of Walter Cronkite and Diane Sawyer, whose images were so familiar to them).

It was an exercise in beach diplomacy, and it worked. At dark, Wendy and I watched pleased as the Irishmen walked down together to the dock and boarded their boat. When they returned to the Kennedy School for the rest of the seminars, Tim saw definite changes in how they acted, speaking to each other more as fellow human beings, maybe because they'd all been together swimming, drinking, enjoying a surprise outing together. It sounds simple, but sometimes simple things work best.

18

The Women's Refugee Commission
Trip to Bosnia

THE REMARKABLE Women's Commission for Refugee Women and Children (now called simply the Women's Refugee Commission) sent four women to Bosnia in April 1996. I was one. Along with me were Catherine O'Neill, the commission's founding chair; the journalist Jurate Kazickas, who'd been one of the few women combat photographers during the Vietnam War; and Nancy Rubin, on the commission board with me before she became an ambassador to the UN.

Yugoslavia had been an ethnic patchwork of Bosnian Muslims, Catholic Croats, and Orthodox Christian Serbs that was pasted together as one kingdom after World War I. From the end of World War II until his death in 1980, the Communist dictator Josip Broz Tito kept bitter ethnic rivalries in check. Into the power vacuum left in his wake, brutal demagogues like the Serbian Slobodan Milošević arose. In 1991, Yugoslavia broke apart into smaller republics, and ethnic violence erupted. Four years of war and genocide followed. A quarter of a million people were massacred, many in mass executions, and another two million were driven from their homes as refugees. Cities like Sarajevo, Srebrenica, and Vukovar were bombed to rubble. In some towns, all the men and boys were slaughtered, their bodies dumped in mass graves. An estimated twenty thousand women and girls were raped. Knowledge of the widespread use of rape in Bosnia, and almost simultaneously in the genocidal ethnic violence in Rwanda, led to its being recognized as a war crime in international law. A new term was coined for the savagery perpetrated against Muslims by the Serbian leader Milošević and his henchmen Ratko Mladic and Radovan Karadzic: ethnic cleansing.

At first, the world, including President George H. W. Bush (Poppy), merely looked on. Bill Clinton took office in 1993 promising to end the bloodshed. In the summer and fall of 1995, a U.S.-led NATO bombardment of Serbian troops forced Milošević to deal. In November, after three weeks of negotiations led by Dick Holbrooke at Wright-Patterson Air Force Base in Dayton, Ohio, the leaders of Bosnia, Serbia, and Croatia came to an agreement known as the Dayton Accords, a step toward peace.

I went to Bosnia knowing that I would not be able to stay with the other three women sent by the commission for the entire time there; I had committed long before to be one of the speakers toasting our dear friend Bob Brustein at a dinner thrown for him by Harvard's American Repertory Theater in Cambridge. Given my upbringing, with its outdated sense of propriety, I felt I just couldn't bow out. And I thought that the chance to speak at Harvard to people of power and influence about what I would see in Sarajevo could be opportune. I was torn, indecisive as I so often was. I wanted passionately to stay, go to the other sites, finish the mission to this area of transition, but I felt, as usual, that I must honor prior promises. Besides I loved (and still love!) Bob. Like Bill's, his anticipated feelings came first.

I'm sure that what I read that night, written on the plane as I regretted having left, must have struck some of Bob's well-wishers as odd. I didn't care. I'd been thinking about it days before, in the rubble of Sarajevo, a setting that couldn't have been more different from the elegant Cambridge ceremony. It began:

> Yesterday, as the sun came up, I went for my habitual pre-breakfast walk. Had it been summer on the Vineyard I would have phoned my pal Bob Brustein and badgered him to leave his beloved desk to join me on the tennis court. Instead I found

myself in a strange city, standing on a pile of rubble in the rotunda of the shelled, flame-consumed, once beautiful library of Sarajevo—a monument to that city's multicultural history and recent ethnic wars. All around me were gouged brick walls, blasted marble columns, crumbling Moorish arches with a faint layer of design. Once Archduke Ferdinand's storied carriage had stopped here. On the ground were empty melted card-file drawers that stabbed me with remembrance of the full smooth-sliding wooden ones in Baltimore's Pratt Library, which opened myriad paths to excitement so many of my late childhood Saturdays.

I kept writing, not saying:

Where stairways had climbed, there were frozen avalanches of mud. Overhead through a miraculously intact iron dome frame hung with char-spotted plastic strips like antique flypaper, light streamed to laser a single high round window whose clinging shards of stained glass held my morning eye: a child's kaleido-scope, or maybe the night's shattered dream. A line from Sea-mus Heaney's "Glanmore Sonnets" surfaced: "and beyond, inside, your face / haunts like a new moon glimpsed through tangled glass."

I recalled the young woman I'd met before midnight who told me she lived across the street from the Sarajevo library and had wept as it burned for three days. Then she watched in horror as men and women and children who entered trying to save some of the books were shot dead by Serb soldiers. Think how many books have been deliber-ately banned or burned, how many decent citizens have been delib-erately annihilated, how many scholars and scientists and playwrights and poets have been imprisoned everywhere for seeking and telling the truth—sacrificed, as it were, on the altar of words.

In Sarajevo, our mission was to determine what kind of help and funding women needed to start rebuilding their shattered lives, their homes and families, to come back and tell us their horrific stories. We focused on the women because in these conflict situations they are largely the ones who take responsibility for the families, for rebuilding broken lives, protecting the children from further abuse and sorrow. The men have all been killed or wounded or are so dispirited by making war that they don't get engaged as quickly in rebuilding afterward. We saw so many ex-soldiers bending silently over their river's parapets . . . At the Women's Commission we tracked this in the Balkans, in Northern Ireland, in Afghanistan, in Sudan.

We flew into Sarajevo in an old CT-43 military cargo jet, wide-bodied and without seats, so that we sat on the floor facing each other, our backs along the gunnels. We knew that the day before, Clinton's commerce secretary, Ron Brown, had been killed when the CT-43 he and others were in crashed in Croatia. But ours landed safely. Sarajevo had been burned and melted into ugly, bizarre shapes. Every building and apartment house gaped and leaked. After 9/11, I visited Ground Zero in Manhattan and was very much reminded of Sarajevo, the same kind of building disfiguration and exposure. But in Sarajevo, it wasn't confined to one site. The entire city looked like Ground Zero. In apartment houses and offices, you had to be very, very careful to step over live electrical wires lying around, and not to step out on a crumbling balcony. After the Dayton Accords, the city had been arbitrarily divided into neighborhoods belonging to one side or the other, Muslim or Serb. You saw kids obviously afraid to cross the street, their mothers pulling them back because they might walk over some invisible border. I couldn't imagine real peace.

Bob Brustein liked my recounting of meeting Mario Vargas Llosa outside the IRC-UNHCR building in Sarajevo, where Mario's son Gonzalo worked. How poignant, I thought, to see each other again, on another continent, through our mutual passions for human rights (and art and words). He was awarded the Nobel Prize in Literature fourteen years later.

Mario was off then to see the suburb of Grbavica, where angry Serbs had fled, forced from their homes after the Dayton Accords. Following lunch with Nancy Rubin and John Fawcett (of USAID) in the teeming main square, John and his Bosnian colleague enlightened us on post-Dayton progress and problems. I then headed to the suburb Lukavica and other enemy-dominated towns with Rada, a lovely young Muslim refugee from Zenica. It was Good Friday and the assistance centers were closed, so we went to the house where Rada and eight others lived, on the tidy first floor, the upper apartments jammed chaotically with their hauled possessions. The walls were cracked and riddled with holes, and all the window frames were covered in plastic. Rada considered herself lucky: Only one of her sisters had been killed on the trek from home. We stood on the little balcony looking out at shelled apartment complexes, at the rusted corrugated barracks that held countless families, and the center for the elderly where perhaps a dozen men and women sat out on flimsy chairs as four figures foraged through a can-filled garbage bin. There was a deep trench below us next to piled orange roof tiles that one family had carried for undetermined distances. I stepped down for a moment onto the patch of grass and was peremptorily ordered back. "*Any* grass could be mined," Rada warned. Imagine. Across the street, teens and children played on asphalt. "The Dayton line runs right through that play area and apartment building and this house," she said, laughing. "They took a territorial map and said Muslims to the left, Serbs to the right. The neighbors are trying to get it moved a hundred yards, to the corner, but so far no one is listening."

Returning to Sarajevo, Vargas Llosa and I compared notes over tea with his son and our delegation leader, Catherine O'Neill. Nancy was at our pensione dealing with a terribly burned, disfigured woman brought for help by a *Stars and Stripes* correspondent named Carlos. Jurate Kazickas was at a women's center observing a puppet theater and then an art therapy and group counseling sessions for depressed teenagers.

We all met at a dinner organized by PEN. Vargas Llosa, apparently pleased to come along as the surprise guest, was eloquent. I sat across from a middle-aged poet who leveled me with her gaze and demanded, "Do you know what it's like to hear six million shells exploding? I scream and scream back to keep my sanity. Why didn't you in the West rescue us?" I tried to explain American confusion, Clinton's goodwill but respect for Europe, to apologize, sympathize, as I prompted her to tell me of her family losses. She smiled a bit, and gave me a book of her verse. Her name was Bisera Alikadić.

Wherever members of our delegation went—to Sarajevo, snow-heavy Zagreb, Tuzla, Banja Luka, to barely habitable suburbs or miserable refugee camps where one could hardly breathe for the thick coal smoke—it was the women who impressed us. They harbored no ethnic hatred. "This was not a women's war," one of them stated forcefully. They wanted to work cross-culturally to rebuild their communities, reclaim childhood for their children, and restore sanity to their families and a sense of purpose to society. Those in their twenties said that with so few men left they did not expect to marry and raise children, so they'd devote themselves to public service. High-initiative urban women from various professions took us through the centers they had pooled resources to start. They stressed the need for funding, for jobs, for teaching English and business skills.

"You could hire ten of us for the salary of one of your foreign NGO workers," one proclaimed. Group therapy for the elderly, get-togethers for teenagers, a puppet theater workshop, and a one-room school for kids, a knitting and craft center were under way. So was a cultural center operated by feminists aware that recovery from "brain drain" (hundreds of educated citizens fled and settled abroad) would be slow. Women shared ideas and personal problems. They listened to scholars and writers. One advocacy group counseled women who had survived genocidal rape.

Sarajevo, of course, was a multicultural capital, not a third-world town, unbelievable as its devastation was now. Its citizens were ready learners, doers, educated. It was different with Srebrenicans. Of fifteen thousand survivors, few were fully educated. Refugees needed schooling and jobs, reconstruction and business skills, a place to go. Employed women didn't want to lose their jobs to men returning; they wanted everyone to work. Everywhere we walked, demobilized soldiers, unemployed, were wandering. Some stared down from a bridge they leaned on, others sat at cafés, drinking. Their frustration, we heard, was giving rise to domestic violence.

In Zagreb, we were moved by the words of tireless doctors who treated the injured and the traumatized. They sought not just money, up-to-date equipment, and unexpired medicines (70 percent of what was donated had to be thrown away) for their decimated hospitals, and sponsors for young victims of a new epidemic, leukemia. They wanted refresher courses that would include the advanced techniques they felt they had lost out on during the war years. They wanted health centers, home care programs, and a clubhouse for their youth.

Driving north toward Tuzla, beyond the treacherous suburbs of

Sarajevo, some of us stopped at refugee camps. They were desperately crowded, with fifty refugees in one schoolroom sharing twelve beds. They needed sanitation and mental health facilities. The few men who had escaped the massacre of males in Srebrenica and joined the women and children bused there were furious that the UN offered their families only potentially dangerous border areas for resettlement. Refugees felt they should be consulted about the places to live out their lives. They wondered why no one was interested in identifying the men they had witnessed from the woods they hid in, executing their kin.

The day after the rest of my group returned from Bosnia, we went on Charlie Rose's show with actress Liv Ullmann, a Women's Commission spokesperson, to relate a little of what we'd seen and heard. Then Nancy Rubin rushed back to D.C., where she immediately went to work on programs to get organized health care going and provide loans so that the women we'd met could form small businesses or cooperatives that would begin to bring their shattered society back to life. Nancy constantly impressed me as an imaginative champion of women in need and of victims of war or abuse as she traveled the world. Her work on the board Women for Women, the ideas and support she gave Amnesty International USA when I'd been appointed chair of its fiftieth anniversary year, her spontaneous gifts of speech and care continue to inspire. She went on to be ambassador to the

Rose in Sarajevo—ruins.

UN, and to found a very important mental health foundation in California, most recently incorporating a suicide prevention center with rooms for educating young and old in its plan for prevention. Catherine O'Neill, who died in 2012, was magnificent, publicly and privately. Jurate and I are delighted still when occasionally our paths cross.

19

Impromptu Dinner Parties, Martha's Vineyard, and Havana

I N WALLACE STEGNER'S NOVEL *Crossing to Safety,* a protagonist notes that "he's the only person who ever had a dinner party change his life." Stegner didn't know me. I'm thinking of one in 1995 at the Styron table in Martha's Vineyard.

In recent years, Cuba has been on many American minds: Obama's welcome diplomatic opening, Trump's threats of closing off relations, Fidel Castro's death, his brother Raúl's ascension with successful plans for tourism, and his announcement in 2021 to step down. What might Biden's policy be now?

My most recent visit to Cuba was in January 2016. I traveled with the Boston Museum of Fine Arts, accompanied by my daughter Susanna, who was still game for a mother-daughter adventure after our dangerous trip to Chile when she was a teenager. This safe (and rain-drenched) excursion generated surprise, delight, and concerns. Many artists welcomed us into their studios, galleries, homes. Several were in buildings converted from the abandoned, half-built structures I'd seen on my earlier trip. We surmised that the arts communities were beginning to flourish because they could sell their work to visitors, exhibit abroad, and on occasion even travel with their exhibitions. A quiet hour spent with our remarkable de facto ambassador at the time, Jeff DeLaurentis, afforded us invaluable insights to Cuba's political and cultural situation. (In Cambridge, just before our Covid years, the DeLaurentises told me, sadly, that the tourist boom declined, and Jeff left the service, along with other Americans. I learned that the escalating repression of civil rights, the curtailing of free expression, the imprisonment and house arrests of artists are presently overshadowing plans for the Havana Biennial. More recently, Amnesty International named two artists—Luis Manuel Otero Alcántara and Hamlet Lavastida—and four others prisoners of conscience, calling for their immediate release along with others who have been jailed.)

In 2016, tourism in Cuba was flourishing. While Susanna and I were there, I often thought back to the amazing experience I had with Bill in Havana at the invitation of Fidel Castro in the year 2000. Its highlight was a long, lively impromptu dinner at the Presidential Palace, which spooled my memory back further to a dinner party Bill and I hastily arranged at our home on the Vineyard. I think now that its diplomatic fallout is what must have prompted Castro to invite us to Cuba five years later. At least a half dozen descriptions of our dinner party have appeared in print by persons who were present or not, each of whom has claimed to have been there. I've read about it in a long article by Gabriel García Márquez, who was our beloved guest, in an interview with Carlos Fuentes, in memoirs by President Clinton and President Carlos Salinas of Mexico, and even in Peter Kornbluh's *Back Channel to Cuba* (not a dinner guest, he kindly corrected a couple of details after consulting me). Harvey Weinstein, giving an interview after Gabriel García Márquez died, pretended he'd been our dinner guest that night. Surely not. How innocent we Styrons were of the international complexities and the secret Latin American mission behind our island evening.

To set that scene: It was a beautiful sun-drenched week, crowded with family and friends, a last summer hurrah. Every day our lawn was filled early with sounds from the Vineyard Haven Yacht Club next door—children taking tennis and sailing lessons; adults preparing a variety of boat and fishing excursions, playing tennis, or gathering for boisterous lunches on the Yacht Club deck, a summer hub for political and social talk. In the afternoons, my grandchildren and their pals would burst through the hedge path and begin games on the lawn, football and milder. Later, our contemporaries might gather for a drink before sunset, or a bite, perhaps before attending a movie "downtown."

One evening, pretty late, the phone rang. I had been sitting alone watching the harbor turn pink, backlit at sunset, then black, sailboat masts tinkling, waiting for moonrise. It was Gabo (Gabriel García Márquez) calling from Mexico City. "Remember you always said I should come to Martha's Vineyard?" he began. "Should I join Carlos Fuentes and come in a couple of weeks?" (As I've mentioned, Carlos and his family came to stay with us each August, and we joined them somewhere in Mexico each New Year's.) I assented enthusiastically. Gabo and I had been friends since we met at Chapultepec Castle in 1975. Carlos had been Bill's friend since an earlier Pan-American writers' conference in Mérida, and we had met very briefly at a gathering Carlos had arranged.

Gabo, before he hung up the phone, and called again later, said, "I'll let you know in a few days if I can make it." The noon following Gabo's evening call, I found myself on a private stretch of Squibnocket Beach in Chilmark (known for spectacular dune views of the sea, even Nomans Land) with First Lady Hillary Clinton and "Les Girls." That day, we had been luncheon guests of Tess Bramhall, a brilliant guardian of this special place, and all our island's land. We swam and explored, ending up atop a high dune that we'd climbed, when suddenly the view was marred by a fleet of cars down on the sand, the pristine silence broken by sirens. Out stepped Bill Clinton and a flock of Secret Service men. Clinton had been playing golf with Vernon Jordan and asked where Hillary might be found, seeking to join her. Tess and Hillary seemed less than enchanted with the intrusion, but of course we descended to greet the president. His buoyant mood was infectious, as always. I was happy to see him.

"I'd love to go in the water," he said, "but I'm in golf clothes and don't have a bathing suit."

By now another friend, Luciano Rebay, a professor who headed the Casa Italiana at Columbia University, had joined us. (Born in Milan, the son of a blind organist, Luciano had experiences as a teenage messenger/activist in World War II Italy that could make as fascinat-

Gabriel García Márquez, Susanna Styron, and Hillary Clinton
in our Vineyard living room, mid-1990s.

ing a book as Italian teen Ginetta Sagan's did.) He was slight, handsome, and an exceptional swimmer—the kind of European man I'd often admired on the Lido.

"Mr. President," Luciano said, beaming, "I happen to have two swimsuits on!" He dropped his loose flowered trunks, revealing a classic Speedo underneath. The president slipped behind a dune to change. For a moment, the Secret Service lost sight of him and jabbered on their walkie-talkies again.

Emerging to swim, Bill Clinton said to me, "I know you're friends with Gabriel García Márquez. He's Chelsea's favorite author, and one of mine. I heard a rumor he might be coming to the Vineyard."

A bit puzzled as to how he knew, I replied, "I think last night I heard that rumor too."

"If he makes it, please invite us to dinner!" And he walked out into the water.

When Gabo heard that President Clinton might be coming to dinner, he let us know how pleased he was. When Clinton was elected president, he ended the decades-long travel ban on García Márquez. Apparently it had been based on Gabo's criticism of U.S. foreign policy. In those days anyone suspected of being a Communist or an intellectual with ideas different from those of our America First defenders was suspect. In my role as chair of PEN's Freedom to

Write Committee in the 1970s and '80s, I had signed petitions to the U.S. government to admit such writers as García Márquez, Fuentes, and Graham Greene—Cold War stuff—with only marginal success. I knew Gabo admired our president. But the U.S. government seemed to be scared that left-leaning wordsmiths might negatively influence American patriots.

At dinner, a week or two later, at 8:00 p.m., seated on my left, Gabo began an intense conversation with Bill Clinton (seated, of course, on my right) about lifting sanctions on Cuba. He described the plight of poorer Cubans and their need for personal and political hope. Bill and I were unaware of his well-planned top-level secret mission. Clinton was sympathetic.

Bill Styron, at the other end of the table with Hillary, commandeered the table, talking animatedly, possibly continuing a conversation started on one of their beach walks together. Next to me, Gabo continued urging the president to ease U.S.-Cuban relations. Cuban refugees had been flooding into Florida in recent years, more than a few perishing on the way. In 1993, Clinton had been persuaded to tighten the trade embargo to get Castro to stem the tide of refugees arriving in flimsy boats on our southern shores. It had not worked. One report predicted that three hundred thousand Cubans would soon be embarking for the States. After perhaps twenty minutes or so, the president appeared uncomfortable at being pressed semi-publicly on the topic. Speaking softly in Spanish, Bill Luers, the consummate diplomat, whom I'd seated on the other side of Gabo (he had led the State Department's attempt to reconcile with Cuba years before), suggested that Gabo change the subject.

Gabo hastily declared how much Castro admired Clinton, that they should meet.

Promptly, Carlos suggested that the new subject should be what book or author had most influenced each of the men at the table when he was young, especially if he had become a writer. Suddenly conversation became cheery. *The Count of Monte Cristo* was augmented by *You Can't Go Home Again.* Suddenly President Clinton rose, pushed back his chair, and said, "Faulkner! I'm a southern boy," and began walking around our long oval table reciting Benjy's monologue from *The Sound and the Fury* in its entirety. Gabo described the hour as "a literary jousting match." Clinton amazed us with the breadth and depth of his reading. We, of course, knew he was a fan of Bill Styron's works because the year before he had awarded Bill the National Medal of Arts. At the White House, he had stated, "I can say that a whole generation of us had never quite found words to give expression to many of the things we had imagined until we read the works of William Styron."

President Clinton years later spoke about Bill and his work at Bill's memorial service at St. Bart's in New York. Clinton said he remembered reading *The Confessions of Nat Turner* when he was a twenty-one-year-old senior at Georgetown University. "I ran out and bought a copy and buried myself in my little house along the Potomac River and did not come out until I'd finished it," he said. "As a southerner myself, a boy from Arkansas, the words of a southern novelist were particularly meaningful to me."

When on that noon beach, Clinton had mentioned that his daughter Chelsea's favorite book was *One Hundred Years of Solitude*. Gabo had joked to the press that Clinton was probably just eyeing the Latino vote. On the lawn when the president and Gabo shook hands before dinner, Clinton assured the writer that he'd meant every word. He then declared that he himself had also read other García Márquez novels, particularly liking *The General in His Labyrinth,* Gabo's novel about Simón Bolívar. A few days after the dinner and meeting teenage Chelsea Clinton, Gabo sent her English translations of all his novels, gratified to learn that someone so young loved his work.

Gabo and Carlos were already impressed with Clinton's knowledge, but then the president astonished them by saying he was currently reading his third in the series of mystery novels by the young Mexican author Paco Ignacio Taibo II.

"Paco!" Carlos exclaimed. He and Gabo had had lunch with Taibo just the week before. They were extremely pleased that the American president was so well versed in current Latin American literature.

The dozen guests around the table continued talking amiably with the president about the books that had meant the most to them. Bill Styron, after his Thomas Wolfe choice, named *The Adventures of Huckleberry Finn*. Gabo declared that *The Count of Monte Cristo* was his favorite (and later wrote that he chose it mainly for reasons of

Richard Dixon, Daphne Lewis, and Bill Clinton,
Martha's Vineyard fried chicken dinner, mid-'90s.

technique). Bill Clinton said his was *The Meditations of Marcus Aurelius.*
Later an interviewer of Carlos Fuentes quoted him explaining his
choice that night: "I was about to say *Don Quixote,* but I wanted to
take the president to the South. I bit my tongue and said, *Absalom,*
Absalom!"

It was approaching eleven o'clock, dessert just arriving, when
Daphne, our summer cook, emerged from the kitchen to announce
that President Clinton had a phone call from Ireland. Clinton rose,
feigning surprise. The caller, he told us on his return to the table, was
Gerry Adams. After decades of the Troubles, peace was tentatively
blooming, and Gerry called our home from Belfast to urge Mr. Clinton to come to Northern Ireland to promote the coming peace talks.
(Although Gerry and I were friends by then, following our meetings in Belfast, Maine, New York, and D.C., I did not set up this call,
and vaguely wondered why he hadn't asked for me.) The president,
secluded on our kitchen phone, assured Gerry he was already committed to helping if he could, and he agreed then and there to try to
step up U.S. involvement. Clinton, returning to finish dessert before
saying good night and stuffing two remaining pieces of Daphne's
fried chicken in his pockets, seemed to be musing—positively—over
Gerry's request that he come personally to Ireland to further the
peace talks. At a different dinner party a couple of years ago at Bryan

and Tara Meehan's in West Chop, I learned from guest Christine Varney that she had been Clinton's young assistant at the time and was in our kitchen with the Secret Service guys, munching fried chicken and waiting for the call that Clinton feigned surprise at. She had already prepared talking points for him.

After dinner, as we sat over late coffee and dessert, Clinton had said he thought he needed to go to Northern Ireland personally. Indeed, he made the historic visit and appointed George Mitchell to be the U.S. special envoy for Northern Ireland. (As I mentioned, on a subsequent trip to Belfast, I watched Mitchell at Stormont, parrying verbal shots between Gerry Adams and Ian Paisley, whom he sat between. They refused to talk to each other directly.)

"That would have been an historic ending to an unforgettable night," Gabo wrote, "had Fuentes not gone one step further. He asked Clinton whom he considered his enemies. The answer was instant: 'My only enemy is right-wing religious fundamentalism.'" A discussion on that topic pretty much concluded the evening.

Years after that dinner, I learned that President Carlos Salinas of Mexico had a behind-the-scenes role with Comandante Castro then. We did not suspect that on August 24, five days before our dinner, Clinton, upset over the Cuba situation (especially the arrivals in Florida by flimsy boats), had called President Salinas, whom he knew was President Castro's favored communicator. Salinas suggested that Clinton and Castro have a conversation, though he suspected neither leader would be willing to do so in public. He then recruited the one person both he and Castro completely trusted: Gabriel García Márquez, a Styron friend, as liaison. Gabo never told anyone. He had been flown on the Mexican presidential plane directly to Cuba to deliver the message that Clinton had given to Salinas over the phone and Salinas had scribbled down. Gabo was then flown back on the plane from Cuba to Mexico, and he then flew with the Fuenteses to the Vineyard to deliver Castro's response to Clinton's message—at our table.

Gabo had long before told us that Castro wanted to meet Bill Styron. He reiterated it that night at our dinner, suggesting that in the near future we find a way to get to Cuba, which in those days was not legal for Americans. Carlos Fuentes had no use for Castro and he couldn't see why Bill would want to go. Gabo, however, had been a journalist during Castro's early years as a revolutionary, and had followed him ever since. They had remained loyal friends, even with their severe differences of political opinion and Gabo's despair over Castro's human rights policies at home. On a nonpolitical note, I suspect that Fidel may have rivaled Bill Clinton in his devotion to books and writers.

In March 2000, the second dinner happened a night ahead of schedule. Gabo was on his annual spring visit to Cuba for the film institute that he had founded in Havana with Fidel's blessing. Castro also wanted to meet our Roxbury neighbor Arthur Miller. While Gabo made arrangements in Cuba, Bill Luers, who had negotiated the potential opening of relations with Cuba when he was at the Carter State Department, said that he'd help organize the trip from the United States if he and Wendy could come along. He was remarkably successful. Because of the trade embargo, the Treasury Department restricted U.S. citizens from traveling to and spending money in Cuba. Bill Luers managed to get us permission to travel as a cultural delegation, which was unusual in those days. He then appealed to the Cuban ambassador to the UN to arrange our visas. There were no commer-

With Gabo the Great Lover, Martha's Vineyard living room right after dinner, mid-'90s.

Gabo García Márquez, Hillary Clinton, Bill, Carlos Fuentes, Patricia Cepeda, dinner, 1995.

cial flights to Cuba, so Bill Luers asked literary agent Mort Janklow and his wife, Linda, to join our group and take us in their private plane. Our party consisted of Bill Styron and me, Arthur Miller and his wife Inge Morath, Bill and Wendy Luers, Mort and Linda Janklow, and Patricia Phelps de Cisneros, an American married to the eminently successful Venezuelan entrepreneur Gustavo Cisneros. Patty and Gustavo had established a philanthropic institution, Fundación Cisneros, to support art and education throughout Latin America, and Patty was very interested in meeting artists in Cuba.

I was particularly grateful to Bill Luers for securing the visas. I had been turned down twice for a visa by Cuba, once when I had hoped to accompany Arthur Schlesinger, because Cuban officials knew of my Amnesty International connections and my friendship with Néstor Almendros, the Cuban cinematographer for *Sophie's Choice,* who had apparently criticized Castro at length. Bill Luers claimed that William Styron couldn't travel without his wife, "a harmless poet."

We arrived and settled in at a charming little hotel on the Parque Central, Havana's main square. A guide met us and took us on a tour to a museum and around the city to see the typical old houses, which were mostly in desperate need of repair. He then showed us a special exhibit that included a model of the city past and present, with future planning. When we returned to the hotel, I thought this would be a fine time to see a highly respected known dissident, Elizardo Sánchez, with whom I had informally corresponded through others. We were not slated to meet Castro until the next evening, and I assumed our time was our own.

Elizardo was the founder of the Cuban Commission for Human Rights and National Reconciliation. He'd been arrested numerous times over the years for his public opposition to Castro's abuses, and he had spent more than eight years in prison, once serving a six-year term. As recently as 2007, the government denounced him as a "mercenary" paid by the United States to spread lies and rumors about the number of political prisoners in Cuba. I knew, of course, that government agents were monitoring all our movements, and that our hotel rooms were surely bugged. But by 2000, Elizardo was such a famous figure internationally that he assured me I would not endanger him by meeting him.

A couple of members of our party wanted to join me. I should have thought twice about that. We went to Elizardo's simple house in Havana. With him was a woman who seemed to be his longtime colleague. We were all sitting at his kitchen table, talking, when suddenly Mort Janklow came out with the question, "Well, Mr. Sánchez, what are you going to do to get rid of Mr. Castro?"

Mort had brought us to Cuba in his private plane, gratis. I could not tell him not to join me. I felt I could not say anything, though I wanted to . . . My mistake.

I realized Mort had no notion of the diplomacy of human rights— and that we were no doubt being bugged. Elizardo replied, "Oh, I don't want to get rid of Comandante Castro. We have disagreements, but I want to work with him. I am part of Cuba. I'm trying to make things better from the inside. Mr. Castro and I have dialogue." Long silence.

For the benefit of whoever was listening in, I filled the vacuum with a positive note, saying that in the last couple of months the case of Elián Gonzáles had been on every TV screen and in every newspaper in the United States. Elián was the little Cuban boy whose mother had drowned trying to escape with him to Florida in a flotilla of boats. He was staying in Miami with relatives who petitioned for

*All dressed up for dinner at the palace with Fidel—(front row) Patricia Cepeda,
Wendy Luers, unknown, Gabo García Márquez, Arthur Miller, Inge Morath,
Castro, Rose, Linda LeRoy Janklow; (back row, from right) Bill Styron,
Bill Luers, Mort Janklow, Havana, 2000.*

him to be granted asylum. (Their lawyer, Manny Diaz, would later
become mayor of Miami; I met and talked with him as a fellow at
Harvard's Institute of Politics.) Elián's father, still in Cuba, demanded
his return, and Elián went back not long after our visit. I invented for
the eavesdroppers something to the effect that because of Elián, the
American people had a much better idea of life in Cuban towns and
had become interested in closer ties with his country.

"It seems to me that there will be much more rapport in the near
future," I suggested.

When we left Elizardo's house shortly afterward, a photographer
was outside waiting. I had no doubt that the government knew where
we were.

That evening we dressed in gala attire and left for a large reception
and dinner held in our honor by the Ludwig Foundation, an excellent cultural organization of German origin, which was founded in
1995 to support Cuban artists. We were having pre-dinner drinks and

conversing with interesting Cuban artists and writers when the president of the foundation, looking disgruntled, came to inform us that Castro had abruptly invited us to dine with him at the Presidential Palace instead. Gabo protested—"Tomorrow night!"—in vain. Of course, no invitation from El Presidente could be refused—by us, or by his cabinet members, several of whom were at the festive event. Those of us summoned reluctantly went off. I was sorry to leave this perfectly planned, sparkling affair—and sorry for its director, Helmo Hernández.

The Presidential Palace turned out to be relatively simple, more like a decorated law office building, one scenic wall mosaic gracing its foyer. It had been designated Castro's official presidential quarters. In an article Arthur Miller wrote in 2004 for *The Nation,* our travel companion described it as "very modern and aggressively opulent with gleaming black stone walls and checkered floors." We had no time to look at the art.

The rest of Castro's cabinet who had been at the Ludwig Foundation reception joined us, none of them appearing too happy to have been forced to leave the event for a dinner with their boss. We were standing around in a group when Castro entered the foyer. I had seen many photos and films of him, always in his iconic military garb. I was surprised to discover him now looking quite elegant, in a handsome pin-striped suit that might have been tailored on Savile Row. He wore an ascot with his trimmed beard tucked into it. As he leaned over to greet us individually—well briefed, assuredly—I couldn't help but think of tall Bill Clinton's attentive demeanor and warm smile when meeting people.

I remember Castro shaking hands with the equally tall Arthur Miller, asking him when he was born. Castro already knew said, "October 17, 1915!" Castro appeared to do some quick calculating in his head and declared, "You are ten years, nine months, and twenty-eight days older than I!" He seemed pleased, too, with this display of math. Arthur nodded, in good cheer, and then we all went into a conference room, where we were seated at a very large table. Our group sat on one side. Castro sat directly across from me, with his deputies lined up to his right and left. At each place was a notebook and pen, which delighted me: I am an inveterate notetaker.

We proceeded to have conversations on various cultural and political topics for perhaps an hour, during which I became concerned at seeing Fidel, across from me, grow increasingly paler and paler. Finally, he stopped the conversation and said, "It's time for you all to go into the dining room. I will join you there." He stood and left the room, looking quite unwell.

The rest of us filed into the dining room, where I saw I was to be seated to Castro's left, with Gabo next to me, and Bill on Castro's right. El Comandante joined us a quarter hour later, looking like a new man, vigorous and pink-cheeked. Gabo confirmed that Castro had just received one of the European "youth" injections he took to give him timely boosts.

Gabo sighed despairingly. He was unhappy about my afternoon visit with Elizardo. That was the reason, he explained, that Castro had suddenly moved our dinner ahead a night; he wanted to see us immediately before anything else got out of hand. Castro began his first monologue. For the rest of the evening, Gabo, forgiving me, I guess, kept passing me funny notes with doodled flowers. I knew Castro had bugged us, and he knew I knew. Touché. Gabo, on my left, had whispered earlier, "It's your fault we're here. Why did you go today? We'll be here till 4:00 a.m.!" And he drew me two hearts on his napkin.

Just behind and between Castro and me sat his incredible interpreter, a woman who I learned had been in this role for a couple of decades. She was so good that I felt I was talking directly to the president and he to me. We could look each other in the eye as she instantly translated. It occurred to me after a while that Castro probably understood and spoke English pretty well. She was his front man and safety net.

Castro turned to me and said, "Did you have a good time in Havana this afternoon?" I said, "Yes. It's a beautiful city."

"I know that from 2:00 to 3:00 p.m. you were at the exhibition, the model for city planning," he said, "and from 3:00 to 4:00 p.m. you were on tour, and from 4:00 to 5:00 p.m. you went to the museum. What did you do from 5:00 to 6:00 p.m.? Were you shopping?"

I grinned and said, "Yes." He grinned back and said, "I don't know if I agree with you about Elián Gonzáles."

The first question Castro threw out to all assembled was what did

Bill, Castro aid, Fidel Castro, Castro aid,
Gabriel "Gabo" García Márquez, 2000.

we think about life on other planets? He explained that he'd just read a couple of books on it. One of them was by Carl Sagan, arguing that there was surely life elsewhere in the cosmos. Castro agreed. From this he went into a fascinating peroration on the history of military leaders, from the Greeks to General Patton, who came to great and deserved power but also made serious mistakes in judgment. He noted miscalculations of his own during the Bay of Pigs and, more recently, when Cuban fighter jets shot down a small plane flown by Miami Cubans—what he termed "the Cuban mafia in Miami." He said that he and Bill Clinton had achieved a verbal rapport before the incident (following our Martha's Vineyard night), and he felt that relations between the two governments were about to brighten when the downing happened. He blamed himself for not warning his air force general not to fire on the plane, that if there were an incident it would not have been choreographed by Washington but by Miami.

After his discoursing on more things at great length, as Gabo doodled on my left, Castro suddenly stopped and asked, "Are there any questions?" Arthur, for reasons known only to him, popped out with, "Why haven't we seen any birds in Havana?"

"Well, we're not rich like you are in New York," Castro replied. "In Cuba we catch and eat our birds." I joined in, asking why we hadn't seen the famed ivory-billed woodpecker. It was thought to be extinct, but there'd been news lately of a possible sighting in Louisiana, causing ornithologists from everywhere to race there to catch a glimpse. The last confirmed sighting had been in Cuba, years before.

Again, to my surprise, Castro replied, "Oh, the ivory-billed woodpecker is alive and well in the forest down at the southern end of Cuba. Would you like to see it? If you have time I'll take you there." And then he went into the whole history and habits of the bird, which he certainly knew a lot more about than I did. When he finished, he turned to the rest of the group and said, smiling, "See? I knew I'd like this woman! She didn't ask me about human rights and democracy, she asked me about birds! So I think we all have to read her poetry."

During a delicious Cuban dinner, Castro picked at a small plate of greens and talked and talked and talked. Eventually, sometime after 1:00 a.m., he paused, took another breath and asked, "Does anyone want to say anything?"

Ever-ready Arthur jumped in: "Mr. Castro, when we arrived several hours ago, you said to me I'm ten years, nine months, and twenty-eight days older than you. Now I'm five days older and I'm very tired, and I'd like to go to sleep."

Castro leaped up. "I'm so sorry. I have transgressed. Please, everyone say good night and go home."

His entourage beamed, having expected hours more at the table. As we filed out, ministers clapped Arthur on the back and thanked him.

The next morning we were taken to San Francisco de Paula for a tour of Finca Vigía (Lookout Farm), the house on the outskirts of Havana where Ernest Hemingway lived for twenty years. I felt comfortable in his parlor. I scanned his bookshelves (I often do that first everywhere when visiting), and recognized scores of titles that had filled my parents' library in Baltimore when I was young and fewer books were actually being published. After Hemingway's death in 1961, his widow, Mary, got permission, despite the frosty relations between the United States and Cuba, to go back to Finca Vigía and ship some of his manuscripts, letters, and other documents to the States. These became the basis of the Ernest Hemingway Collection at the JFK Presidential Library and Museum, where I joined the Hemingway Council. A major project of the council has been digitizing and preserving the hundreds of letters and manuscripts Mary Hemingway saw left behind at Finca Vigía, still stored in a dirt-floored basement where I had seen them and worried at the mold and their possibly perilous condition. Thirteen years later, a new cache of Papa's papers arrived at the library from Havana. And the Cuban curators visited the next season to discuss the entire collection, which was sorted and displayed handsomely in 2016.

After Gabo amiably led us through Finca Vigía, including a tour of Papa's moored boat, we were taken out to the countryside to a coffee finca, an estate with fine high views, where two tables were set for our lunch on a broad, shaded verandah. As we ate, we heard a profound rumbling coming up the hill toward us. A black Cadillac tailed by military vehicles pulled up. President Castro emerged from the Cadillac in his more familiar full military uniform, despite the hot day. He strode toward us carrying some wrapped boxes. Soldiers preceded him, using their rifles to push goats and other farm animals out of his path.

"They told me you'd gone to the Hemingway house, but when I got there you'd left. So I came here," El Presidente explained.

He had come mainly to see Bill. He wanted to speak with him about American literature. He sat at our table and the two of them discussed American presidents and heroes, and books, especially from the nineteenth century. Castro said he was going to place a tall monument to some nineteenth-century American heroes in the Parque Central. Abraham Lincoln would be the central figure, but he wasn't sure whom else to include. When someone in our party mentioned Bill's *Confessions of Nat Turner*, Castro perked up and began to quiz Bill about Nat and his rebellion. After Bill briefly told Nat's story, Castro cried, "That's wonderful! I will put him right under President Lincoln on the monument." Bill winced and demurred, firmly. Others explained why a man who had caused the massacre of innocent victims, even in a conceivably just cause, might not be the most appropriate figure for a monument to American heroes.

They continued to discuss books, and I realized that although Castro didn't know much about contemporary American literature (unlike Clinton on Latin American volumes), he really wanted to. He knew European, especially Hispanic, literature quite well, and clearly felt a gap in his knowledge of American writers. He kept us there most of the lovely afternoon. Eventually, he rose and distributed his large packages to each American couple.

"In here is the elixir of life," he said. "It's what I take to keep myself in good shape. There are enough doses here to make you all as healthy and happy as I am."

When we parted company with him later, Bill took one look at the box and said, "Throw it away." He didn't want to have anything to do with it. I kept saying maybe we should take it home and have an American doctor look at it. Bill was adamant. The package made it as far as the airport, where he tossed it. I never did see the contents, and have not forgiven myself for not quizzing our companions about their experiences with their boxed gifts. Did they try them?

As we prepared to leave the finca, Castro invited Bill Luers to ride with him in the Cadillac. Our diplomat later said they had a long and fascinating conversation in Spanish about Cuba's various military and political interventions around the world.

Back at the hotel, Wendy, Patty, and I stepped out onto the balcony that connected our rooms facing the square. Looking down, we were startled to see soldiers lift and aim rifles at us. We didn't know if they were there because of Patty and her husband, who were certainly not revolutionaries, or if they were aiming at us simply because we weren't supposed to be seen or perhaps observing something from the balcony. Whatever the cause, it was a graphic demonstration of the tight security and surveillance that prevailed. We retreated instantly into Patty's room, shaking our heads in amusement at this incongruity.

At one point during our visit, Bill and Arthur went to speak to a group of Cuban writers, artists, and theater students. I wasn't there. Apparently it did not go well. The audience was stiff and reserved, no doubt aware that the event was being closely monitored. They seemed to expect Bill, as the celebrated author of *Sophie's Choice* and friend of President Clinton, to have come with some great message for them, which he had not. Arthur's feelings were evidently ruffled when the theater students seemed to know him not for his plays but simply as a husband of Marilyn Monroe.

Thinking back on it today, I smile realizing there was more than one parallel between these successive dinners.

20

Bill's Second Depression

I HAD LIVED with Bill threatening suicide in 1985. The depression he wrote about so candidly in *Darkness Visible* he thought was permanently conquered. But his second crash nearly destroyed him fifteen years later. Coupled with his physical illness and frailty, it was much worse than in 1985. And he couldn't shake off his guilt for having promised readers the beast was conquered.

Bill began to have trouble sleeping in the 1990s. He went to the Martha's Vineyard Hospital, and a young doctor there gave him Halcion again. When he stopped taking it in 2000, the withdrawal was rather like his withdrawal from liquor in 1984, and it led him to a second crash.

A few weeks after we came home from Cuba, Bill started saying, "I feel I'm going down again." We went to see Dr. Malcolm Bowers at Yale New Haven Hospital, who had been his excellent psychiatrist in '84, bringing him through with the prescribed MAO inhibitor. But Bill had written quite negatively of his experiences with another psychiatrist or doctor. Perhaps now Dr. Bowers was being overly cautious.

He asked Bill what medication he wanted to take. Bill and I had no idea.

"Well, a friend of mine, Luciano Rebay, did very well on Wellbutrin," Bill managed to suggest. Dr. Bowers consulted the physician's manual on his desk. "Fine," he said. "Let's try it. Here's a prescription."

Wellbutrin turned out to be a disaster. Bill declined within a few days. Apparently Wellbutrin has an antihistamine base, and Bill was allergic to antihistamines, which apparently wasn't noted in his medical records.

Mia Farrow visited Bill often during this period, both at our home and when he was in the hospital. One afternoon in Roxbury I asked her to stay with him while I went to pick up one of his prescriptions in New Milford. She remembers that while I was out of the house he was "fretful, walking around and around." At his request she sat at my computer and tried to find information online about electroshock, which he had read was often recommended for depressive patients over seventy. Mia said she researched several accounts on the computer, many negative, but Bill wanted to read only the positive ones, reaffirming his instinct to try ECT. Mia remembered that Dick Cavett had had the treatment. She called our mutual friend Carly Simon, who put her in touch with Dick. Mia put Bill on the line with him, and Dick was comforting, helpful. He relayed its success for him.

"Bill had it in his head that he needed this," Mia told me recently. "He was so afraid of free fall. He was really doing his best. And he thought maybe shock treatment would do it. Our hearts went out to him. With all his might he was trying to stop what he felt was inevitable."

I happened to go to Wellesley the Friday after our meeting with Dr. Bowers—for my fiftieth class reunion weekend. I was scheduled to give a talk on Sunday morning at chapel. Late Saturday afternoon Bill called and said, "This isn't working. I'm crashing."

I told him to call Dr. Bowers right away, and let me know later how things were going. He called that night and said he felt worse. The next morning, I gave a very shortened version of my planned speech and went home. Monday we saw Dr. Bowers again.

Bill said to him, "I think maybe I want to try electroshock."

"Well, if that's what you want I'll put you in touch with a doctor who does that," Bowers said.

We went to see Dr. Robert Ostroff at Yale New Haven. He knew who Bill was and welcomed us. When Bill said he wanted to try electroshock, Dr. Ostroff said, "If I give it to you, I'm going to have to write that it was elective. You were supposed to have tried all the available drugs, and if they'd failed to help, I could then positively recommend it."

Bill insisted that he wanted it. Other than Dick Cavett, we knew no one personally who had tried it, but Bill, through reading in his panicked state, was convinced. Dr. Ostroff took over. He was careful, great actually. When Bill started the treatments, I went with him each time, as far as the door of the treatment room. It was at the Yale Psychiatric Institute, in a building designed by Frank Gehry, interesting outside, but for patients it was a nightmare of design and execution inside. The team put Bill in a too-short wooden bed in a crowded space. It was humiliating, disgusting. The radiators failed on two cold days. I brought him blankets and pillows and commiserated with him on the lack of comfort and privacy, then brought blankets to other patients. Dr. Ostroff had thoughtfully, as I understood, just applied ECT to one side of Bill's brain so as not to disturb the creative side.

They were to give him a series of seven treatments, one every few days. After the first couple of treatments they thought it was working. But after the fourth one he panicked again, scarily.

"I can't do this anymore," he told me. "It's not working."

I told Dr. Ostroff, who insisted he couldn't stop in the middle of the series. He said the effects would be much worse. I appealed to him, explaining that Bill didn't want to continue. Ostroff simply said, "Go with him and make him do it."

I went down to the treatment chamber with Bill, saying, "I don't like this any better than you do, but we put ourselves in the hands of a good doctor and I've been asked to please go down with you and make you try to finish the process."

In what seems to me still the worst moment of my life, he said, "You're killing me." He walked through the door, and I fell apart.

The treatments continued. I was miserable, he was miserable. The doctors seemed to be nowhere around. Susanna and I, with family consultation, decided we had to get him out of there.

In effect we kidnapped him, with the compliance of a nurse who agreed with us that he was getting worse, not better. I traveled back to the Vineyard and chartered a small plane. I'd taken many flying lessons in the '70s, and soloed, but traveling for Amnesty plus being a wife and mom meant I never got the hours needed to secure my pilot's license, though I copiloted often. This time I flew to New Haven as a passenger, with Alexandra as passenger too. Our friend Bill Madden drove with Susanna to the hospital to get Bill. The nurse arranged for him to receive a certain medication before he left, to help keep him calm during the journey home. It may or may not have been administered as he went out the hospital door. It surely did not work fast enough. As Susanna and Bill Madden drove him to the airport, where I waited anxiously, Bill panicked. In the middle of New Haven traffic, he suddenly opened his door and got halfway out. Susanna threw her arms around him from the backseat, pinning him until Bill Madden could stop and close and lock the door. Eventually they arrived at Tweed Airport—at the same moment that Connecticut senator Joe Lieberman, who had just been tapped as Al Gore's vice presidential candidate, was also arriving. Our pilot took one look at super-agitated Bill and said, "I'm not flying with *him*."

Susanna and Alexandra took Bill to a room at the terminal, hoping to quiet him down. When Lieberman and company finally disappeared, we helped Bill walk down the runway to the plane and the pilot—acquiescing but nervous still—took off. Alexandra wrote about this episode in her memoir *Reading My Father,* perfectly capturing the chaos of the moment.

When we finally landed at the Martha's Vineyard Airport, we found ourselves part of another politically inspired farce: President Clinton and Hillary were flying out after a long visit on the island. Our pilot was instructed to taxi and park at the far edge of the airport. I remember thinking and maybe even saying desperately something like "The Clintons are friends of ours! They'll let us through!" But there was no way we could get out of the plane until Air Force One had taken off. Would Bill stay calm? Try to run? An anxious stillness seized each of us. It was some time before we were safely home. The electroshock, it seemed, had done serious damage. Bill kept saying, "They have stolen my brain." I would counter (not soothing him, obviously), "But you remember every fact, every place, every name." I had always counted on his extraordinary memory and needed him to be okay almost as much as Bill needed to believe he would truly recover.

"Yes, but they've stolen my *narrative*," he insisted. I thought he meant he could no longer write fiction, which he actually never did successfully again. Was it Bill's own story he felt he could not relate to or remember or tell? Had he lost his sense of self? Whenever anyone came to visit, whether it was for an interview or just a friend coming by to talk, Bill always asked me to be there. He didn't trust himself to recall or say things in the right order or depth, which was pretty awful for a man who had always been known for his fine conversation, his wit, his ability to enchant by speech and the written word.

For me, one of the worst side effects of the ECT was that it stimulated in Bill a pathological guilt about all the ways he thought he had wronged the family and me over our many years together. Though my suffering was nothing compared to what he was enduring, I had lost my equilibrium. I took one hour at a time. His going over his affairs, his selfishness, his cruelties felt overwhelming and unbearable. It was too hurtful to keep remembering. I'd long before tried to put such things behind me. I'm sure it was harder for the children. And of course we had lived by our code of silence. I had always needed to look forward to keep our glass half full. I don't know how the children handled his confessions. Were they as painful to them as to me? We all just tried to keep our heads above water. I regret having said over and over, in effect, that everything had been okay. Pollyanna couldn't handle it.

Jorie Graham is right when she says that Bill got the therapy, but we both got the shock. Jorie, who wrote a fine poem for Bill, "Physician," that's in her book *Overlord* ("My person is sick. It trembles . . ."), commented thoughtfully that I had always wanted to free prisoners of conscience because I felt in some ways imprisoned in myself—as a poet, a wife, whatever. I usually agree with Jorie—I so admire and trust her—but I really don't believe this is true. I'm such an escape artist. Perhaps it's that skill that has enabled me to help others escape. But I couldn't escape this crisis by leaving for an Amnesty mission or a wildlife adventure. I needed to stay with Bill and do what I could to protect him and help him through.

We were most often inside our comfortable living room that hot August. Friends came to visit and I'd seize a chance to get outdoor time, occasionally tennis, plus a swim. Bill Luers and Bob Kiley were first among Bill's loyal friends who came to sit with him or take him for an occasional careful walk.

· · ·

The morning of 9/11, I was in my tennis clothes, ready to go off for a competitive game. As I was going out the door, marvelous landscape painter Kib Bramhall called me and said we had to cancel. "Why?" I asked. "Go turn on the TV!" he said. I asked if there'd been some terrible accident on the Vineyard. He said, "No," then again, "Turn on your TV." I could scarcely believe what I was seeing and hearing. I woke Bill up and we sat together, glued to the television for the rest of the day. My daughter Susanna, who by then had returned to her home in Nyack, went down to the disastrous World Trade Center site and helped to translate for and take care of people who couldn't speak English. Polly and Tom were at their respective Connecticut homes. Bill and I returned to Roxbury the following week. The whole time is a complete blur.

From 2002 to 2005, Bill was well enough to begin traveling again. Our only important foray was to London to see the world premiere of the opera *Sophie's Choice* at Covent Garden in December 2002. At home, Bill almost always listened to classical music or opera, or sometimes folk, as I mentioned, in the evenings, after he finished writing. Yet he never much liked attending concerts or opera or theater or sitting through any kind of live performance. I never quite understood why. I usually went to the theater without him. This venture, an opera based on Bill's work, of course promised to be special. The composer was an Englishman, Nicholas Maw, who was on the faculty at the Peabody Institute conservatory in Baltimore, where as a teenager I'd studied singing. (I could still break into "Vissi d'Arte," but my children would object.)

In fact, the way we learned about the opera's imminent performance in London was through a Peabody alumna, an administrator at Camp Jabberwocky in Vineyard Haven. She happened to say to me, "I'll see you in London." I was baffled. Bill's agent had never approached him to say the opera was in the works, and so nobody had told us Covent Garden was scheduled. Then I opened the mail one day and read in a Johns Hopkins alumni letter that they were taking a large group to London for the premiere of Professor Maw's opera *Sophie's Choice*! I called a woman I knew at Hopkins, who gave me Maws's telephone number in England, and I rang up Nicholas.

He was startled to hear that we hadn't been informed. Bill's agent, Don Congdon, had earlier told him Bill wouldn't be interested in the opera. (How dare he! Untrue!) Maw was delighted to hear that we would surely come.

So we gathered our kids and their spouses and trekked to London for a glorious opening night. Surprisingly, Wendy and Bill Luers and Peter and Maria Matthiessen and others came too. *Sophie's* had an extraordinarily lavish and complex December-long production directed by Trevor Nunn, with twenty-one scene changes, from Sophie's father's study to Coney Island to Auschwitz, complete with a rattling simulated train heading to the concentration camp. At four hours it was perhaps a bit long for some. Not us! It was stunning.

Every performance and scene was breathtaking, the music intriguing. Simon Rattle conducted brilliantly. Bill adored, as did all of us, the soprano Angelika Kirchschlager, who came from Vienna to be Sophie. She amused us at lunch one day, describing how she was made to study the part dramatically for a week or two before she was allowed to sing a note. She is an incomparable soprano. Nicholas Maw and his wife were charming, inclusive. We enjoyed a lively, long lunch with them all at our hotel restaurant the noon after the first performance. Bill was moved, truly delighted, especially with Angelika.

From London, Bill and I went on to Berlin, where we were thrilled to see and hear Simon Rattle conduct the Berlin Symphony Orchestra. We spent a week at the American Academy in Berlin, where we'd been invited as scholars in residence. It was an energizing experience. Bill spoke to the fellows more than once and I gave a roundtable talk. We explored Berlin together—the art and history museums, the Reichstag newly wrapped by Christo. It was one city now, quite marvelous, not the tense, Wall-divided one I'd last visited with Kurt Vonnegut on our mission for PEN in 1985. Bill and I returned to London for *Sophie's* closing night performance in Covent Garden. Bill stood to receive much rewarding applause, and subsequent kudos. He was a happy man. I was exhilarated and breathed a huge sigh of relief. It was one of the most rewarding times of our marriage. We were closer than ever, joyous, content.

In the fall of 2004, we were on Martha's Vineyard. I had to go to Connecticut for a whole day, and I didn't like leaving Bill, who at that moment seemed to need me more than ever. A valued friend of mine on the Vineyard was psychiatrist Charles Silberstein.

"We'll take Bill to the Vineyard Hospital," Charlie said. "I'll look in on him. He'll be fine for the day. We'll just let him rest and feel safe."

I settled him into a light, airy hospital room. Charlie and a nurse I knew assured me he'd be fine, I should just go.

I left for Connecticut midmorning. At two o'clock I got a call.

Charlie said, "As you know, we took Bill in early. I went back to see him after lunch and he wasn't there."

"What?" I cried.

"I am distressed to tell you that the admitting doctor decided he shouldn't be there, because, he said, Martha's Vineyard Hospital is not a mental hospital." He was referring to the doctor who had advised Bill he could take limitless doses of Halcion. I never liked or trusted him. I guess it was mutual.

"He sent Bill off at noon by ambulance, by himself, to Massachusetts General in Boston."

By the time they got him there Bill was in such a state of panic that he'd gone catatonic. He was like a puppet, immobile. He couldn't move his bent arms and legs. They put him straight into the psychiatric ward and locked him up. I found him there that evening. I was horrified, unable to help. I cried and cried.

The most awful couple of weeks ensued. My anger at that Vineyard doctor, and the consequences for Bill, were unmitigated. If he hadn't pulled rank unadvisedly I would have picked Bill up in the late afternoon and he would have been fine. When I visited Mass General daily, orderlies would wheel Bill out and he'd sit in the waiting room with me, completely out of it. It was agonizing. He was still catatonic. This had surely never happened during his first breakdown.

Gradually Bill got a little better, and the medical team started giving him electroshock treatments again. The ward doctors said there was no other way to get him out of his extreme depression. The electroshock did bring him around, enough so that he and I thought maybe he'd gradually become okay. He was visibly much thinner, and less vocal. The *Paris Review* was going to honor him at a gala event that November and he really wanted to be there. The Mass General doctors warned against our going, but said if we did go to New York,

Bill should see a psychiatrist and check in at a hospital as soon as we arrived, to ensure his safety and keep tabs on him.

Unfortunately, the psychiatrist to whom we were referred was absolutely the wrong one for Bill. She was a lovely, caring person, but she must have seen Bill as a near-hopeless case. She couldn't have been nicer, but she didn't understand him. Instead of the daily exercise regime I'd arranged for him at a hospital near the little apartment we rented, she firmly suggested total rest, only expensive home care, and she insisted we alert Columbia-Presbyterian doctors (way, way uptown) in case Bill had an emergency.

It became another nightmare, but as much as Bill disliked New York City, he insisted on being there for the *Paris Review* celebration. The previous January, I had rented us a charming little one-bedroom pied-à-terre. We and the Arthur Millers had given up the studios we each rented for years on East 62nd Street. Then Arthur found a larger place, and Bill could no longer manage the steep three flights of stairs. We settled farther uptown in a building with an elevator.

Bill did make it to the gala, the wonderful annual *Paris Review* Fall Revel at Cipriani on 23rd Street. A lot of our friends were there to toast him. Though we missed George Plimpton (he had died the year before), Peter Matthiessen came, and Tom Guinzburg, Kurt Vonnegut, Gloria Jones, Frank and Ellen McCourt, Mike and Mary Wallace, Ed and Helen Doctorow, Bob Silvers, our children and grandchildren, also young writers, actors, musicians. There were toasts, as photographs and film clips of us flashed on the wall. Favorite actors Ed Harris and Maggie Gyllenhaal read selections from *Lie Down in Darkness*. Cancan girls paraded. The editors presented Bill with the Hadada Award, a statuette of an hadada ibis christened with the birding nickname that Victor had given to George on one of our wildlife tours. (George and I had once spotted an hadada—a particularly large ibis—on a beach during a trip in Africa. After George died, his wife, Sarah, created the Hadada Award in his honor. The bronze sculpted ibis resides on our Vineyard piano.)

The party was joyous. Bill was quiet, smiling, walking with a cane. He wasn't up to making one of his funny, eloquent speeches, but he did thank everybody. And didn't want to leave.

We were advised by a Columbia-Presbyterian doctor to continue staying in New York for regular appointments with a psychiatrist. Bill wanted to return to Roxbury, but we spent the rest of that winter in New York, eager to go home.

At first the psychiatrist suggested we hire a full-time home care nurse. There was only the one bed and a couch in our apartment, and the nurse and I took turns sleeping on the couch or sitting up in a chair. I was tired. Soon I gave up and found a larger apartment on Park Avenue. I shuddered at the address. It was expensive, owned by a woman we deemed, possibly unfairly, a "madam." She was sweet and absolutely beautiful, probably in her fifties but looking a seductive thirty-five. She met me in a glamorous bathrobe at noon after I replied to her ad in the *New York Times*. The apartment was unique. There were large frescoes of bewigged ladies in French gardens, pale damask seating around the living room, and every kind of furnishing from rococo to Napoleonic, gold lions fronting the shiny black arms of the most promising chair. She cautioned that we must cover the white damask couches and matching side chair with towels before we sat, to protect the delicate fabrics. I was totally smitten.

It was advertised as having three bathrooms. I saw a bathroom near the one bedroom, and a little bathroom by the study. There was a small room in the back with a satiny couch where the nurse could stay. But I couldn't find the third bathroom.

She said, "It's right there. You just passed it." I looked in. The bath was completely disguised. There was a large damask-covered cushion and back cover hiding the toilet, so that it looked like a comfortable chair. She'd made a little stage out of the tub, with white damask curtains and another big white damask cushion over the tub. The apartment's kitchen looked as if it had never been used. A giant wine rack pushed against the shiny black stove made our attempts at cooking a challenge. Bill and I laughed often, later, at our choice of digs.

No peace, no privacy. More than once I answered the phone when a gentleman caller asked for the woman who had sublet to us. I learned she had moved to Connecticut temporarily with an earlier "client." It was a long winter, but our landlord and the doorman and a physical therapist who cajoled Bill into taking walks with him five days a week made it work.

Bill had two episodes that necessitated taking him by taxi to Columbia-Presbyterian. Both times he and I sat up all night without attention in the emergency room. A doctor finally saw him both mornings, recommending brief stays. In May, we returned, thankful, to Roxbury.

Bill never fully recovered after that. He had his upswings, but he was pretty weak physically during his last two years. Our dentist discovered a cancerous growth at the base of his tongue. It was painful and difficult for him to swallow, and it sometimes compromised his speech. For a man who, as I said, loved good conversation and loved to cook and eat, it was demoralizing. Back on the Vineyard by summer, we made an appointment with a recommended specialist, and Bill began a regime of flying or taking the ferry to Hyannis five days a week, for seven weeks. An organization called Angel Flight flew him for free whenever weather permitted. At one point another organization, MedFlight, flew him from Martha's Vineyard Hospital to Mass General, our first harrowing experience with transporting him off-island at night. MedFlight took turns at different hospitals and was supposed to bring Bill to one in Worcester that night, but we were determined Bill should go back to Mass General, where Dr. Welch, whom we'd come to value, could attend him. Frantic calls, finally one to Carly Simon (who probably called her close friend Dr. Richard Kohler), facilitated the change of route, and Bill landed safely on Mass General's roof. Carly, like Mia, was ever concerned for Bill. At the depth of his depression, Carly brought him a Bose CD player, and beloved music, exceptionally well sounded, lifted his spirits.

Soon Bill began to have terrifying nightmares of himself dangling alone in the abyss after he died, Satan condemning him, God abandoning him, and he being all alone forever in a pit deeper than Dante's hell, a void somewhere lower. The origins of such condemnation must have been from his Christian upbringing, the "void" unlike a benign Buddhist transition to a new life.

Bill had always had a huge dream life. After a particularly grand one he'd wake me and describe it. Some were terrifying in their message of betrayal. My own dreams were always rather pedestrian. I remember his dreams much better than mine. Some were pretty grand. (In my recent "single" life, my dreams of being stranded in strange, usually crowded exotic places, unable to find Bill or my companions, my planned destinations, or my way home, are memorable only for being endless, maddening.)

Bill had dreams about Nat Turner from his teenage years on. Signs near his Virginia home marking Nat's revolt haunted him till he began to write Nat's imagined story. Another was, famously, a dream about his year in a Brooklyn boardinghouse and a young woman from Poland who had lived there. That one got him started immediately on *Sophie's Choice*. I still smile at the memory of Bill—barefoot in a short, open wool robe—appearing in the living room at 10:00 a.m. one day (he rarely rose till noon) and announcing that his dream had made him decide to abandon the marine novel he was writing and start pronto on what—after seven years—became *Sophie's Choice*. He was so involved in his story that if I needed him to weigh in on a plan or help with the kids or the house, I'd endeavor to adopt a Polish accent, which got his attention. Pretty comical!

Bill also had many dreams that involved the presidents of his lifetime—FDR (who as a boy he admired), John Kennedy (with whom we had an ongoing relationship), Ronald Reagan (whom we had dined with at Kay Graham's and joined at the White House), Lyndon Johnson (who invited Bill to the White House for the signing of the Civil Rights Act), and Bill Clinton (a friend on the Vineyard and in Washington). In the dreams, he was always conversing with or advising the presidents as though he felt he needed to warn them about the brutal and treacherous world that Bill saw, worse than the one he wrote about in his books. (Might he have anticipated Jack's assassination?) He'd tell these dreams to me in incredible detail. As dreams do, they mixed fantasy and reality, events and places from our lives together and from his boyhood. In listening to the dreams, I shared his experience of them in some way. Each might have made a good short story.

As I said in my poem "Beacon Hill," we strolled the cobbled streets by Boston's Louisburg Square, villages in Virginia, and the ruins of Rome. Kennedy, Johnson, and Reagan passed us in cavalcades on Charles Street as Bill approached them to pronounce the world's horrors moving closer, experiences of slaves, trying to appeal to the presidents to take actions that would lead to a haven of justice. With Bill, I felt the anguish of a friend's betrayal, a tyrannical childhood bully, the balm of *Amos and Andy*, and Brahms's Alto Rhapsody soaring:

BEACON HILL

I have inherited your dreams.
What is this foreign Beacon Hill
we stroll all gaslit night?
Amos and Andy radio voices spar
window to elegant window
across the narrow cobbled streets
by Louisburg Square—
villages of Virginia, ruins of Rome
rolling away.

We are slim, fit, eager,
exploring New England's darkness
for the first time—no dogs,
children, lazy sun or pilgrim fires
in sight. Presidents Kennedy,
Johnson, Reagan go by in a cavalcade
down Charles Street at the bottom
of the hill. Each pauses, waves.
You hurry closer, give them one by one
advice for the world, in oratorical tones:
its horrors, distant, coming closer
slave and prisoner of every hue
burned, beaten, under cross and star
fleeing, coming closer, standing
in the dock, hugging a tree's shade
coming closer, seeking, somehow
a paradise of justice.

The carriages disappear.
On the corner, a boy from the old South
plays marbles in the dirt yard.
Amos and Andy, Brahms' Alto Rhapsody
soar, end. Deep silence
pierced by a bully's senseless tirades
refuses to let me wake.

An old tyrant's words echo
refusing to let me wake.
A friend's betrayal lingers
refusing to let me wake.

Bill's last public outing, his last hurrah, was in September 2006 at
the Kennedy Center, where we flew to see the American premiere
of *Sophie's Choice,* produced by the Washington National Opera. Art
Buchwald came along with us, with the Kennedy Center and its director graciously covering the costs. Bill and Art were both on the Vineyard, both in really bad shape then. But they so wanted to go that
while any sensible wife might have stopped her husband, I encouraged him, and with our assistant Christina Christensen's inspired
help, we made arrangements. Apparently, when I was out, Bill began
to tell Christina (over and over) that he was not up to going, and
wouldn't. I was used to Bill not being able to imagine traveling, facing
an unknown scene. I'd do my best to reassure him, though I often
failed, and the best of plans (to Israel, to China, to Adriatic waters
and more) dissolved at the last moment. In this case I was not there to
reassure him, and Christina, who had spent time reading the newspapers to Bill and turning on his beloved music, took him quite seriously
and conveyed his message to the Kennedy Center's president. "What
can we do to get him here?" the president asked. "Send a jet," she
replied. And by God he did. They had already booked rooms for us
at the Hay-Adams, a favorite hotel of Bill's. Of course Art Buchwald
was included in the plane journey, which turned out to be pretty jolly,
thanks to Art.

But things deteriorated quickly when we settled in at the hotel.
Bill's pretty, lively, favorite nurse Dianne Cabelus had called at the last
minute to say she couldn't accompany us. Her willing replacement
was not a nurse, but an attractive, sociable Wampanoag leader from
Aquinnah, June Manning. She had on several occasions helped out
Art in his weakened physical condition. But she had no experience in
handling Bill. She tried, but the night and day at the hotel were filled
with anxiety and problems. More than one well-wisher stopped by
hoping to chat with Bill, but he stayed in his room in physical and
psychological discomfort. As the important evening approached, he

cheered up, and said, "Let's go." I'll never forget the sight of Bill
and Art watching the performance from their twin wheelchairs, front
row, side by side. Everyone but I (I presume) hugely enjoyed the
performance. I remembered the splendor and complex details and
easy pacing of Covent Garden. The original cast, including the stellar
Angelika, had come together again for this special performance, but
the new German director, who had taken the opera successfully to
several continental European venues, had cut too many scenes and
drastically scaled back the production in order to tour it.

The twenty-one magnificent settings that we had enjoyed in London had devolved into two drab, cardboard-looking backdrops, no
furniture, and much awkward sitting and rising, Sophie's high-heeled
feet dangling over the platform that divided the past and present of
the script. Still, both Bill and Art had a great time. And so, relax-
ing after the performance, did I. Surely beautifully clad June Manning enjoyed herself too. At the dinner afterward the performers
and musicians visited our table one by one to talk with Bill. Placido
Domingo toasted him handsomely. Angelika kissed him. Bill was a
happy man, once again! One last time . . .

During his last months, some friends, such as Paul Theroux, Mia,
Peter, and Carly, visited Bill. Philip Roth stayed away. The kids came
with their families as often as they could. In September and October,
Bill was blessed to be on brief upswings. I was shocked when the end
came. The only time I planned an overnight away that final year was
when I traveled to New York for a weekend in late October to help
Ed, Alexandra's husband, with her fortieth birthday party. I left late
Friday, Bill chatting on the phone with Peter Matthiessen, in the care
once more of his favorite nurse Dianne, who promised to stay over
the two nights while I was away. I planned to return early Sunday.

Bill, the gourmet, had stopped eating anything but the softest food
by then. The emerging cancer at the base of his tongue proved more
than annoying. He insisted on leaving a feeding tube in longer than
a doctor recommended. In my opinion, that mouth cancer was what
killed him in the end. The acid—real and emotional—just backed up
on him. That late October Saturday morning Dianne woke and went

into the next room to check on Bill and found him barely breathing. She and he were raced by ambulance to the hospital. Christina received a call saying Bill wanted to see his dog. When they appeared in his room, Bill said, "Lady Bird, I think we're both done for." And though he didn't want to eat, he asked Christina to read the most recent food section of the *New York Times*. He was definitely still with us!

In Manhattan that day (Saturday, October 28) I had offered to run around town picking up mammoth balloons and small glasses and funny party items Ed had ordered as part of his smashing celebration plan. It was 5:00 p.m., time for me to get dressed for the party, and I went back to the spacious, empty apartment Don and Sue Rappaport (friends from D.C. and Martha's Vineyard) had recently inherited and offered me. So far it was furnished with a bed, a table and chairs, a fridge, and a working telephone. I was so glad to stay there. Just as I was ready to leave, I heard the apartment phone ring. An ominous voice from Martha's Vineyard Hospital relayed this message: "Your husband has been brought in. He's dying. We don't think we can keep him alive much longer. We have his signature on the paper that says 'DO NOT RESUSCITATE.'"

That document was perhaps two weeks old. Peter Matthiessen had come up from Sagaponack to visit, and he and Bill had agreed it would be a good idea to sign the DNR, lest they put a tube down his nose and throat that couldn't legally be removed, as in the Terri Schiavo case. Bill would never talk to me about wills, even living wills, or about impending death, his or kin's, or funerals. I think we were both in denial, but I hadn't questioned his signing the DNR at that time.

"You just disregard that document!" I exploded. "He wasn't in his right mind! Keep him alive any way you can until I get there. Don't you dare let him go. Resuscitate him three times if you have to." I went on and on. At some moment then my cell phone rang. I answered it, not hanging up on the hospital line. It was the Edgartown vet. "Mrs. Styron, your dog has just been brought in. She was in the hospital with your husband and she collapsed. We feel we must put her down."

I shouted, feeling as if I were in a Jules Feiffer comedy on a divided stage, "Don't you dare put her down. Keep her alive until I get there!"

I hung up the phones simultaneously and, clearly not in my right mind, went to the party with the rainbow of outsized balloons streaming from the taxi window. I mentioned nothing about my phone calls.

Storms were fierce up and down the coast that weekend. Calling the airport and the Steamship Authority from the taxi, I was informed there were no flights and there would be no ferries to the island until Monday. Somehow I ended up in the loft Ed had rented for Al's party. The celebration was fabulous—all my children and favorite young people, Al's friends, recent and from long past, in attendance. Drinks, food, music, funny skits, a wealth of roasts befitting the birthday girl paraded.

Near the end of the evening, I spotted Michael and Sydney Barclay, lovely young friends of Al and Ed's who have a Vineyard home and a little plane. I explained a bit about needing to get back to Bill and begged Michael to fly me up the moment the storms abated. He looked dubious, saying he might try from Westchester after the 6:00 a.m. weather report Monday. And he *did,* calling me at 6:05.

As I recall, we left Manhattan, arriving at the airport before another living soul, and climbed into Michael's single-engine plane. I was glad to be in my copilot mode again. He turned on the ignition. The engine turned over a few times, and then it died. He tried again, then looked at me.

"I'm really sorry, but we have to wait until the airport opens so somebody can come give me a charge," Michael said.

We sat impatiently. Then he gave it one last try, and the engine suddenly kicked in. We were off. An hour later, almost within sight of Martha's Vineyard, he got on the radio with the airport and was told that due to clouds and fog then just beginning to lift, they'd have to talk him in. "It's fine, we'll be in contact with them the whole way," Michael assured me. And then the radio died. Apparently we had enough electrical power to fly, but not to work the radio too. Michael started to look unhappy, sweat beading his brow. He seemed much more upset than I was.

"Don't worry, we'll get in," I kept telling him. "I've been in many plane fixes worse than this." Which was true.

Of course, I was thinking at that moment of John Kennedy Jr., and I'm sure Michael was too. It was inevitable we would. But I was convinced Michael was a good pilot, and he managed a fine landing without any contact with the tower. I am forever grateful to him.

I went straight to the hospital. I had missed two days with Bill, but we had this whole day together. All that marred it for me was the hospice care workers insisting on coming in and sitting with me, telling me it was time to let Bill go. I didn't want them there. I admire hospice workers and respect their goals, but I certainly didn't want to hear that. "It was good that you'd gone away," they said. "That's when they let go, when you leave. He needed to let go, and it's a good thing you left him." That wasn't the way I felt about it. And I wanted to be alone with Bill, at least for a few last hours. The hospital had a free bed down the hall and I spent the night.

Bill was quiet the next morning. I called the kids early, urging them to come. The only time Bill spoke was when Polly called to say she was on her way. As I held the phone to his ear, Bill suddenly opened his eyes and said emphatically, "Hurry, darling!"

The children each rushed to the Vineyard and arrived for a last visit. Bill would open his eyes and smile. I don't remember any conversation. There were no beds available for us. That evening the four went to our Vineyard Haven home to sleep.

At 10:00 p.m. I'd been sitting with Bill all day and I started nodding off. He was awake and suddenly said, "Why don't you go home and sleep?"

"I hate to leave you," I countered. I had a feeling that I really should stay. But I couldn't keep my eyes open.

"You can come back in the morning," he persisted.

"If you're sure it's okay, I'll go home," I said. "I'll come back first thing."

I called a taxi, went home and straight to sleep. At the stroke of midnight I woke from a terrible nightmare of being strangled by Daphne (our Jamaican summer cook who adored Bill). I sat up in a panic and called the hospital.

"You have to let me speak to my husband," I said.

"It's after midnight. He's asleep," the voice on the line replied.

"I have to talk to him," I insisted.

It was too late to call a taxi. I knew I shouldn't drive at night (I was recovering from shingles in my left eye), but I got ready to. I called the hospital again, insistent. They got Bill on the line. I told him I was worried and was on my way back to the hospital.

"No, don't try to come back now," he said. "Come back in the morning. I love you, go to sleep, I love you, I love you."

Those were the last words he said to me.

At 5:00 a.m. the hospital called and said he was slipping away. I drove there as quickly as I could. Bill was lying still, unable to speak. He squeezed my hand, but he was barely there. He lived almost another full day, time for the four children to come and say goodbye. He died in the dark, November 1, 2006. He was eighty-one.

21

Bill's Burial and Memorial

W E BURIED BILL in the little graveyard up the road on Main Street known as the West Chop Cemetery. One book I read said it was the oldest cemetery in Massachusetts, but research shows that might not be quite true. The graveyard is tiny, shaped like a slice of pie, some of its dwellers dating back to the eighteenth century according to their headstones. I'd discovered and tarried in that old green graveyard on a walk during one of our first summers renting in Vineyard Haven, before we bought and settled on High Hedge Lane. On occasion I would stroll and settle there and write poems. Following Bill's, Mike Wallace's, and Art Buchwald's mental crashes in the winter of 1985, each had returned to Martha's Vineyard for the summer and Art made them take a walk together every morning. He insisted they go even in the rain. They called themselves the Blues Brothers. Susanna took their picture at the West Chop Cemetery gate, looking comical in the bright ponchos Art had bought them that morning, and the photo was used when they went on tour to talk with Americans suffering from depression. Art had commanded Bill and Mike to get special permission to buy plots in the cemetery so they could "go on talking to each other underground," as they had on their daily walks.

Bill's burial was a small and eclectic event, which pleased the fam-

*Three Depressed Men—Mike Wallace, Art Buchwald, and
Bill—Martha's Vineyard, 1991.*

ily. We decided to invite a few close Vineyarders and no one from
off-island except for Peter Matthiessen, who would officiate. We were
within walking distance of the graveyard. I had called the Veterans
Association to ask if a bugler could come to play "Taps" because
I recalled how moved I was at James Jones's funeral in 1977, when
the bugle sounded and we hummed, "Day is done, gone the sun . . ."
As the children and I approached the graveyard, walking together
from our nearby houses, we got two surprises. I saw beyond the white
fence at least a dozen khaki-uniformed backs, some more than a bit
bent, and I thought, "Oh dear, I forgot it's Veterans Day. It must be
someone else's ceremony still in progress. We'd best return for our
funeral later."

But it was ours. The entire Martha's Vineyard Veterans Association had decided to attend. Unexpectedly, so did four dear Connecticut neighbor-friends, Wendy and Bill Luers and Ellen and Frank
McCourt. They had chartered a plane from Oxford, Connecticut, and
told the pilot to wait till they returned to the airport. Dick Widmark
was upset for weeks at not having been alerted and given a ride. I
apologized later, saying I hadn't invited anyone from off-island.

Officiating at the gravesite was Peter Matthiessen, who had visited
Bill less than a month before. A bluebird suddenly flew overhead as
if signaling Peter to begin to speak. He offered a wondrous blending
of his Buddhism and the Christian tradition that Peter and Bill had
both been steeped in as children. I remember the ceremony as full of

soothing words and readings and the lowering of the ash-filled urn. Tom, Peter's godson, recited a poem by Rumi. He doubtless consulted Polly, our Rumi expert. Someone told me recently that I read a poem I'd written for Bill. I don't remember that. Together the family recited Emily Dickinson's "Ample make this Bed." Then we threw shovels full of dirt and rose blossoms into the grave.

Carly Simon led us all in "Swing Low, Sweet Chariot" and the bugler sounded a soulful "Taps." On time, the bluebird, singing his song, flew back over us. Later Bill's grave would be marked by Christian White's beautiful stone with a bright gold star and Dante's words: ". . . and so we came forth, and once again beheld the stars." Christian's artist parents had officiated at our wedding in Rome.

Bill Luers recently reminded me of amusing memories of the day. First, Peter had to try again and again to get his incense to light. Then, toward the end of the ceremony, he doused some of the roses in water and went around to those assembled to shake rose water on us. The rose heads kept coming off their long stems, hitting people in their chests and faces. We were all chuckling. Bill would have too.

The one moment I personally recall occurred when my daughter Polly and I emerged from the cemetery's gate. We had waited to leave till all other attendees had walked back to the house. The big black funeral van that had delivered Bill's urn of ashes was still parked across the street. The van driver jumped out and announced, "My car died! When you get home could you call a tow truck?"

In the sadness of the day, we laughed and assented. Our mood lifting for a moment, Polly and I walked back to High Hedge Lane, where we gathered for a lovely lunch prepared by Annie Foley.

I don't remember well the days that followed. I wanted to be alone or only with immediate family.

VETERANS' DAY

Bluebird across the graveyard sky
startles us, orange breast bursting,
singing: the burial can begin.

Gather for the Buddhist prayer
the Christian hymn, the poems,

the swinging low again of Sweet
Chariot as your ashes are
lowered carefully by your son,
his godfather, strong loves.

Then Taps—
the young marine, gazing up
through shovelfuls of fresh rich
earth, rose-strewn,
at the bits of sky, too soon
left alone under a blanket
of drying grass, wet snow,
and the blossoms. Look.

That poem has been set to beautiful music by composer Joel Mandelbaum and performed in churches in New York and Martha's Vineyard on or near Veterans Day these past few Novembers. Coincidentally, James Lapine's film on me, *In the Company of Rose,* was shown on Veterans Day in New York 2022.

When Bill died, our dog Lady Bird knew it. She had been taken from Bill's hospital room to the vet the day of Alexandra's birthday party and was returned home two days later. She was frantic. For days she ran all over the house, up and down the stairs, hiding under the adjustable bed Bill last slept in. She was inconsolable, acting wilder and getting sicker. Before the month was out, it was clear I had to put her down. She would go out on the lawn and walk around in circles, always to the right, but mostly would stand rigid, or fall down, or pee and pee in the kitchen. The vet came to the house and I held Lady Bird while he gave her the fatal injection, by the kitchen table. I remembered Bill saying, as Lady Bird had lain beside him day after day, "She has the same problems I do." I had smiled to myself, but . . . I don't remember where she was buried. I was too sad to consider getting another dog, ever. Thank heaven Al and Ed's yellow Lab Dixie made this her second home. She kept me company through most of the pandemic. I had lucked out, and now miss terribly her licks, antics, couch snoozes upside down. We were golden oldies together, I once thought.

. . .

There were two memorial services for Bill. The first was arranged by the New England chapter of PEN and held at the Boston Public Library on December 13, 2006, six weeks after he died. It was a heart-warming appreciation of Bill's life and work. I was quite surprised to see Norman Mailer come to the podium. As I've said, he was Bill's on-and-off pal and tormentor, a long-term, self-styled angry competitor. He walked gallantly, with canes. His amusing address was actually on the competitiveness of writers. He cited Bill's supposed rivalry at croquet. Norman was full of false stories, putting unimaginable words in my mouth and claiming incidents on the lawn in Connecticut, where we did play many games of American croquet and occasionally roque. He even declared he wished I'd been *his* wife. (Horrors!) Our dear friend Bob Brustein also spoke, and wonderful writer and beloved Vineyard neighbor Geraldine Brooks, both movingly. Several scholars added thoughts about Bill and his work. I was cheered, impressed, and most thankful for the day.

Soon I arranged the second memorial, a larger one—at St. Bartholomew's Episcopal Church on Park Avenue in Manhattan—to take place on February 2, 2007. It was much more personal, an occasion for family and friends to remember Bill from the altar, to tell some favorite stories. Susanna, her older daughter, Emma, and Alexandra spoke, and Teddy Kennedy and Bill Clinton, and Bill's editor Bob Loomis and Mike Nichols, our neighbor and old friend Philip Roth, who had refused to come to see Bill his last few years despite Mia Farrow's pleading, turned up and, uninvited, sat down in the front row with the speakers. (Though Philip told his biographer, Blake Bailey, that I had forgiven him, I hadn't. Bill was truly saddened by Philip's absence. Anyone who's read *Selected Letters of William Styron* can tell what exceptionally good friends they had long been.)

Sadly, Bill's pal Art Buchwald had died just two weeks earlier. They now lie near each other in that little West Chop graveyard in Vineyard Haven, as Art had planned, along with the third Blues Brother, Mike Wallace, and my longtime girlfriend Mary Yates Wallace. Mike and Mary Wallace have twin marble pillars on their graves. The left says for Mike, "Tough but Fair." And on the right, Mary's reads, "Fairly

Tough." I'm sure Mary—knowing she would be buried too soon, next to Mike, invented the inscriptions. Two-thirds of the cemetery includes new markers of our friends: neighbors John and Barbara Hersey, and later Sheldon and Lucy Hackney and their daughter Virginia, right next to Bill and his unique marvelous tombstone. When I visit the cemetery I see more and more stones on top of the Wallace pillars, a Jewish tradition that I only learned of recently. I wonder who the stone-placers are . . .

At St. Bart's, Peter Matthiessen spoke about the first time he and his first wife, Patsy, met Bill in Paris. "In the spring of 1952," he said, "a woebegone young man turned up at the door of my small borrowed flat in the railroad neighborhood of Montparnasse. Here he was, a complete stranger, unheralded and all alone on that lightless, cheerless top-floor landing. A young novelist as it turned out, who had had the terrible misfortune of arriving in Paris weeks in advance of his own acclaim for that superb first novel, *Lie Down in Darkness*. That first evening we gave him drink and took him out to supper at a small Breton café around the corner, where in due course, having polished off his first platter of large fresh beautiful Belon and a bit more than his fair share, perhaps, of the rough, bad country wine, he confessed to a fatal homesickness ('I just want to go back to Virginia and grow peanuts!'), whereupon he fell forward at his place and lay there lachrymose amongst the oysters."

Peter paused, then mused, "I think Bill would've kind of liked that, 'lachrymose amongst the oysters.'"

Yes, he certainly would have. He valued Peter as a wordsmith as well as his special friend. Peter went on: "On that homesick first evening, years ago, Bill confessed that he had very little tolerance for change, 'no more resistance to change than a snowflake' is how he put it. I think Bill never lost that snowflake aspect of his being. That fragile, unspoiled quality that made all of us indulge him no matter what. And as we know, that 'what' could be quite something! But if you'll forgive me, we all spoiled him. Everybody but his kids, perhaps, in those years when they were growing up at home. We wanted to spoil him. Why? Was it simply because we recognized instinctively that William Styron was a great artist who needed to air out all that pent-up creativity and therefore required special handling out of our respect for his rare gift? I suppose so. And later on, after we'd spoiled him, it was easier and easier to take no notice, let it go. But that metaphoric snowflake, that delicate undefended sensibility, explains much, I think, about why we always sheltered our old friend and why we loved him."

How that resonated for me.

Should *I* have indulged him as I did?

22

Past Missions
and Moving Forward

ROXBURY: JANUARY

An early poem
teases, but is not
daybreak's song
by the kitchen window
that signals home.
How shall we raise him
how fill his cup . . .

AFTER BILL'S DEATH, I stayed on the Vineyard, writing poems every morning, creating a year's diary of grief and healing noted from the window of our bedroom overlooking the ever-changing harbor. Ferries, sailboats, fishermen, swimmers, gulls, crows, ospreys, on the water. Starlings, cardinals, sparrows, at the lawn feeders. The Vineyard Haven Yacht Club next door was being redesigned with vast solar panels across the long roof. The builders' hammers and voices were a welcome distraction. Fat squirrels climbed the birdfeeders daily. One got himself caught upside down, tail flailing for quite a while. The garden shone till snowfall, with late roses, dahlias, lavender, zinnias. The sun rose farther to the right each dawn and still farther right behind our big hazelnut tree dockside. No house lights shone anywhere except behind and beyond our hedge, at the Hackneys', where my closest friend, Lucy, stayed the year, watching over her daughter Virginia, who died the next summer. Virginia is buried between Bill and, too soon afterward, Virginia's father, southern historian Sheldon Hackney, in the West Chop Cemetery. To my ongoing sorrow, Lucy is at rest beside them. I was blessed that Elizabeth Hackney, their older daughter and our Al's best Vineyard friend, moved into the house, husband Brian and four grown children appearing often through our hedge, our only close winter neighbors. Tragically, as I write this, in February 2022, the splendid historic Hackney house somehow just burned to the ground. Men and women I met on the Hackney porch and lawn—from Alabama, Washington, abroad . . . What a history lost!

Returning briefly to Roxbury in late spring, we scattered a saved part of Bill's ashes across a field we loved, on a hilltop by the dirt strip on Upper County Road, where Bill had walked his series of cherished dogs nearly every day in spring, fall, winter. I had often come along. Polly chose the site and planted Russian lilacs at the field's entrance. She and the Widmarks, Brooke Allen, and Peter Aaron helped me toss Bill's ashes to the welcoming wind one noon. A long chapter of our lives closed there.

Following the memorial services, I went into hibernation on Martha's Vineyard. How I missed Bill and our life together. Surprising memories surfaced during the months following his death. I began thinking back to our meeting in Rome and our trip to Paris that Christmas of 1952 to meet the *Paris Review* friends Bill had made before his Rome Prize would begin. In his "Letter to an Editor" in *PR*'s first issue, he wrote of a writer's duty that "he must go on writing, reflecting disorder, defeat, despair, should that be all he sees at the moment, but ever searching for the elusive love, joy, and hope—qualities which, as in the act of life itself, are best when they have to be struggled for."

I chronicled Bill's last year, his death, and burial in my volume of poems *Fierce Day,* published a few years later. Bill surely struggled more than I did. I could not conjure biblical phrases about God's power and mercy to tease or comfort him with. For the first time, he had wanted me to read and reread my poems to him. I was pleased, grateful. I felt closer to him than ever.

Poetry proved to be a comfort during those painful months. It helped me to know I was alive, to think, to continue to see beauty around me. I retreated from activities I had always enjoyed and saw only family and very few friends. I wanted to be alone with my memories. Poetry from my favorite authors (Keats, Yeats, Dickinson, Hopkins, now Jorie Graham, for instance) helped my grieving. The sadness was enormous. I lived with it a long time.

Unlike my years working for Amnesty, when I stopped writing poems because the suffering of others became central, now I needed to read poetry and to write it. Looking back, I realize that during the years I was on Amnesty missions, I perhaps did not write because I could not allow myself to fully feel what I witnessed and what I learned about the plight of the imprisoned and tortured. It was horrifying, over and over again, in different countries. I had to rein in my emotions in order to write effective journalism about what I now

Amnesty Media Spotlight Awards—Kenneth Cole, Muhammad Ali, Maria Cuomo, Rose, Kerry Kennedy, early '90s.

knew. Often part of my missions was attempting to persuade political leaders and prison chiefs to alleviate the plight of individuals or groups or whole segments of the population. The grief following Bill's death was a separate world. Poetry, as one friend pointed out to me, was a lifeboat, along with the lifeboats of my family, my close friends, and the Vineyard itself.

Bill had loved poetry, but, as I've said, he didn't want to pay attention to mine or talk to me about what I wrote. Until he asked me to read my poems to him a few years before he died. As I've already said, we talked about *his* writing. It was complicated for a little while, but I understood his need for total concentration on what he was going to commit to paper. He didn't focus on what many of his friends were writing, either. Perhaps he was afraid I would take up his time, his focus, his energy. In the beginning I minded, but I got over it. It's interesting to me now that in the '90s, after working with Amnesty for twenty years, I needed to be in the midst of poetry, and I connected first with like-minded poets at Squaw Valley. Following Bill's death, poetry flowed once more. I moved full circle back to my poet self that existed before I met Bill, though its raiments were, of course, different.

Gradually, over a couple of years, I began engaging in activities again. It's a matter of pride, and some disbelief, that the psychiatry department at Mass General Hospital once adopted me as its official poet. It was headed by Jerry Rosenberg and fueled by Maurizio Fava and its star writer-neurologist Alice Flaherty (who best understood and counseled Bill and whose visits kept both of us above sea level for years). They are/were among the cutting-edge physicians whose generosity in time, knowledge, and caring I was fortunate to be a part of.

I spoke at MGH and Johns Hopkins Hospital about Bill's depression and his fifteen-year regeneration that permitted the writing of *Darkness Visible* and *Tidewater Morning*. The process of writing *Darkness* and the top-drawer response to it was certainly healing for Bill, as were his personal connections with the depressed or their loved ones. I tried to convey the ways in which the second crash undid him, including the dramatic change in our lives then, in order to offer medical practitioners, family members, and sufferers of depression's particular personal insights. While it's obvious that each person endures depression differently, my hope was to help others find ways forward by speaking of my experiences with Bill.

One of the best afternoons on our Vineyard lawn was an MGH celebration. The most recent innovations in each sub-field of psychiatry were spelled out to interested Vineyarders, intriguing us all.

In 2008, I received an unexpected gift that surely enhanced my life for the better. Jim Leach, the head of Harvard's Kennedy School Institute of Politics, encouraged me to think about a fellowship, based on conversations we'd had at the JFK Library and during a ride he gave me to Cambridge. I said I had no idea how to teach, but he asked me to send a letter about our conversation on the intersection of art and politics, which I did. I also, at his request, went back to Harvard from the Vineyard to talk with a student committee that had read my letter as if it were a proposal. I suspect its members were the brightest and most committed of Harvard's undergraduates who one day might seek political leadership. The committee helped to choose future fellows at the Kennedy School. The Institute of Politics was the one division that accepted dedicated undergraduates who did not seek credit. The students asked me questions that sparked my thinking, my memory, my imagination.

I felt it would be fun to be more closely connected. Jim asked me to apply formally. Shy, I did not. But in the fall, Eric Anderson, the IOP program director I had liked so much on my spring trips, called and asked me to reconsider, to send a brief proposal including suggested topics for eight to ten study group sessions, half or more with guests. Not really wanting to keep going to New York for board meetings or face sympathetic friends and colleagues or travel to Connecticut to enter our lifetime home alone each night, I agreed, pretty sure nothing would come of it.

In November, Eric asked me to come up to meet a few students on the committee and the new IOP director, southerner Bill Purcell, who until recently had been the popular mayor of Nashville. I enjoyed that day immensely, and Bill Purcell phoned me in early December to say they wanted me to teach in the spring term of 2009. He and I became frequent dinner companions when his wife was busy at home in Tennessee, and truly good friends. He always says that I answered his first phone call by saying, "You're making a big mistake!" I don't remember, but I don't doubt it. I rarely censor my thoughts before speaking.

In late January 2009, I arrived at a comfortable apartment provided by the IOP. Five "Spring Fellows" had identical ones in two small new buildings next to each other on Grant Street in Cambridge. A sixth was reserved for a part-time fellow or two, or Washington exiles spending a few weeks teaching. It was at most a ten-minute walk to my grand office, next to Eric's, overlooking JFK Street. I found it hard to write. Mainly I think I chatted with smart, friendly staff, lively visitors, and a famous pundit or two and received wonderful students who signed up for my posted office hours or just dropped by. Intellectually substantive lunches and dinners supplemented the exceptional public forum events across the hall. Everyone involved was interesting. Some made me talk about myself, which I was most reluctant to do, but soon realized it had to be a component of my prize. Forgotten tales emerged willy-nilly, sudden portraits of the players well known to our generation, though not often familiar to the students.

Then I wrote a formal outline of what I would teach: the influence of writers on public policy and political leaders' influence on the engaged writer, from Thucydides to Émile Zola, Jefferson to Obama. I met with the key students, confessing I'd never taught before and asking if they'd like to comment or offer advice. One said, "Cut the history. We get that in all our courses." Another said, "How about including other artists and lots of guests from drama and film and music and painting?" I definitely cheered up and agreed. This would be fun. I could invite some creative friends who had helped move lawmakers to change society in one way or another. Harvard would put them up at the perfect Charles Hotel almost next door, and pay for intimate dinners that I would arrange between guests and students. I was also given six special student liaisons (who had chosen me) to help me prepare for the Tuesday afternoon study group titled Art and Politics. They were terrific: Tyler, Rachel, Eva, Kostya, Obi, and Chase (the last three, guys from Russia, Nigeria, and China). I felt each was becoming a real friend. Tyler Brandon remains in my life like a fourth daughter. Chase Hu still contacts me—most recently about his wedding.

I accepted invitations to join them and other IOP student officers whenever I could. I went with student leaders Kenzi and Taylor to Club Passim, where my friend Joan Baez first performed under the auspices of Joyce Chopra, my Roxbury neighbor who had been a Harvard senior then. I played pub trivia at Saunders Theatre, almost never living up to their expectations for my answers. I talked about my human rights adventures to student advocacy groups. (Unlike many campuses, Harvard did not have an Amnesty International chapter.) My students even arranged for me to speak to eleven-year-olds at a charter school and to seniors at Boston Latin. It was a pleasure, day after day, for four months.

A warm late spring with its sailors and rowers along the Charles was also serendipitous. So was coffee with Drew Gilpin Faust, Harvard's splendid new president. I'd been riveted by her moving book *The Republic of Suffering* and hoped to discuss it with her. I had long heard about Drew, the Virginia family rebel, from her close cousin, actor/minister Connecticut neighbor and pal Jack Gilpin. Her elegant Virginia family teased her by calling her Ben Franklin. I was told it was because of her round glasses, her haircut, the clothes she wore, and her intellectual proclivities. Drew did not enlighten me literarily but graciously asked about my course, Art and Politics. By then, after my modest solo sessions, a number of friends I'd invited to converse with my study group spoke on public platforms across the building, with audiences often in the hundreds: Mike Nichols, Gerry Adams, and Ken Burns perhaps impressing them most. Poet Jorie Graham, who had succeeded Seamus Heaney as Harvard's top poetry professor, had the study group spellbound. Mia Farrow and son Ronan Farrow were especially popular too. Drew was promoting the arts, and soon added requirements of community service for each Harvard student. It was an exciting time for the university, as well as for me.

One week Rory Stewart, the thirty-seven-year-old British genius who had walked across Afghanistan, founded a native village organization there, and had written a first-rate book about it, began attending my study group. He had recently been appointed head of the Kennedy School's Carr Center for Human Rights Policy—taking over for Samantha Power, who'd gone to Washington to serve on Obama's national security team, and Michael Ignatieff, who'd gone to Canada to lead its Labour Party. Rory invited me to be a fellow for the 2009–2010 academic year at the Carr Center. I think he particularly liked guest conversationalists: Peter Matthiessen, Charlayne Hunter-Gault, Carlos Fuentes, Sergio Ramirez, Bill Luers, Jorie, Gerry, Ward Just, and surely Mike Nichols, whose announced appearance necessitated two moves to larger venues as attendance swelled.

Neither Sting nor Frank McCourt, scheduled late in the semester, actually made it for medical reasons, nor did the painter Shepard Fairey, who had been arrested for creating unsolicited poster art on a Boston building. Famous for his ubiquitous image of Obama, he had mounted a vivid retrospective at Boston's Institute of Contemporary Art, much of it protesting tyranny.

Gerry Adams came last to speak to my students, after attending a St. Patrick's Day reception in the Obama White House. At an impromptu Boston Harbor breakfast, as I mentioned earlier, he read me three of his poems in Gaelic, then translated them. I was pleased he'd agreed to be my guest, curious about what he'd say. He gave an extraordinary talk on how he began writing—and thinking through his strategy for negotiating with the British—when he was in prison, not much older than my students. He concluded with a searing ballad Bobby Sands wrote in his H Block cell not long before he died on his famous hunger strike in 1981.

After class, Gerry spoke at the Kennedy School Forum. Just a week earlier, a militant IRA splinter group had killed two British soldiers and a policeman in Northern Ireland. Informed people had voiced their worry that the Troubles might return. But Gerry assured us, "Let there be no equivocation, ambiguity, ambivalence about this. If anybody is concerned that this is the start of the Troubles again, that we're going to slip back into war again, that will not happen. Be sure of that." The fringe IRA would not be tolerated. He was right.

I thought back to when a fierier Gerry Adams had spoken at the forum for the first time fifteen years earlier. I heard he'd had to sneak in the back door for security reasons then, a blanket over his head. Many people (most vocally the president of Boston University) still considered him a terrorist. Now he was being feted as a man of peace and international stature. Both he and the impressive Martin McGuinness traveled the world, helping to negotiate peace in conflicts probably as long-standing and entrenched as the Catholic-Protestant one in Northern Ireland once was. Both were elected to high offices in a more united Ireland. Later that year, I sat between them at Ted Kennedy's Boston memorial.

As part of my second Harvard fellowship year at the Carr Center (where I really missed the anticipated leadership of Rory Stewart, who'd decamped to run for office abroad), I invited Sting's wife, Trudie Styler, to discuss her film about Tiananmen Square, *Moving the Mountain*. I'd first met Trudie when I was part of Sting's Rainforest board (she'd recently become a clothes-shopping companion in Bergdorf's cheaper upstairs corridors, enjoyably). The film was shown across JFK Street at the Kirkus House, where I frequently dined. My hope was that Li Lu would introduce the film, but he was busy leading Warren Buffett through the China he had sworn never to return to. The screening was a gratifying success. The students' positive response was audible, perhaps bringing the reality of Tiananmen Square and the courageous Chinese students into their Harvard consciousness. My Wellesley experience, learning about Yenching University's students' plight, returned to haunt me.

Before I went back to the Vineyard, I spent a few Saturday hours at Wellesley for its reunion weekend, which brought me back to the reunion I'd attended when Bill frantically called asking me to return to Roxbury as he spiraled into his treacherous depression. The only classmate I knew who would be attending the 2010 reunion was my Baltimore pal Kitty Lou Dandy Gladstone. She'd enlisted me as speaker and advisor years earlier when she started a Peace and Justice program at Wellesley. Now Peace and Justice had morphed into a course major, sparked by inspiring professor and minister Victor Kanzanjian, who invited me to speak to his students. He had recently hired the program's first full-time professor. Kitty Lou and my class raised money annually to fund the program. I looked forward to its 9:00 a.m. meeting, hearing the experiences of its recent award recipients, especially those from abroad. We walked through the glorious but sweltering arboretum in bloom, and I remembered this was why I'd chosen to attend Wellesley: for the beauty of its campus, which I'd continually inhaled during my student years.

Today, Wellesley's still all-female student body is much more diverse in backgrounds racial and geographic, as well as interests. They are more politically motivated and publicly engaged than my classmates were. Do any of the students spend half as many hours playing bridge on the floor at night, avoiding earliest classes, and sprinting to Harvard as we did? I sincerely doubt it.

In the half century since college and marriage, it never occurred to me I'd return to academia, even for a while. Mildred McAfee Horton, once head of the WACS in World War II, welcomed me to Wellesley; Drew Gilpin Faust welcomed me to Harvard. Both were exceptional presidents and women. After fully enjoying the stimulating experiences with my Harvard students, I developed a new understanding of why so many of my Vineyard pals teach. How often I regret I am not qualified for a full appointment. I confess to being jealous of my friends Geraldine Brooks, Jorie Graham, and Peter Sacks, among others, even with their online class struggles during the pandemic. Today I regret not having attended storied law school classes taught by Laurence Tribe, as I did the extraordinary poetry classes by Peter Sacks in my fellowship years. I often wish I had become a teacher, though I never regret where the path I *did* choose took me.

23

Selling Roxbury,
Life on the Vineyard Full-Time

I WAS NOT HAPPY being in the Roxbury house without Bill and the children. After Bill's death, I spent a lot of time on the Vineyard and stayed in Cambridge for most of the two years at Harvard for my fellowships. It didn't occur to me that I could keep the house. I loved every corner of it. It was full of memories. If I'd had a partner or a kid who wanted to live there, I never would have sold it. But to be there by myself made no sense. Before I put the house on the market I contacted the Mark Twain House in Hartford about their acquiring it, and I was in touch with Yale about the university using it for faculty and graduate student housing, and possibly hosting lectures and outdoor theater performances there, as they'd done in the past. If Yale had worked out, I would have stayed. But it didn't.

We had lived in the house since 1954, most of my adult life. I still miss our huge high-ceilinged living room that I designed a few years after we moved in, with its floor-to-ceiling bookcases on the fireplace wall, a built-in windowed plant area, and the floor-to-ceiling glass doors that opened onto a terrace on the back side of the old house. We lived in that room. Arthur Miller built stairs up to the little balcony. We had my mother's baby grand there. Aside from Lenny

Bernstein, there were other stellar pianists who'd played it from time to time (when I remembered to have it tuned). The piano was in one corner and a bar in the other.

Often I think of Bill sitting at that bar at the end of the day, reading over what he wrote and pouring his first drink as he awaited dinner with me and possibly friends. I miss the pond at the end of the pine-shaded path across the unpaved road, and the tennis court. I miss the walkways into the woods. We put in a big pool in our backyard. I spent hours there almost daily, exercising, and using its heated extension under the old toolshed. Poppies, iris, peonies, and roses bloomed in the garden after the hundreds of daffodils came up each year from the bulbs my mother sent to me from Holland. I would fling them helter-skelter down the long green lawn that sloped downhill. How I miss being with my children when they were very young: Polly and Susanna rolling down the lawn among the daffodils; Tommy riding his little red go-cart on the narrow path at the bottom of the lawn below the yellow blooms; and later, Alexandra trotting on her pony in the Carlsons' field below.

These are my happiest memories—being a mom, growing with them, sharing their new passions and playmates and glowing in their accomplishments, their kindness, compassion, moral fiber. I thought myself the luckiest mother in the world. Sometimes I think of the blossoming grape arbor between our house and Bill's studio. And the Norway maple outside the kitchen window, reputedly the largest in Litchfield County. It had been struck by lightning, half of it falling on the house and crushing a piece of the roof, but, against advice, I refused to cut it down. It bonsaied itself to live and shelter us for another decade, at least.

For some reason, I was obsessed with wallpaper in early Roxbury days, although I honored the plain white walls in the two living rooms. The dining room, kitchen, and stairways up to the bedrooms and the bedrooms themselves sported floral, scenic, or subtly patterned wallpaper that I bought repeatedly when visiting New York showrooms after museum excursions with friends. I particularly loved one single large panel of a white unicorn in its green garden, which our kitchen table pushed up against. I wish I could find a photo I took of Yevtushenko resting his head against it.

I'm content here on Martha's Vineyard. I don't think about Roxbury often, but when I do, I of course recollect my friends there as well as the house. None of the longtime Roxbury pals of our generation are still alive. There are a few special friends nearby, a bit younger than I, still at home in Bridgewater and Washington—Mia, and the Luers, who were always part-time but have been living in their splendid country home through the pandemic. I still speak at length on the phone with Mia and we reminisce. She was the closest to Bill of any woman, I believe. She was invaluable as my pal when I had to pack up the house, helping physically on long summer days. She recently reminded me and sent wonderful photos via email.

I was surprised and disappointed that there were no offers on the house for several years, so I took half the asking price when a couple from New York said they both so admired Bill's work and would be honored to be in his home and surroundings. Our children needed the money, shared chiefly in Bill's and my wills.

I sold it in July, and the day after we signed, I asked if I could wait until September to move everything out of the house, since I was going back to the Vineyard promptly. I suggested they enjoy Bill's extensive library, our special Italian-designed dining table, even a brand-new king-sized bed. I proposed that by Labor Day we would choose what to keep, what to give them, what to sell. I thought the new owners would be pleased, hearing how much they admired my husband's work and valued living in his home. That was not the case. They said they wanted everything out of the house within a week or two. Now I realize I should have made the arrangements before we closed, and wish my Realtor had clarified everything with me at the time. I was unhappy about the arrangement but legally had no choice.

So Polly, my assistant Christina, her family, and her friend Caroline stayed with me for a week, going through the attics with the stacks and closets full of my mother's, the children's, our family's papers. To say nothing of my own past writings. The kids' childhood objects were all there: ski equipment, ice skates, roller skates, first sports teams' uniforms. There was a separate closet filled with my silk and organza dresses that I wore to formal New York and Washington occasions (mice, I discovered, had made colorful nests in some). Christina took many dresses to the dry cleaners and then my granddaughters and daughters selected what they wanted. I donated daytime outfits to Equality Now, which raised money for women in trouble, and hoped some of the women could wear them as they applied for jobs. A selection of the dresses, such as a beautiful black-and-white gown I wore to Kay Graham's and Truman Capote's Black and White Ball, went to a vintage shop in Washington.

After the family selected their most treasured books, the rest were packed up and sent to the Strand Bookstore. I confess I kept more than a hundred of my favorites and those by our writer friends along with Bill's myriad translations that now crowd the bookcases and floors in my much smaller Vineyard home. I hope, still, some foreign-language libraries will house them. (Any offers?)

When the frantic packing and moving was over, I found myself thinking of the different houseguests who stayed with us in our main house and the Little House during our Roxbury years. The *Paris Review* guys visited us, often staying in both houses. Ralph Ellison and his wife, Fanny, came to stay with us in the main house and we had such an enjoyable visit that Ralph said they wanted to look for a house to buy in Roxbury. I called the real estate broker who had sold us our house and asked if he could find a dwelling nearby for our friend, who I explained was a prominent Black writer. He said yes of course. Malcolm Bray picked up Ralph and Fanny, who left their dog with son Tommy to look after. They disappeared for many hours, which gave Bill and me hope that they had found a house in the neighborhood. When Malcolm dropped them off in our driveway, Ralph was in a terrible mood, came in, collected his dog, and he and Fanny went to their car. Bill followed hastily and asked what was wrong. Ralph said, "Your real estate agent took us to a town more than an hour away, which he deemed 'suitable.' He would show us nothing in Roxbury. I'm never coming back." The next Sunday when I entered the Episcopal church, people on opposite sides of the aisle were arguing about whether they should drive the real estate agent out of Roxbury because of his treatment of the Ellisons. Very soon Mr. Bray was gone. We were not sad about that, but we were about Ralph and Fanny.

I do not miss the kids' things, my papers, the clothes, the full attic, the basement Ping-Pong table that (after the kids grew up) I piled high with everything I was not using. Now it's actually funny to remember the mice that nested in the Roxbury closets, repeatedly eating through many of the electrical wires. Bill was not amused at the time.

The silver lining of the move: I like living simply. (Though I realize, often in despair, that I still don't want to take the time to sort through and throw out old things. I seem to use my time barreling forward.) Years ago a truck arrived from Colorado to pick up all my Amnesty and related human rights papers in Connecticut: the tape recordings, the many folders of meetings and missions. They were driven to Amnesty's archives at the University of Colorado in Boulder, and later moved with all the Amnesty archives to Columbia University. I've never been there to look at it all. I've wondered if they've digitized my materials or possibly abandoned them. I'm glad that the Schlesinger Library at Radcliffe will at some point house all my remaining papers.

Nearly all of Bill's papers are at Duke University. We are in the process of raising money for a William Styron Writer's Prize to be given there, and soon a stipend for a visiting Styron professor. A ceremony in October 2022 at Duke, launched by the Bostock Library and involving the Rubenstein Library, where Bill's papers reside, was very special. I was amazed to see among Bill's papers—so marvelously set out for me on the afternoon tour by Robin Rosenberg, who flew down and led me through the pages—Bill's teenage writings his father must have sent, and the childish handwriting that preceded his beautiful adult script.

Throughout our Vineyard years, lots of writers came to visit and spend a few days with us on High Hedge Lane as well. Philip Roth stayed with us a couple of times with different girlfriends and wives. He treated us to his singular wit at more than one hilarious dinner chez Styron. The last time, he arrived with Claire Bloom, which didn't go so well. They parted soon afterward. When I opened the new issue of the *Paris Review* recently, I recalled reading the "over the transom" (as we called them), unsolicited manuscripts submitted to George in the early *PR* days. Philip had sent in the only two stories I enthusiastically recommended to George, who published them promptly. Phil credited me with "discovering" him, although within a year a national magazine printed another story, and he was off to writing *Portnoy's Complaint.*

As a child, I had total faith in the American government. Having grown up during World War II, a champion of the Marshall Plan, I assumed that is the way we Americans would always behave toward those people less fortunate than us. In the Trump era I experienced the diminution of not only my trust in our government but our global position. I remember being quite undone in my early Amnesty days, going into countries where there were tyrants and no democracy, trying as an American to help people who had fallen prey to such extremism, even though I realized in Chile, in my 1974 awakening, that the United States did in fact support tyranny and encourage it if it strengthened our financial and political interests.

My admired friend Bill Luers, after years of hard work, led the devising of a successful policy for our moving forward with Iran. Unfortunately the political complications of that agreement have recently been challenged. Now I worry about Afghan citizens who helped us maintain peace while our troops were there, and I am desperately concerned about the women whose hard-earned status has been summarily taken away, their education, careers, and independence apparently soon to be gone. Our greatest current worry is Ukraine. What will Putin and tomorrow bring? A world at war again in my lifetime?

Sometimes I walk to the West Chop Cemetery and wonder what Bill, Mike Wallace, Sheldon Hackney, and Art Buchwald are saying to each other about the political situation today. I miss their insights, their company. There are days when I'm struck with nostalgia, wishing they could reappear.

On my fridge I have a picture of my three favorite guys in stylish suits, smiling: Bill, Mike Nichols, Peter Matthiessen. I don't remember where they were or what they were doing when the photograph was taken. While memories of many of my pals come and go, Bill, Peter, and Mike are always nearby. Bill is of course my eternal loss. It occurs to me that Peter was my longest-standing guy friend (sixty-two years, we noted cheerfully as 2014 began). He was a cohort, inventing one extraordinary adventure after another, leading me into wildlife and into his Zendo and his mesmerizing books. Bill, too, came to regard Peter as his best pal. We three (I'm smiling) even shared each other's honeymoons in Italy and Venezuela.

Peter's moving last book, *In Paradise,* came out three days after his death. He was at home in Sagaponack with Maria. I read it in galleys and talked with him about it by phone, but I regret I did not hurry to write to him in depth or insist on visiting. I am ever slow to make choices or consider intruding, always Victor's scarlet tanager, putting off decisions like Scarlett O'Hara.

I was moved when Terry Malick showed me the excellent rushes of Peter for his film *Knight of Cups* when I visited Terry and Ecky in Austin at the end of my last book tour. I was staying with the Malicks, and mentioned that Peter had confided in me that he hoped he could see some footage "but might not have much time left." Terry promptly made a DVD to send. The film was begun not much more than a year before. Alas, it did not arrive in time.

The landscapes Peter and I shared, from Europe and Africa through Asia and the Americas and at sea in the Mediterranean and Caribbean, stream through my memory now, on this sunny day on the island, with news of the Arctic melting. A migratory snowy owl is perched on our dock. Sixteen robins have flown into the large seaside tree that months ago held a murder of crows day after day, munching and spitting out late crabapples from the smaller, shapely tree across the lawn. I was surprised to see two dozen mallards swim near the beach, escorted by a flock of resident eiders. Every April a pair of mallards who adopted us five or six springs ago (Pete and Re-Pete, my kids named them) return to rattle our birdfeeder before the front porch. Each year, Mom Mallard prepares her nest under our dock, protected fiercely by her staunch mate. I watch cheering when the babies flap their wings, dive, and follow her across the water.

My friendship with Peter was literary, social, political. Not romantic. Though we were on an island together once and were tempted, we decided we were both devoted to our spouses and should keep our friendship as it had long been. He and Bill and I were happy together, particularly after Peter married Maria.

In addition to the wildlife trips Peter and I went on together, I joined him as he worked hard to get Leonard Peltier freed from prison. Peter thought that on Bill Clinton's last day in office, Peltier would surely be among the people he pardoned. Peter constantly went out to see Leonard, and he had already bought a ticket to meet him, expecting the release. But Leonard got stiffed by the FBI because two of their guys who were involved in shooting Native Americans on the Pine Ridge Indian Reservation in South Dakota were shot and killed, and the FBI claimed that Peltier was responsible. Leonard had been in charge of the whole place when it happened, so he was accused, tried, and convicted—though he hadn't done it. Someone else did and apparently eventually confessed. It didn't matter. The FBI threatened Clinton: If he pardoned Peltier on his last day in office, they would find a way to accuse him of more than the reputed misbehavior with Monica Lewinsky. So that was the end of the pardon. Today we hope President Biden will rescue Leonard, who is recovering from a severe case of Covid. I stay only tangentially in touch with Leonard, recently through messages via an active writer-advocate.

Mike Nichols and I had long-term fun, we had friends in common, we had our word games together, and he came up to Cambridge because he was interested in my teaching at Harvard. I so admired him as a director of captivating plays and films, and still listen to my old records he and Elaine May made together. Our friendship was social. As far as I know Bill never was jealous of Mike and Peter. He had his own "guy relationship" with each of them.

What I remember best about the summer I first met Mike is that he, Lenny Bernstein, Bill, and I played anagrams a lot, usually after I took up a rug from the living room floor. Mike and I also played word games that we made up, just him and me. Sometimes we wrote them down on paper, sometimes we played them in the air on the dock. We had such a good time together. At one point he even playfully suggested that I run away with him and leave Bill, who kept going back to work.

The next year he married Margo and brought her to the Vineyard. When Mike and I played tennis, often doubles, occasionally singles, Margo would stand on the side, beautifully dressed, wearing gloves, keeping score, raising her hand to show who had made the last point. It was bizarre and charming. A year or so later she had their baby, the adorable Daisy. Someone said she tried to stab Mike right after that. Surely they had a terrific quarrel. They didn't stay together long. Margo and Daisy went to live in France and Mike paid for the two to come back annually so he would have Daisy with him for at least a little while every summer. And Margo could go off and do whatever she wanted to.

Then Annabel Davis-Goff came into Mike's life. He visited us on Rucum Road and asked me to help him find a house. I got a real estate agent (not Malcolm Bray as I did for Ralph) and we went through Roxbury and the neighboring town of Bridgewater together. There we entered a spacious run-down country dwelling on the water. It was the end of January. When we opened the door we were smitten by the heat, which was set at ninety degrees. The couple had apparently turned it up and then left after they'd had a fight on Christmas Eve, a month earlier. They had thrown the lipsticks, rouge, and foundations from the wife's upscale cosmetic company at each other. Melted red marks were smeared all over the purple flowered wallpaper that complemented the purple Naugahyde chairs, purple couches, purple rug, and lacy window coverings in the downstairs living room. Mike and I had a good laugh at the scene. I advised him not to buy the house. He ignored me, as Kay had, and promptly bought it, turning it into a pristine, charming, purpleless welcoming home.

Mike built stables for his white Arabian horses. I understand that he rode daily. He said he had been some sort of jockey when he was young. His Hollywood and New York friends would come, and he'd invite them to ride or to watch. Then he would invite me over to keep them company. Warren Beatty and Buck Henry, for instance. We'd lean on the fence outside to watch the horsemen together. It was a lot of fun. Warren became a special friend.

When Mike wanted to marry Annabel and needed a divorce, he asked me to testify in court to his admirable behavior since he and Margo had parted company, and he wanted me to say there was never anyone else in his life. I agreed to. I sat in the first row at the small courthouse in Litchfield, the county seat. There was a full Litchfield audience. Margo came in from the right, tall, striking, dressed in a chic suit with a wide skirt and high heels. She was with an even taller imposing lawyer from New York.

Mike, a bit plump at the time, came in from the left, wearing a Chinese jacket with a high round neck and brass buttons all the way down the front (very popular that season). Following him was a thin, black-haired, short lawyer from Waterbury. The lawyer was dressed identically, brass buttons shining. I burst out laughing but then tried to keep quiet as the scene progressed. I was not needed as a witness. The judge and the entire audience were in favor of Mike. The judge pronounced them divorced and said Mike didn't have to pay Margo a nickel, but Mike was so embarrassed by this that he paid her a lot anyway, with the proviso that she bring or send Daisy for many succeeding years. He married Annabel and they had two terrific kids, Max and Jenny, whom I don't see often enough now.

Then, years later, the kids grown, he fell for Diane Sawyer and divorced Annabel, who became a valued teacher at Bennington. I never saw Mike as happy, as calm, and as productive as he was with Diane, perhaps the happiest he'd ever been, for the rest of his life, as Teddy had been with Vicki. I don't recall even the slightest reprise of his depression during those years. He and Diane got married at a church in Edgartown, and they both wanted Bill and me and Carly Simon and her new husband, Jim, to renew our vows with them. Bill and I had never done that in church. Diane made beautiful wreaths to circle her hair and for Carly's and mine. We all got married (us again) and went out to dinner afterward.

Bill and I would have a wonderful time when Mike and Diane came up to the Vineyard in the summers. They bought a spectacular property called Chip Chop, and we had many small dinners with them there, often playing a complicated game of Dictionary we loved. On the eve of the twenty-first century, the four of us had supper at our house, and we each wrote down all of our hopes for the new century.

Diane put them in some kind of tubular container and buried them outside under tree roots. Neither Diane nor I can remember where. I checked under the roots of a battered tree taken down near our kitchen, but no luck. Maybe some great-great-grandchild will come upon it.

Mike used to come over a lot in Roxbury. He and Ken Burns came at the same time at least once and talked (I listened) instinctively about film. In much earlier days, Mike and neighbor Lew Allen went up to another town in northern Connecticut to see what was apparently a lousy production of *Annie*. They decided they could do a really good musical, and took it over. That was the start of many early runs of *Annie*, which I saw the first productions of as they were preparing for Broadway. A few years into its Broadway success, Alexandra actually tried out to replace a star Annie, but though she was a good actress (how I cheered from the bleachers), her voice was not a superbly trained one.

Lillian Hellman adored Mike and he respected and valued her. She saw him through his girlfriends, even traveling with the couples from time to time. But I gather from a guest at Mike and Annabel's wedding that Lillian's nose was pretty out of joint. Once when Bill and I and Mike and a girlfriend had sailed from a Caribbean isle, planning a week's jaunt, Lillian called Mike and persuaded him to come back to the island we had just left and wait for her to join us. We did. She did. A storm came up. We never left the island port and a grumbling captain managed to eat most of the good food. Lil was smart, a great hostess, often lots of fun and (as I've said) lots of trouble.

When Mike came to meet with my class at Harvard, I recounted a story I thought would amuse him after many years. Bill and I, Jim Jones and his wife, Moss (Gloria), came into the city to see *Who's Afraid of Virginia Woolf?* We were up front in prime seats, and after the first act Bill and Jim left to go off for a drink, never to return. Moss and I stayed, both of us enthusiastic about the play. At Harvard, Mike seemed not to think that was funny at all. I wasn't okay with Bill and Jim's boys-will-be-boys exit, but I guess the wives of writers were expected to have thick skins, to placate on behalf of our spouses. I believe things have changed.

The last time I saw Mike was when he gave a whole program devoted to *The Graduate* at the Martha's Vineyard Film Center. He and Richard Paradise, the founder of our fine film center, talked back and forth onstage. Mike charmed us when he spoke about his casting indecisions before choosing unheralded Dustin Hoffman, whom he'd seen off-Broadway playing a transvestite Russian fishwife. He added that there was never a question about casting Mrs. Robinson. It had to be Anne ("Annie") Bancroft. The *Martha's Vineyard Times* quoted Mike describing her as "all the things that arouse the senses and give you hours of joy and kill you slowly."

Mike looked thin. He hadn't been out in public for a long while, but he recounted many funny events. Everyone was laughing. When he couldn't remember the name of the person or place he was talking about, he would point to Diane in the first row, and she would prompt him. How I wish I had a Diane to prompt me as I try to recall the name of someone I'm reminiscing about at a dinner table these days!

I knew Mike was not well, but I didn't know how sick he was. I realize as I write this that my response perhaps echoed my willful disbelief about Peter's and Bill's deaths. Maybe I just couldn't bear to let go of the men I loved most. Soon after that special evening, Mike died.

As I reflect on my relationships with others my age, I am faced with so many who are no longer around. The girls I was so happily close to in Baltimore, for instance. My Roxbury pals Jay Allen, Jean Widmark, Inge Morath are gone too. And Mary Wallace, Lucy Hackney, Kay Graham, to whom I was closest on Martha's Vineyard. But girlfriends (long-term and short-) keep me enjoying life still.

The women whom I became really close to for the first time during the pandemic are widowed, divorced, or single, mostly writers, artists, musicians, and fine filmmakers. And activists, some actually neighbors. We are in different stages in our lives of recovery and reshaping. We each push forward in different ways. Our conversations are intimate. We talk about childhoods, how we feel now, what we felt in the past.

After visiting Sundance a couple of times in recent Januarys and heading to Los Angeles and the Palm Springs Valley for the Rancho Mirage Writers Festival, I totally enjoyed time with my special West Coast girlfriends Nancy Rubin, Aileen Adams, and Mathea Falco, who, married, came to play with me on the Vineyard in pre-Covid summer.

Belatedly, then, I am attached to women friends, for fun and comfort. One-on-one, we reveal new and often surprising insights into each other and ourselves. It's a plus of aging, an even bigger plus for those of us aging solo. Often I think we're revealing long-kept secrets. Privacy and protection seem so much less necessary now. Besides, telling stories often long buried—and hearing them—is rewarding.

My life is so different from my decades as WIFE. I am still plagued by my ancient upbringing, in which wives took care of husbands, not assuming we could go to starry events without our spouses. It was a couples' culture.

I still attend and host lots of events. Of course I welcome visits from my children and grandchildren, who take turns living across the lawn and in my one guest room. People stop by while I'm on my porch (often trying to write this memoir), and I enjoy their local news, their company, their fresh outlooks on national and international politics, reports on birds they've seen on the island, their advice about books to read, movies to watch, people to pay attention to. I know at my age how lucky I am.

Before the pandemic, Mia Farrow and I had a few afternoons alone on her lovely property. No spouses or kids. We sat quietly by the lake, reminiscing. A confirmed activist by then, not acting very often, she was usually just back from Sudan or Chad via UNICEF expeditions on behalf of human rights. She had often taken her brilliant youngest son, Ronan, along. I found myself thinking about the dinner party at our house when she met Philip Roth and Václav Havel, who both promptly fell in love with her. She had been dressed in a special leather outfit and gold earrings. Philip and Václav were smitten. Mia had long liaisons with both, longer with Philip. I advised her not to marry him, having known details of his life with previous girlfriends and wives. She was with Philip I believe until he died, and, perhaps more than fifteen years ago, saw Václav until he married in Prague.

During my visits with Mia, I found myself thinking about her Bridgewater house as a miracle. We inspected every absent child's room. They were shrines, really. Today two of her sons and their children are in residence on the property. We visit too rarely. In a recent phone call, Mia told me she bought a little house in Roxbury near where we lived so she could have a small place entirely her own, by a stream, and give the children her big house, which she can visit or move back into whenever she wants. Carly Simon and I miss the frequent summer visits she used to pay us on the Vineyard.

Unfortunately I haven't seen Carly this year. She had some leg problems and was less mobile and even more Covid-protective than some of us. And I never went to swim at her welcoming pool where we might possibly have visited. I hear she has designed and put up original wallpaper with her own floral patterns around her house. Could the wallpaper be as beautiful as her uniquely designed silk scarves I wear? My Roxbury wallpaper penchant resurfaces . . .

Carly and I met each other when Bill and I first came to Martha's Vineyard in the early '6os. Bill had known James Taylor's father in the South, and Carly and I were introduced when she was engaged to James. After James's parents were divorced, his mother, whom everyone adored, lived alone on the Vineyard and traveled happily for decades. Carly's mother imported a very attractive young lover who lived at home with her and her three growing daughters. It was complicated. Carly and I got to be friends, James and I got to be friends, and Bill was friends with each. Bill and I saw Carly often when she was married to James. After their split, we enjoyed her partners Jim Hart and Richard Kohler. James remained our valued friend. For a short time, James and his next wife were our Roxbury neighbors. Carly is a much more frequent companion who continues to live on our island, but I delight in seeing James occasionally from afar. I am so sad for Carly this winter: she lost both sisters, a week apart.

A few years ago, Carly Simon published a book about her friendship with Jackie Kennedy. Daughter Susanna was recently looking at the signed copy Carly gave to me and was startled by some notes on the Styrons. Even I was startled. It made me think back to encounters of my own with Jackie, whom I was surely not as close to as Carly was.

Carly's memoir brings back my experience of standing at the edge of Squibnocket Pond nearest the ocean. It was Memorial Day 1994. I was looking down at deer tracks, crab tracks, when a noise from the sky took my gaze to the far side of the pond. The sand, sunlit at seven, was cool beneath my feet, bared for the year's first visit to the beach at Gay Head, quite a ways across from Jackie's house. Flying over the center chimney of Jackie's home and heading directly for me, flapping its great wings, was a pure white swan. It landed and settled briefly three feet away on the unsettled water, ruffled its feathers, rose up again, and started back. I had this crazy, overwhelming feeling that it was Jackie, or Jackie's messenger from the realm of her endless, superior imagination.

The last time Jackie and I were together, we were leaving for our separate winters, she to New York City and I to Roxbury, knowing that we might see each other on some special occasion and doubtless keep track through the close friendship of our daughters Caroline and Alexandra, but basically saying goodbye for the season.

"Damn," I remember having uttered then, "I never made it up-island for my kayak lesson."

"Next summer, first thing," Jackie replied.

I confessed to her that I had stolen a book from her library shelf during her annual Labor Day picnic. Robert Hass's *Earthly Pleasures*. I promised to return it as soon as I got to Connecticut and my own copy.

"Just bring it next summer," she said, and smiled.

I'd mailed the book back to Jackie months later and received a prompt note of thanks on her thin blue paper. "Next summer: earthly pleasures?" It must have been written shortly before she died.

On top of the stack of books I started sorting through is Thomas Christopher's *In Search of Lost Roses*, which Jackie had inscribed and given to me. The quote on the cover begins, "through ghost towns, graveyards, wilderness . . ." Like most of her friends, except the closest—I wish I could claim to be among them—I had no idea how soon this quote would seem fateful. The art of losing *is* hard to master. At my age I am trying to, but it takes its toll.

24

Vineyard Celebrations

I REALIZE THAT I'VE ONLY really lived in three homes in over nine decades: my childhood family home in Baltimore, my married family homes in Roxbury and Vineyard Haven, with brief dwelling places in Rome, Ravello, New York City, Long Island, Cambridge. Elizabeth Bishop's poem "One Art" rings true when she says,

> *I lost my mother's watch. And look! my last, or*
> *next-to-last, of three loved houses went.*
> *The art of losing isn't hard to master.*
>
> *I lost two cities, lovely ones. And, vaster,*
> *some realms I owned, two rivers, a continent.*
> *I miss them, but it wasn't a disaster.*

She was right on the mark, losing it all wasn't a disaster. Though in the final moments of the Roxbury home it felt like one. Christina arranged a surprise party after the sale. About a dozen people attended. Mia came with Ronan. Months later, I found out that the new owners didn't preserve anything in the house. I also learned they had three or four other residences in the United States and abroad. Bill's home was not as precious to them as I was led to believe. They refused to let me leave even a plaque near Bill's study door, just as Ellen McCourt had placed one on Frank's outdoor work spot.

I like having my mother's desk and dining table and my grandmother's breakfront overfilled with china here in Vineyard Haven. Every so often I glance at the breakfront and remember crawling toward it, pulling myself up on its leg, staring at the dishes through the glass door, turning, and taking my first steps toward my father's outstretched arms. My mother's long, narrow dining table has four leaves and fits perfectly here. If I use the kitchen chairs to supplement the eight unpainted larger ones purchased from Bloomingdale's countless years ago, I can have fourteen around the table, which I last did when the family gathered for supper on a windy night during Covid's latter year.

Before our long, shining brass-topped coffee table broke under the weight of new books, I enjoyed sitting and perusing their contents most evenings. Now the books are in piles in the little adjacent office off the living room, along with manuscripts friends have sent me and pages of this memoir. I have read part of many of the books and look forward to finishing them. Plus volumes of poetry, art books, collections of letters, and tomes about the natural world. The poets whose published treasures are visible on top: Anna Akhmatova, Seamus Heaney, Mary Oliver, flanked by biographies of Mike Nichols and Philip Roth.

The kids despair of my living room, but I think it's fine. Now I have books piled everyplace else. Bill and I had plans to enlarge the living room and the porch, then he got sick and we didn't go ahead. My daughter Susanna, the boss of the family now, brought her architect son-in-law to the Vineyard to arrange adding a downstairs bedroom and bath for me when climbing the stairs to mine may become too arduous. The sight and sounds of it progressing now are an unexpected pleasure.

I feel lucky to have lived with my family in the Roxbury house for nearly sixty years, and I am lucky to live on this little unpaved byway where I can see the Sound and some of the Elizabeth Islands from my upstairs bedroom. Of course my favorite spot is here on the porch, where I can sit in nearly all seasons, writing, reading, welcoming Scrabble players and our favorite visitors.

Everyone teases me about being ridiculously social still. They say

Family portrait, Martha's Vineyard, August 2022.

they expect me to turn up if there's an island party. And of course I take great pleasure in inviting friends and friends of friends here for spontaneous or planned dinners, lunches, even breakfasts on High Hedge Lane. Especially in summer.

Home now is obviously Martha's Vineyard. We've had wonderful gatherings here in Vineyard Haven, with special moments and some sad ones as well, such as Bill's sixtieth birthday when for the first time socially he didn't seem himself. He was heading for a depression. For much of the afternoon, he sat with a big stuffed bear (a gift) in his lap.

Many mornings, as I pause in the living room, on my way to the kitchen for a first cup of coffee, two objects I treasure greet me from the mantel: a beautiful small bronze dancer inherited from my mother and a little hunched clay figure that was a gift from Peter Matthiessen, found on one of his far-flung adventures. Since Covid, I relish the drop-in breakfast visits on my porch, especially now by Craig McNamara from his California olive and walnut orchards, and Tony Marks, who heads the New York Public Library, and other old friends once again on-island. I look forward always to James Lapine's arrival with goodies.

My concerns for political and climate and green disasters and rights removal keep me (night owl still) watching hours of late news, and in constant correspondence with friends surely brighter and more connected than I. I managed three off-island trips that intrigued and satisfied me no end: Peter Sacks's art show at Brandeis's Rose Art Museum, Ben Zander's earlier Mahler concert in Boston, and James Lapine's (embarrassing but admirable) movie about me at New York's documentary film festival. Twenty twenty-two's farewell.

The light on the Sound brings back a splendid, sunny, peaceful June Sunday when I sailed *en famille* on Robert Douglas's *Alabama* not too many seasons ago. The Douglas brothers built it and more or less presented it to the island along with its twin vintage-style sister ship, built first, the *Shenandoah,* soon after we began our summer residences. Its weekly or daily chartered voyages bring enviable views from our porch. Often there were special learning cruises for students. That day the ship had been chartered for a surprise party on Carly Simon's birthday. Special-to-Carly Vineyarders attended, family, old and young, including Sally and Ben Taylor and their musician pals. It was, as they say, *magic,* as my blessed sail on Nat Benjamin's *Charlotte* had been. The night before, a score of old friends had gathered at the Bramhalls' to celebrate the full moon and forty years of camaraderie, much of it on unparalleled stretches of sand in Aquinnah, Chilmark, or West Tisbury. Will we do a big picnic on Squibnocket Beach or Black Point or Seven Gates again? How I wish it could be before another harvest moon.

Acknowledgments

There are so many amazing friends I want to thank for making it possible for me to have found the time, space, and ease of daily life—to say nothing of the inspiration—to write prose solo in my Vineyard home that I hardly know where to begin.

I guess I'll start by sending heartfelt thanks to those without whom this memoir could not have been written:

First: my extraordinary editor, Victoria Wilson, who grew up on the Vineyard, and who prompted me to start looking back at my beginnings, and to keep going, embracing memory uncritically for a long while. It was my old friend Jane Friedman who introduced me to Vicky on my porch one afternoon.

Second, to Christina Christensen, my husband's and my spectacular multitasking assistant of twenty-three years. Her company, good advice, and careful arranging of my daily hours in Connecticut and Martha's Vineyard and sometimes afar have been my anchor. Only Christina could have managed to transcribe my left-handed pen, my endless handwritten pages that resulted in this text.

Then to Bill Madden, who at our home and in the car has—during regular visits—made my life safe, met my appointments on time.

Dana Morris, everyone's dream of a caretaker, who has given me a home base that works and thus the hours for writing.

Carla Paizante, whose cleaning and organizing expertise means my surroundings are pleasurably inhabitable.

I could not look back without counting the years when Daphne Lewis managed our Vineyard Haven kitchen full-time in summer, often arriving in Connecticut for holidays and eternal special attention to our youngest, Al. She lives in Canada but is well remembered by islanders. We talk on the phone. She keeps saying, "I'm so bored!" Daphne was never boring.

I want to thank the many bygone friends mentioned throughout the pages of this book who meant so much to me and contributed so wonderfully to my lucky life. Particular friends I miss most are Peter Matthiessen, Jay Presson Allen, Mike Nichols, and Mike Wallace. My brother, B, is foremost.

How often I look forward to Vanessa Martins's arrival for currently invaluable PT and to mornings with Cathy Ashmun, embracing her years of strength training and care and friendship. Also to Tara Ledden's visits (with daughters and pup) to do my hair and more, and to talented Jodi Baron, who brightens whatever day she chooses to come to help in the office or with a party.

Regular communiqués that bring me great satisfaction and keep me abreast of contemporary affairs, raising my consciousness of national or world problems and their possible easing are welcomed via correspondence with Harvard Law professor Laurence Tribe and his partner, Elizabeth Westling, and with Margaret Marshall and Vineyarder Ric Patterson and his wife, Nancy Clair. Meetings with Bryan Stevenson have given me valued insight into Black history.

Moving on: my dear girlfriends, writers Brooke Allen, Jenny Allen, and Vicki Riskin, who looked at early draft sections and encouraged me to ask patient, imaginative Jan Freeman to help me finish, via Zoom, after an eye accident, were invaluable. Brooke, who since her childhood in Roxbury, Connecticut, has been almost a daughter to me and sister to my brood, said she laughed a lot reading a long recent draft, which was my first encouragement.

Also: friends who insisted I keep writing during the Covid quarantining months: Californians seasonally in Menemsha Aileen Adams and Geoff Cowan, closest neighbors Sue Bailey and Rex Killian, who invite me to breakfast in town with Ken Berkov and others, precious pals Doreen Beinart and Bob Brustein, and long-term island friends Kib and Tess Bramhall, Phil and Penny Weinstein, and Dave and Betsy Weinstock. Also traveling companion and Kennedy colleague Caroline Croft, and admired local friend Laurie David. Special, endlessly caring pals Gogo Ferguson and Dave Sayre, plus marvelous Charlayne Hunter-Gault and Ron Gault. Also inimitable Skip Gates, Jim and Carol Gilligan, Susan and Andy Goldman, Cris and Ben Heineman, Injy and Jason Lew, Paula Lyons, Bob and Dale Mnookin, Sandy Pimentel, Tamara Weiss, and New York's Robyn and Doyle Newmyer . . . and more (too many to list here, I'm advised).

My weekly Scrabble partners and lunch devourers Tess Bramhall, Kathy Newman, and Penny Weinstein give me exceptional cheer and further winter gossip anticipation.

Other special women I bonded with during this writing, one on one, even outside, bundled up in the coldest weather, made daily life particularly interesting as we learned about each other's lives, past and present, and our plans for the future. I often thought more deeply about my own life as a result. Geraldine Brooks, Sarah Catchpole, Judy Crawford, Anne Luzzatto, Paula Lyons, and especially Phyllis Segal have stimulated me at mealtimes, and long after . . .

So has meeting with friends who were memoirists too: Craig McNamara, Laura Roosevelt, Phil Weinstein. When possible, I've attended Phil's wide-ranging off-season literary lectures in our towns, stretching my knowledge and imagination.

Then there are the summer and fall visitors I value, who keep me away from writing when we do get together: Ann and Ted Beason from Georgia, Carol Biondi from L.A., Tamara and Joel Buchwald from D.C., Billy Collins from Florida, Constance Ellis from New York, Mathea Falco from San Francisco, Elena and Norman Foster from Europe, Jane and Michael Horvitz from Cleveland, Bryan and Tara Meehan from Ireland via California, Robin Rosenberg and Michael McAuliffe from Florida, Connie Royster from New Haven, Jill and Paul Ruddock from London, Moira Shipsey from Dublin. Extra-special are my oldest friend, Connie Ellis, of New York and the Vineyard and San Francisco's Victoria Pearman, whose summer conversation and swimming companionship I enjoy almost daily. I've been so surprised and pleased to welcome on the Vineyard, recently, old Amnesty colleagues Larry Cox and Bill Shipsey, their current lives an inspiration to me, their memory-prompting rewarding! And, in my new winter Florida habitats, early Amnesty leaders David and Joan Libby Hawk. Two Sarasota winters reconnected me wonderfully with Britishers Margaret Jay and Michael Adler.

And I so look forward to beautiful Geralyn Dreyfous's impromptu arrivals, bringing as guests exceptional, interesting filmmakers, artists, and philanthropists as well as food and flowers! Famed orchestra conductor Ben Zander has consequently become a welcome visitor on his own. My first post-Covid trip was to Boston for his unmatched Mahler concert, accompanied by Geralyn. My second was to Brandeis's gallery with Peter Sacks to marvel at his remarkable portraits of world-renowned creative leaders.

I'm incredibly grateful for the November 2022 launch of the William Styron Writing Prize at Duke University, which I attended. It included a fruitful Durham hour poring over Bill's impressively laid-out special papers in the Duke Rubenstein Library. The Bostock Library's founders, Merilee and Roy Bostock, generously initiated the prize. I'm planning a longer library trip there.

I look forward to phone calls that refresh my favorite memories, like a recent call from Pam Belafonte, wherein we reminisced about our trip to Dublin for Harry's Amnesty International Ambassador of Conscience Award and subsequently visited Yeats's grave in Sligo. That sparked happy memories. And made me think again how prescient Christian White was in fashioning Bill Styron's gravestone with the comforting quote from Bill's favorite writer, Dante: "And so we came forth and once again beheld the stars."

I'm happy when Pam and Nat Benjamin invite me for cozy dinners, or Roger and Elizabeth Hunt celebrating. And last but not least— in fact FIRST and MOST IMPORTANT TO ME ALWAYS—my sweet, admired, caring-for-me family: filmmaker Susanna, dancer/choreographer Paola, writer Alexandra, and professor of clinical psychology Tom—plus their ever-attentive spouses Phoebe Styron and Ed Beason, and my grandchildren Emma (and, of course, her husband, Wade), Lilah, Tavish, Tommy, Lulu, Gus, Huck, and Sky. They are each special to me and brighten my days, here and beyond, season after season.

A NOTE ON THE TYPE

This book was set in Garamond, a typeface originally designed by the famous Parisian type cutter Claude Garamond (1480–1561). This version of Garamond was drawn by Günter Gerhard Lange (1921–2008) and released by the Berthold type foundry in 1972. Lange based his Garamond revival on a combination of models found in specimen sheets from both Paris and Antwerp.

Claude Garamond is one of the most famous type designers in printing history. His distinguished romans and italics first appeared in *Opera Ciceronis* in 1543–1544. While delightfully unconventional in design, the Garamond types are clear and open, yet maintain an elegance and precision of line that mark them as French.

Composed by North Market Street Graphics, Lancaster, Pennsylvania
Printed and bound by Berryville Graphics, Berryville, Virginia
Designed by Maggie Hinders